How to Rapidly Scale Your SaaS Business

by

Nick Brown and Phil Pearce

Copyright © 2020 Nick Brown and Phil Pearce.
All rights reserved.
ISBN number: 9798617390935

This book is dedicated to the fantastic team at Accelerate and our amazing clients.

Foreword

This book was written for digital marketers working within the SaaS industry and managing those unique challenges. However, the strategies and broader tactics are suitable for any marketers wanting to grow their online business.

The aim is to provide SaaS marketers with a set of proven tools and methods, tried and tested, ones that we use every day. Combined we have more than 30 years' experience working in SEO and Analytics and have seen the landscape change and develop over the last couple of decades. The content in this book comes from our work with clients, ranging from global blue chip to SMEs, and what has created success for them.

At Accelerate, we're big on being open and transparent on how we do things, so that our clients can understand what we do at every step. It works, and our clients trust our expertise as they are with us at every step. We also get them great results, using the methods in this book.

Digital marketing is a fast-moving industry and the challenges to grow a SaaS business are getting harder as the marketplace grows. Carving out a space in the noise is paramount, and we hope this book will help you raise your business's profile and get the recognition you deserve.

Nick and Phil

Accelerate Agency, Bristol, 2020

Content

Chapter 1: Getting traffic to your site
1.1 12 tried & tested SaaS marketing strategies that just work
1.2. Where to promote your SaaS company
1.3 How to develop a content marketing strategy
1.4 Essential guide to guest posting
1.5 Best social media channels

Chapter 2: How to get paying customers
2.1 How to run retargeting ads
2.2. How to set up email marketing campaigns
2.3 How to run webinars
2.4 6-figure payday: a proven five-step online sales strategy

Chapter 3: How to keep visitors on your website
3.1 11 SaaS landing page examples and why they work
3.2 4 free website management tools you can use to generate more sales
3.3 10 AB testing examples that will help you improve your website

Chapter 4: Retaining existing customers
4.1 10 essential SaaS metrics every employee needs to know
4.2 Customer churn prediction and analysis
4.3 17 ways to reduce your customer churn

Chapter 5: How to secure investment or a sale
5.1. A beginner's guide to the 5 steps of startup funding stages
5.2 Top 25 VC investing in SaaS companies
5.3 The definitive guide on how to value your SaaS company
5.4 27 unbeatable pitch deck templates you can use for your startup

Appendix

Authors

Chapter 1: Getting traffic to your website

Software as a service (SaaS) is a business model that is becoming ever more popular. Recent statistics[1] forecast that the SaaS sector could be worth as much as $623 billion by 2023. If yours is a SaaS company, then you're certainly in a booming industry. That means you have plenty of competition, and the competition is only going to increase.

What you need is a way to stand out from the crowd. You need a SaaS marketing strategy that works. One which can help you with the tough job of selling your services to prospective customers. You don't have a physical, tangible product to show off and promote.

What follows in this ebook are the tried and tested elements of a marketing strategy for a SaaS business to stand out from the competition. The first two chapters are dedicated to getting traffic to your website through organic and paid methods. They cover content marketing and adding value by using lead magnets. Later chapters will cover how to keep those customers once you have converted them, how to measure your success at customer service and finally how to secure investment for your business to go to the next level.

1.1: 12 tried & tested SaaS marketing strategies that just work

In this section are 12 elements of a successful SaaS marketing strategy. None of them are too complicated, and all are proven to deliver results. You can pick and choose or implement them all. Either way, these SaaS marketing strategy gems can help you win over new customers.

Tried & tested SaaS marketing strategy

There are two main parts to marketing SaaS. First, you have to get as much traffic to your site as possible. Then you need to promote and show off your service effectively. We've arranged our 12 tried and tested SaaS marketing strategy points by breaking them down into these two parts of the process. We will start by looking at how to get more traffic to your SaaS site.

Generate more site traffic

There are five tried and tested ways to get more traffic to your SaaS site. We will cover some of these in greater depth about some of them in later chapters. For now, here is a whistle-stop intro to our first five SaaS marketing strategy tips:
- Utilising content marketing
- Spending time on your site's SEO

- Investing in Paid Search & PPC
- Intelligent referral marketing
- Getting industry exposure

1. Utilise content marketing

Content marketing is a proven model of lead generation for any SaaS website. At the most basic level, getting more traffic to your website involves publishing high-quality content on your site. The topics you choose to write about should align with the interests of your audience. For example, if you had a Facebook marketing SaaS, suitable topics for your content could include:
- Facebook marketing strategy
- Facebook marketing for small business
- Facebook marketing cost
- How to use Facebook marketing for business

The list of suitable topics you can choose is extensive. You can use a tool like Keywords Everywhere to identify subjects to write about based on search volume.

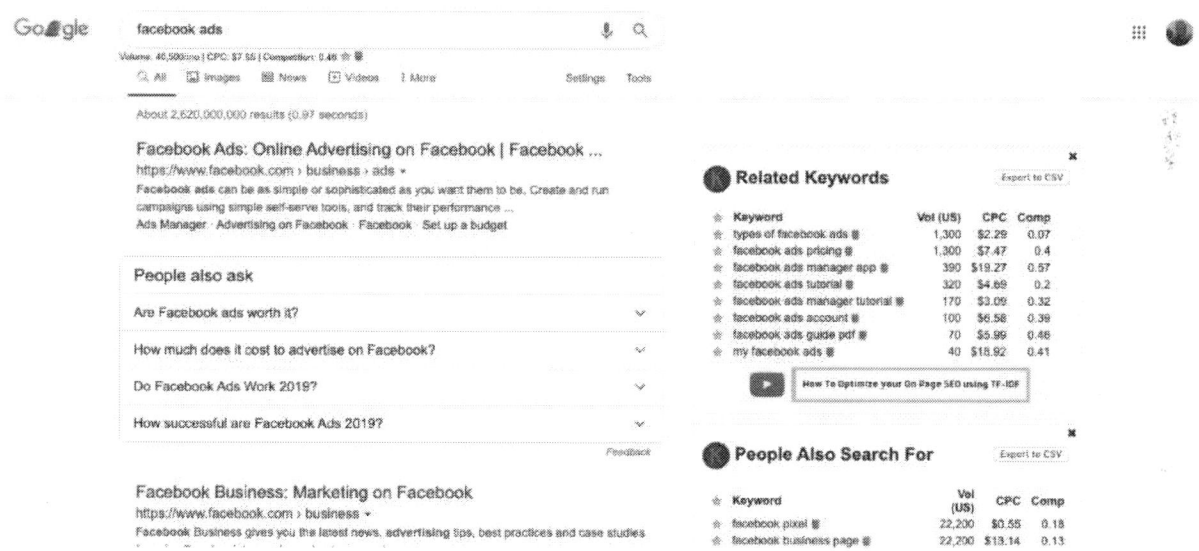

You need to optimise the content you create on your blog for both user intent and keywords. By this, I mean the content needs to answer the query a person using Google was looking to receive. So, if they were looking to purchase a service, then users want to see a sales page. On the other hand, if searchers are doing an informational search, they will want to arrive on a blog post.

In addition to creating great content, you need to generate backlinks to the content for it to rank. To understand how many backlinks you need, you will have to do a backlink analysis of ranking content. Once your content starts getting noticed your business will develop a reputation as an authority in your field.

2. Spend time on your site's SEO

Nothing works as well for boosting site traffic as a comprehensive search engine optimisation (SEO) strategy. SEO is complex and goes hand-in-hand with content marketing. The basic idea is a simple one. You need to tailor and tweak a site so that it appears as high as possible on search engine results pages (SERPs).

The higher your site ranks, the more traffic you'll get. There are a vast number of strands that combine to make for good SEO. Some SEO tasks and efforts work better for SaaS sites than others. Some of these – like guest posting and using social media for SEO – will be covered later, in subsequent sections. For now, suffice it to say that investing in top-quality SEO will do wonders for your site traffic.

3. Invest in Paid Search or PPC

Paid search or pay per click (PPC) advertising is another avenue worth exploring. As a SaaS marketing strategy, you shouldn't see it as an alternative to content marketing and SEO. What it can be is an excellent complement to those two processes. Particularly if you're looking to achieve some quick traffic wins.

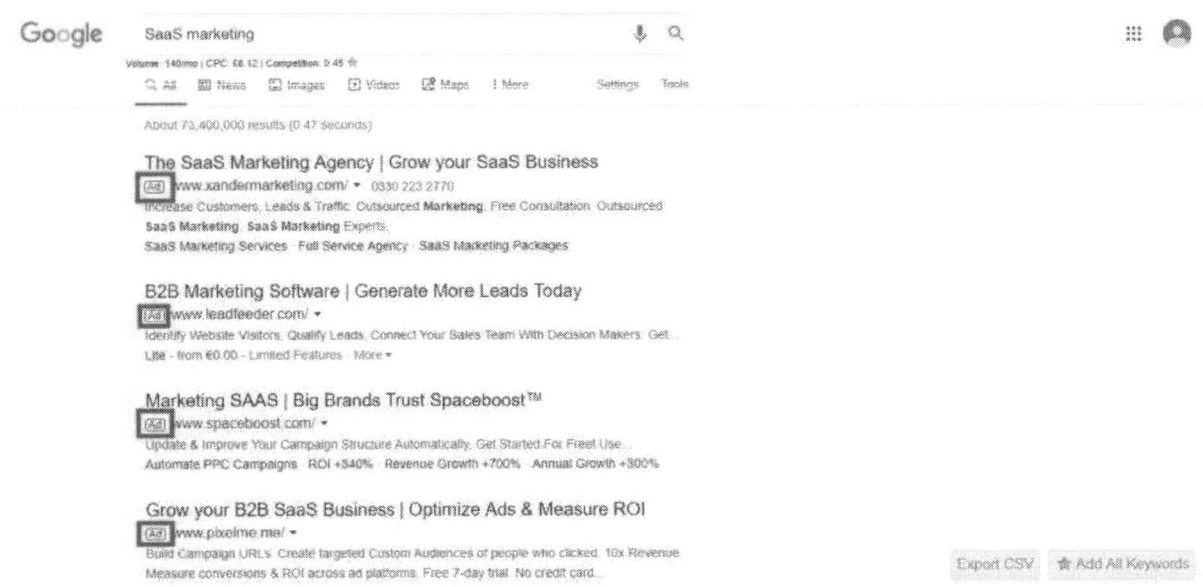

You should always set aside a marketing budget for branded search terms. These are terms that include your company name. Branded search terms are results competitors are likely to pay for, and if they do, you need to have a budget to get those clicks.

If you do invest in PPC ads, you want to get as much bang for your buck as possible. Your ads need to be engaging and attractive. They should convey your service's benefits. The best way to improve the conversion rate of your ads is by repeated testing. Create lots of variations of ad copy and research plenty of keywords to target. That way, you can mix things up and experiment until you find your perfect combinations.

4. Undertake intelligent referral marketing

Referral marketing is like the digital equivalent of word of mouth advertising. It involves getting current customers to recommend your service to people they know. It's an effective SaaS marketing strategy. Referral marketing gets your name out there to new prospective customers. It also ensures that you come with a stamp of approval from someone they trust.

Even your most satisfied customers may need a little push to refer you to friends. That's where smart incentives or rewards enter the picture. Offering access to an extra feature or a higher level of your software in return for a referral is a good example. Dropbox, for instance, gives users extra storage space if they invite friends.

5. Generate industry exposure

People put a lot of stock in reviews. A BrightLocal study[1] found that 91% of 18-34-year-olds trust online reviews as much as personal recommendations. It's critical to get your SaaS business industry exposure on one of the many SaaS review sites around. G2 Crowd is perhaps the best example:

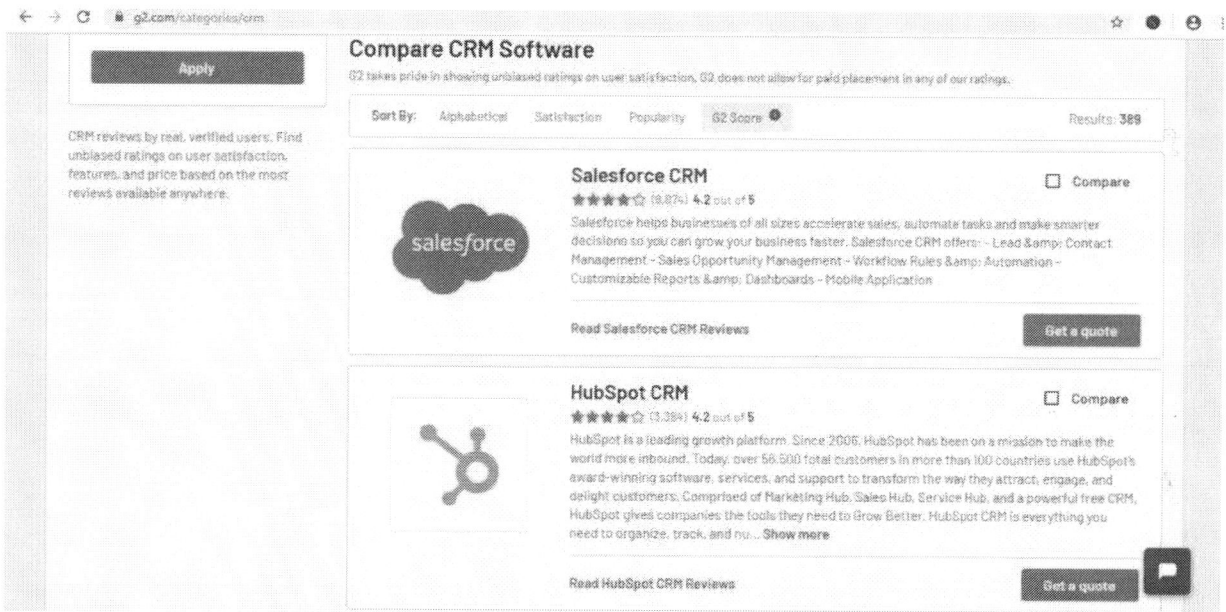

A positive review on a review site will help with site traffic. It's an effective SaaS marketing strategy to get a listing on as many review sites as possible. You may not get featured by all of them, but it's worth a try. Having a presence across sites helps convince potential customers of the viability of your business.

How to sell your service

The next stage of marketing SaaS is to turn site visitors into customers. Without a physical product to sell, this can seem easier said than done. The following seven hints and tips can improve this part of your SaaS marketing strategy:
- Don't provide too much choice
- Don't be coy about pricing
- Offer free trials
- Make it easy to sign up
- Enhance user experience
- Introduce deals & discounts
- Utilise clear CTAs

6. Limit customer choice

At first glance, this piece of SaaS marketing strategy may seem counterintuitive. Surely you want to offer customers as many different options as possible? Actually, no. It's better to limit the range of options as this simplifies the choice.

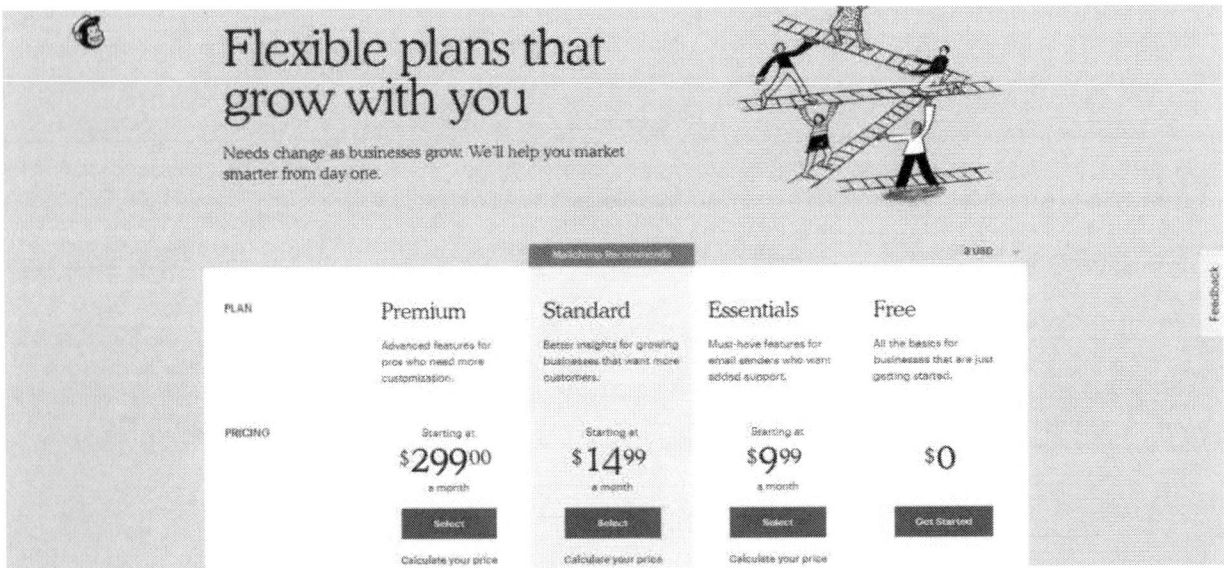

The email marketing software platform Mailchimp is a good example. Their software provides users with loads of different features. There are only four separate plans to choose from, however. Prospective customers can see what each one offers and choose between them - as with many things in business - keeping things simple pays dividends.

7. Don't be coy about pricing

Some SaaS businesses make it difficult for site visitors to see how much their service costs. The idea is presumably to get visitors more interested in the service before revealing the price. As a customer, a lack of transparent pricing can be frustrating. Think about when you head to a site thinking of buying something. What would your response be if you can't see how much it costs?

More often than not, you'd leave the site and find somewhere else to make your purchase. Hiding or obfuscating prices makes prospective customers suspicious. Instead, be open about the cost of your service. Make sure that your pricing strategy makes it easy to show how each plan or package delivers value.

8. Offer free trials

Free trials are a mainstay of SaaS marketing. You'll struggle to find a SaaS business that doesn't offer a free trial. That's because free trials are massively effective in selling SaaS. A free trial helps users understand how your software works. Alongside how efficiently it can solve their problems. That's why leading SaaS companies feature free trials so prominently on their sites:

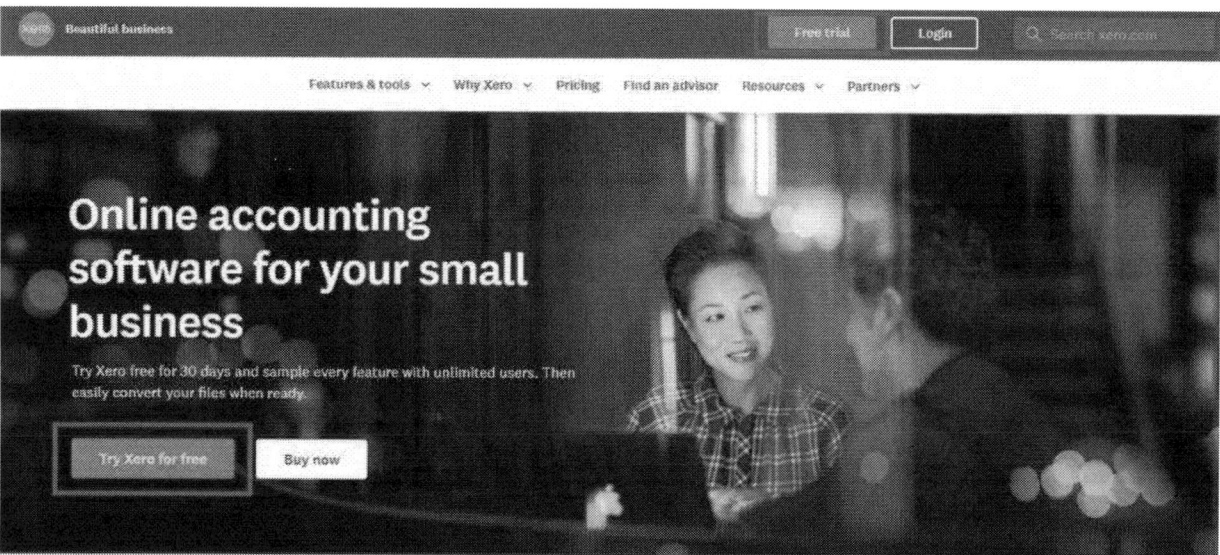

While you can't do without free trials, you do need to be careful as to how you pitch them. What you have to avoid is letting prospective customers use your service for free *instead* of buying it. Your free trial should either last for a limited time or include only core features of the service. That way you're giving customers a taste of the benefits they'll get by signing up proper.

9. Make it easy to sign up

Speaking of signing up, doing so should be as quick and easy as you can make it. You've worked hard to get people onto your site. You've made sure your website sells your service and makes it sound irresistible. That's convinced a prospective customer to sign up. From there, you want there to be as few obstacles as possible.

A long and complicated signup form is a no-no. People often abandon these when they're faced with them, even if they had every intention of signing up. Make sure your sign-up forms are clean and efficient. Don't ask for information that isn't critical to getting a new customer registered. Give those prospective customers as few excuses to change their minds as you can.

10. Enhance user experience

So far, we've talked at length about marketing and selling your software. About how to make potential customers aware of it and to best persuade them of its benefits. It's important to remember that there is another 's' in SaaS. The second 's' is for service, and delivering excellent service to customers is critical.

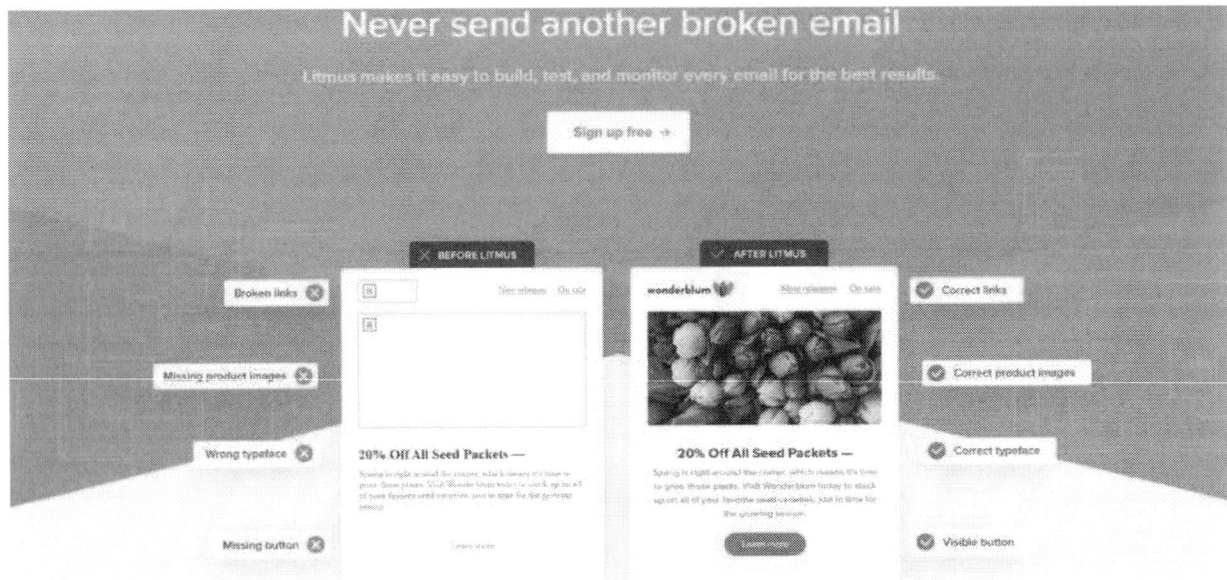

Unless you're fortunate, your software will often be pretty similar to that of other firms in your niche. You need to find a way to differentiate yourself. First, you can show customers how your software will improve their life or their business as in the above example from Litmus. Second, you must ensure it does so, by making your customer service top-notch. Ensure you enhance user experience every time a customer interacts with your firm.

11. Introduce deals & discounts

Deals and discounts are also crucial to your SaaS marketing strategy. For the same reason, that good customer service is. You have to differentiate yourself from your competition. Offers can help show prospective customers that they can get higher value with you. What deals and discounts are also great for is upselling and cross-selling.

While you can profit from running deals and discounts, make sure you only run them on occasion. If people are offered discounts all of the time, they stop perceiving them as a special offer. Instead, people will view these deals and discounts as the regular price they expect to access.

12. Utilise clear CTAs

You should organise your site in a way that makes moving around it as frictionless as possible. You want the process of becoming a customer to be as easy as it can be. Clear calls to action (CTAs) can help with this. Take this example of the Mailchimp website:

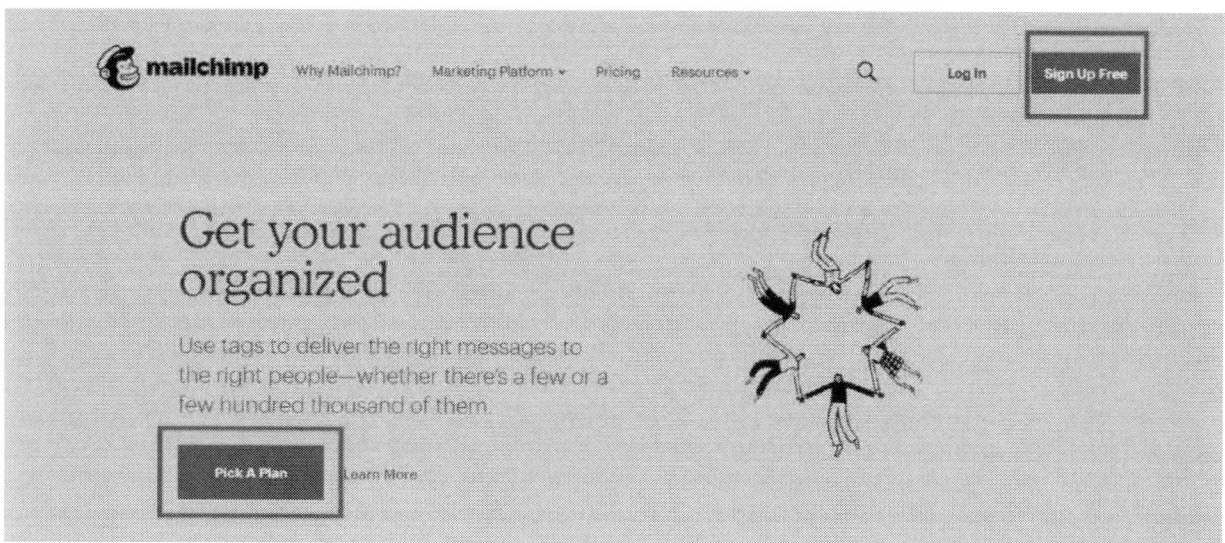

The email marketing company makes a visitor's next steps clear. They can choose to 'Sign Up Free' or 'Pick a Plan.' The explicit anchor text and prominent positioning of the CTAs are key. They make it more likely users will progress through the site. Almost before they realise, they'll find themselves at the point of signing up.

In this section, we've given a very broad overview of the strategic tactics that you need to consider for your SaaS business. These are tried and tested tactics that work to drive traffic to your website and then position your offering once they are on the landing page. In the next sections, we'll cover content marketing. We'll talk a bit more about improving user experience and sales copy in Chapter 3 but for now, let's look at places you can promote your SaaS to a wider audience using platforms that already have traffic.

1.2: Where to promote your SaaS company

Early adopters are important for any company. They can provide you with insights on how to improve your software platform and feedback regarding the pain points they are experiencing. Just as importantly, they can help spread the word about your platform.

To help you get more early adopters, we created a shortlist of 15 of the best sites for promoting your startup. The sites are a mixture of forums and platforms. The top five are sites we recommend any SaaS business to look at using. The rest are also useful and low-cost options to think about. Let's get started.

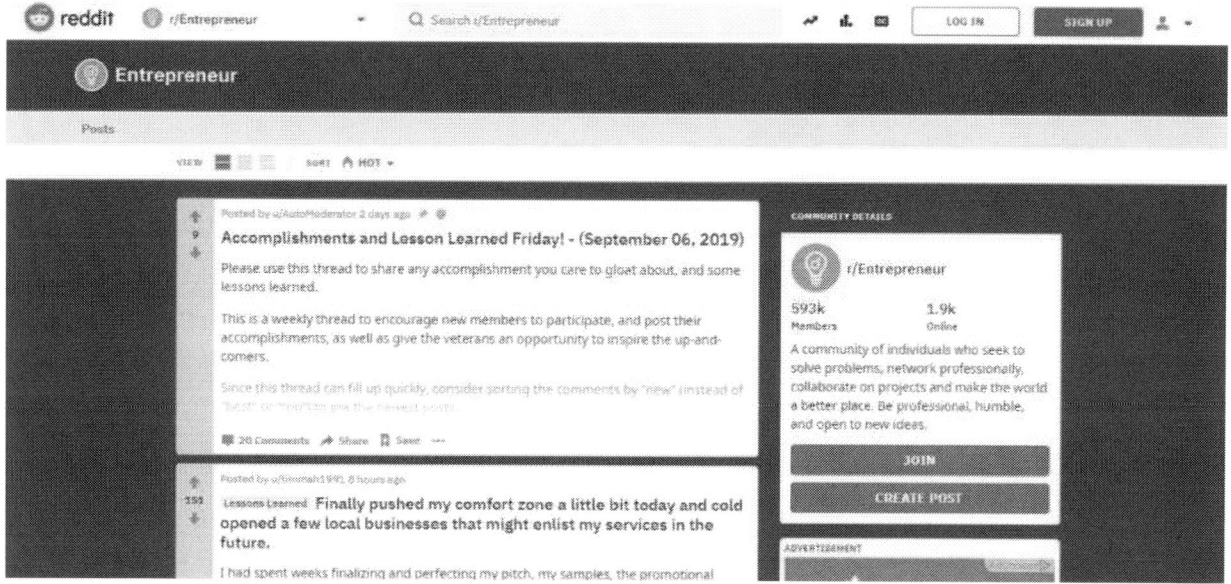

1. Reddit – Entrepreneur

Social media platforms are a great place to promote your startup. They're also effective for supporting your SEO efforts. As any content marketer will understand, with the correct approach Reddit can send thousands of qualified leads to your site. The platform achieves well over one billion visits each month, after all.

You can't simply *promote* your SaaS site on Reddit. Reddit is not a channel that takes kindly to direct marketing. To harness the power of the platform's huge community, you must become an actual part of it. Participate in discussions and hold back from sharing links to your site for a while.

You need to become a trusted user and discover the best way to introduce your site to discussions. Neil Patel does a great job explaining the intricacies of using Reddit to get more site traffic. Including how you should target the right subreddits for your business.

Reddit – Entrepreneur is one of the best subreddits on the site to use to generate buzz about a SaaS business. r/Entrepreneur is a Reddit community designed for professional networking. You can't submit your business to it, per se. What you can do is share news and stories about your firm to a sizeable audience.

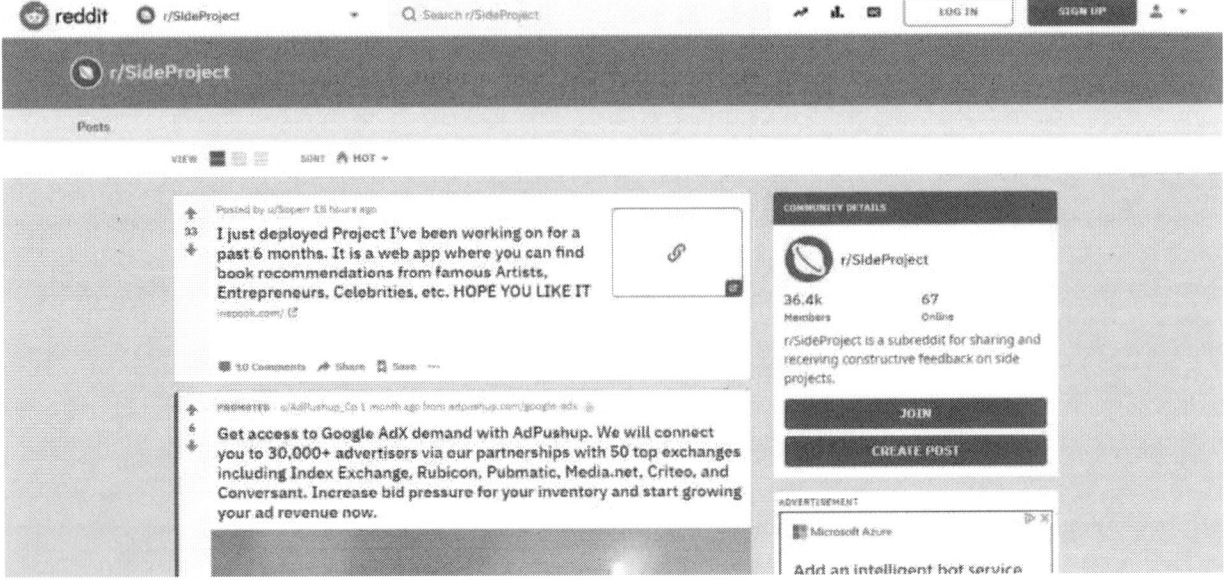

2. Reddit – SideProject

Another sub-reddit where you can promote your startup is Reddit SideProject. This group is great when you're just starting out. You can engage with the community to get the word out about what you're doing and receive feedback from other users.

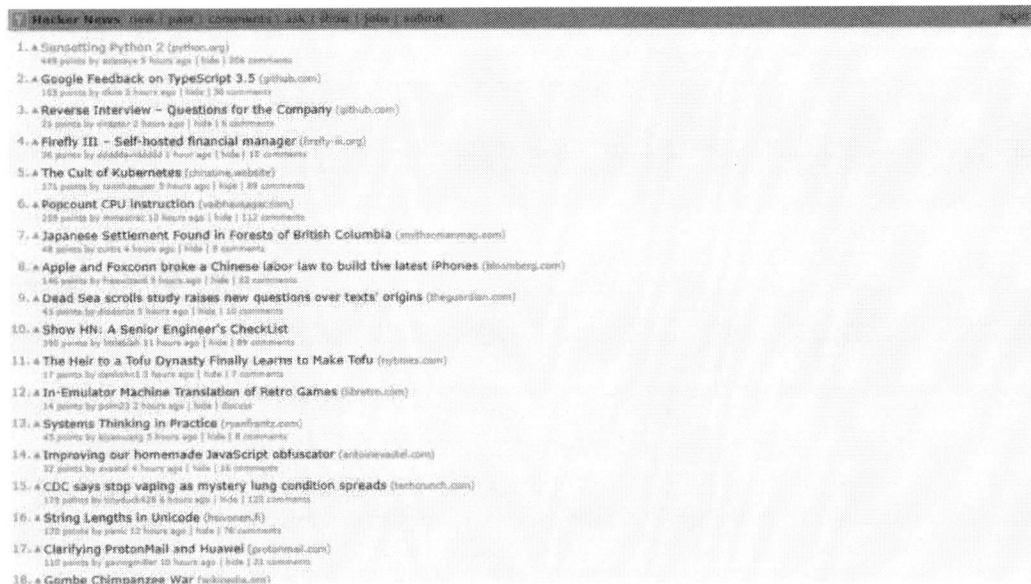

3. Hacker News

Hacker News is a forum for people who love technology and entrepreneurs. If your SaaS company will be serving that kind of audience, you'll want to get involved. It's quick, easy and free to start engaging with people on Hacker News.

You can create an account and submit news or announcements you want to share. Whatever you share has a chance of reaching a big portion of the 150,000 plus Hacker News subscribers. Those subscribers are also highly engaged with the forum. Hacker News gets an extraordinary 13.5m monthly visits.

When it comes to promoting your site on Hacker News, you need to treat the forum like any other social media channel. Be sure to become a genuine user of the site. Listen to what other users are interested in and promote content that fits the bill. Don't just post what amounts to a link or advert to your site.

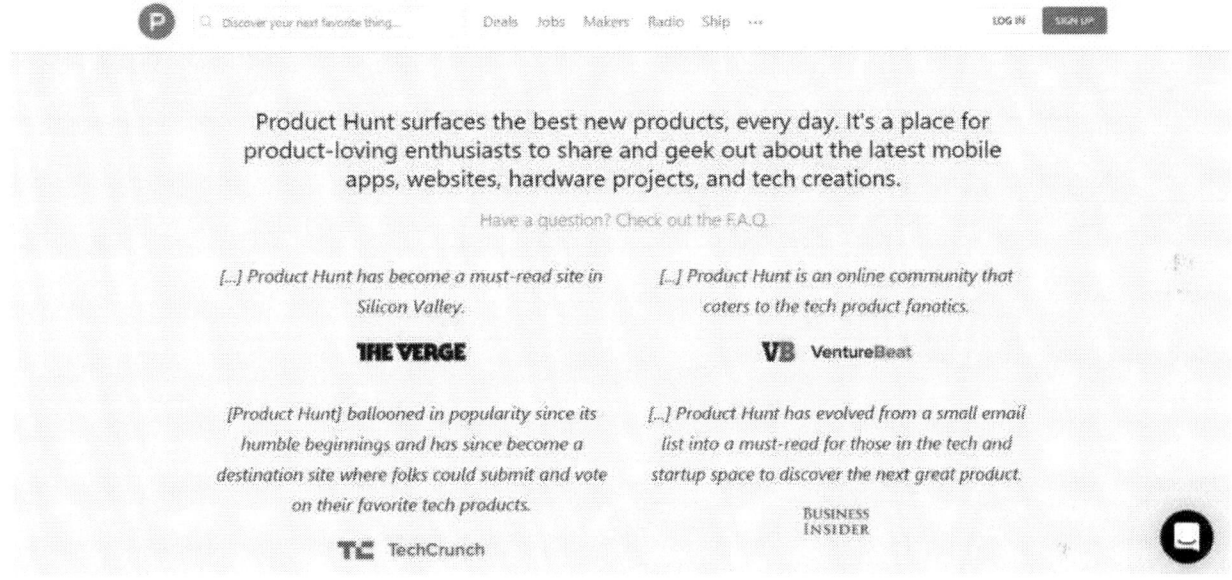

4. Product Hunt

Product Hunt is an active community where people share news about and discuss new tech products. Subscription to the service is free. It has one of the largest active communities of beta users on the net. In fact, the site gets a mind-blowing 6M+ monthly visits.

If you want to generate immediate exposure for your SaaS company there are few better places to do so on the net than Product Hunt. If your announcement and your service capture the imagination, you're pretty much guaranteed 500+ visitors a day to your site for 3-4 days.

The best way to ensure you do capture the imagination is to hit the Product Hunt front page. You can only do that if you fully understand the site and how it works. You have to tailor your product launch to best suit and appeal to the site's users.

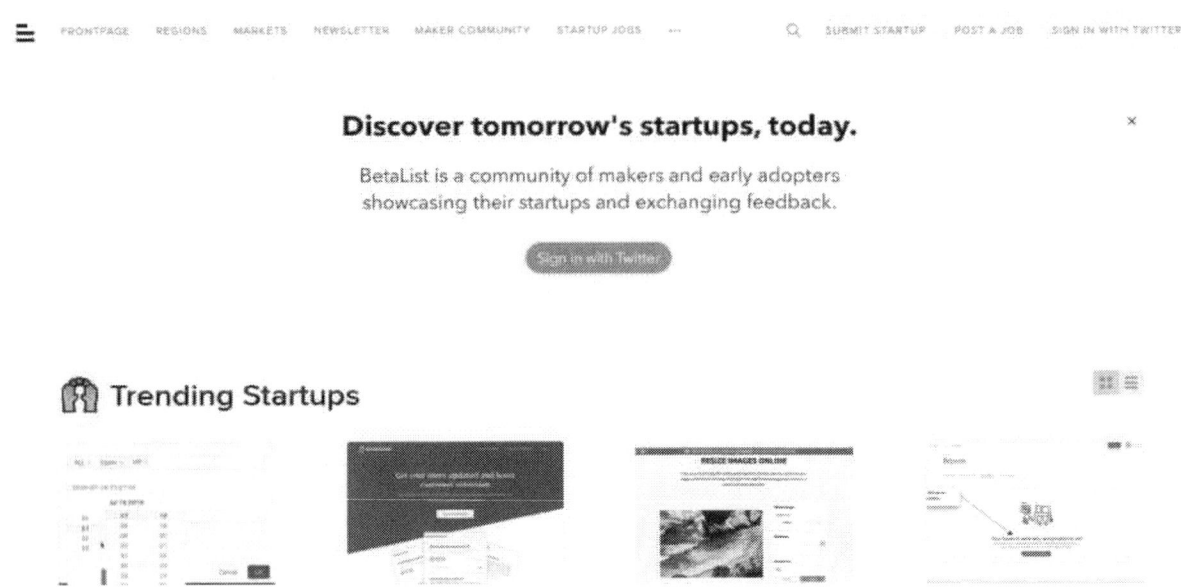

5. Betalist

Betalist is well known as the place to go to find hot technology startups before they hit the open market. Successful brands like Pinterest and Nuji were introduced to the world on the site. That reputation explains why the site gets over 120,000 hits every month.

There are two listing options available for software companies that want to appear on the site. With the free listing service, you can expect to appear on the site within two months of submission, though they reject the free listings more often than the paid ones. The fast track version, which will see your startup featured within 48 hours, costs $129. In general, though, it's worth it.

6. AngelList

AngelList bills itself as 'where the world meets startups'. That makes it an obvious candidate as to where to promote your startup. The platform is designed to help startups get funding or hire skilled employees. Even if you're not looking for those things, it's still a good place to list your firm.

You can sign up for free. Appearing on the site will get your name out there to people all around the world. The site gets a hugely impressive five million monthly visits! If you can get even a small number of those site visitors to view your site, that's a massive boost to your traffic.

What's more, AngelList has a social aspect. Through the platform, you can get in touch with all kinds of people who could help your company.

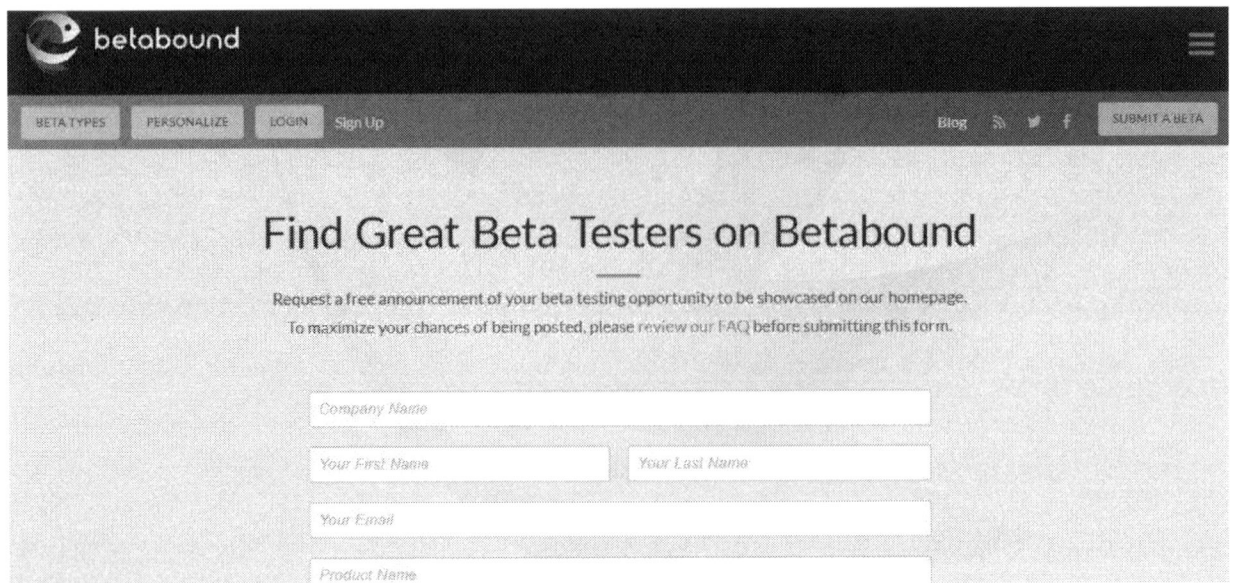

7. Beta Bound

Before you fully roll out your SaaS platform you need to iron out as many of the glitches or kinks as possible. You can do a fair bit of that in-house. Having a legion of beta testers to report issues to you, provides you with valuable additional feedback.

Beta Bound is a community of beta testers. You can list your SaaS company on the site. There are paid and free listing services available. The site enjoys traffic of over 110,000 monthly visits. A listing will certainly help to get your site noticed.

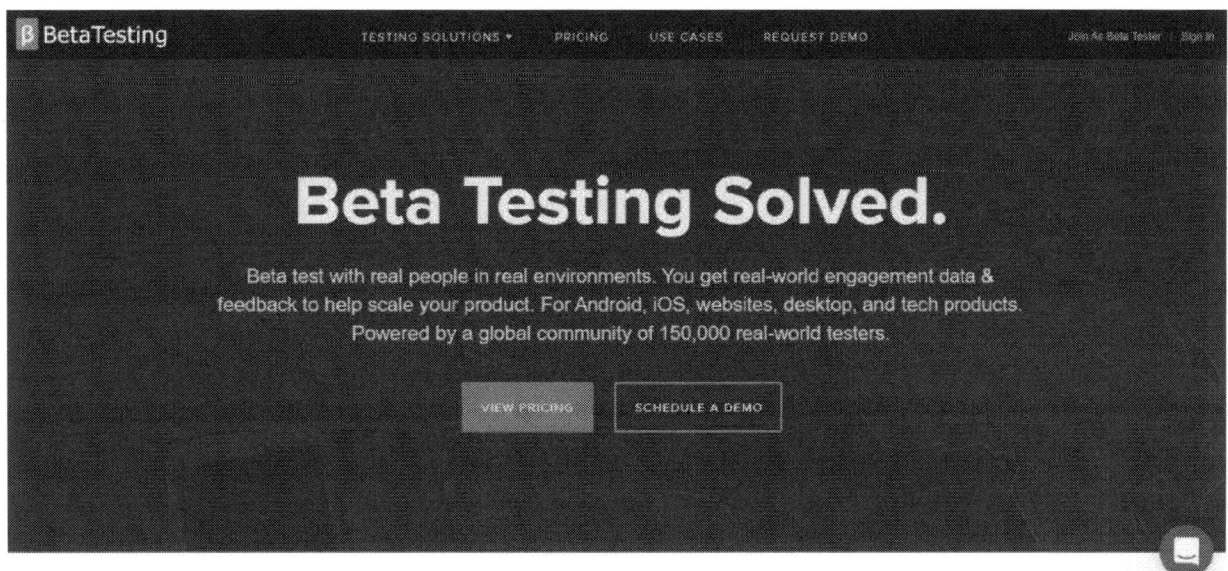

8. BetaTesting (Formerly Erli Bird)

Set up in 2012, BetaTesting was one of the first sites linking startups and beta testers. Originally named Erli Bird, the site did indeed catch that particular worm. Today, the site is home to a community of 150,000 beta testers. That's a significant number of people to promote your site to.

BetaTesting can cater to Android, iOS, desktop sites and other types of software. It then put firms in touch with knowledgeable early adopters.

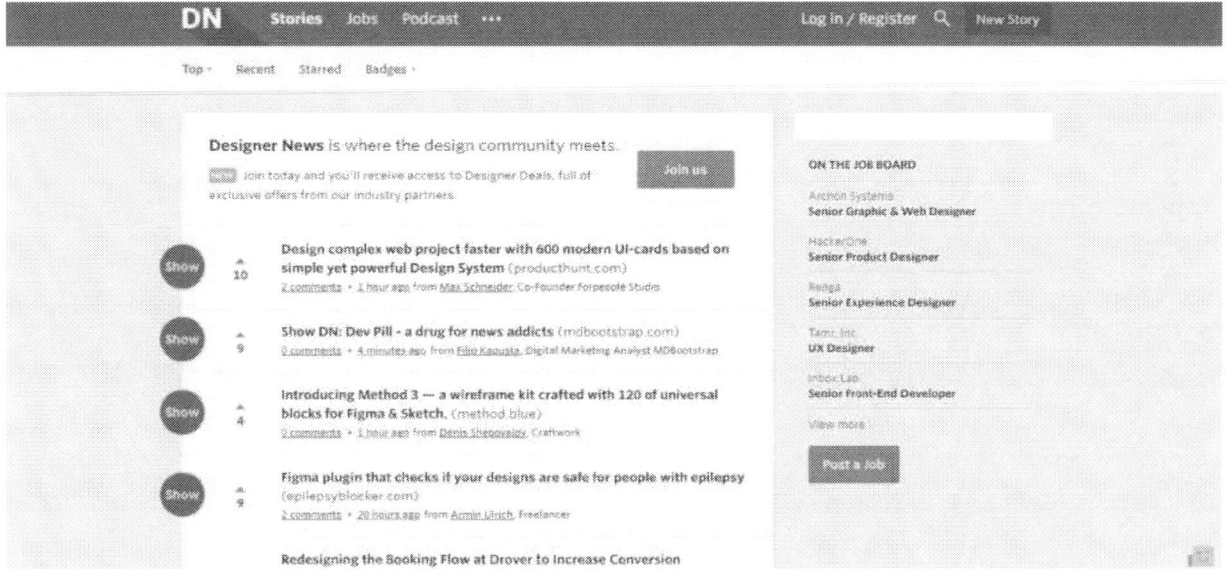

9. Designer News

If your SaaS offering has design implications, there's no better place to promote your startup than Designer News. The site is a forum and platform for people in the design community to get together and share ideas.

Through signing up you can reach close to 20,000 Designer News subscribers with news of your new company. Those subscribers help the site to achieve over 330,000 unique site visits each month. What's more, the platform fosters community engagement, so you can communicate directly with people interested in using your platform.

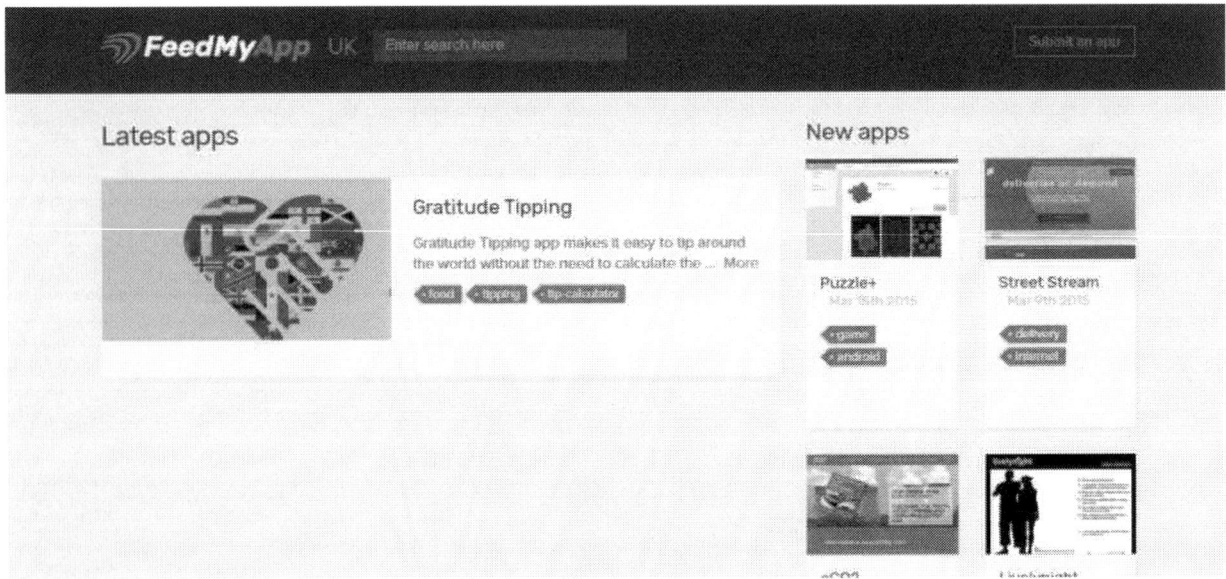

10. Feed My App

In the digital world, few apps or platforms work in complete isolation. There are loads of different apps designed to work with major social media platforms. There are also plenty of tools that work with services like Google Analytics.

Our sixth place to promote your startup is perfect if your software fits that category. Feed My App is a place to showcase your new app.

You can submit your app to the site for just $1.90 and get exposure to the service's growing user base. That user base is perhaps not as large as that of some of our listed sites, but it's still a pool of people worth reaching. For a fee, starting at $9, you can increase the exposure that your app receives.

11. Index.co

Index.co is an online service dedicated to showcasing what tech companies are up to. The site aims to be a one-stop-shop for information about all kinds of businesses in the tech industry.

If you want to list your company on index.co you will need to first create an account. Once you have created an account you can promote your startup on the site. With over 110,000 monthly visits to the site, it offers a good number of people for you to promote it to.

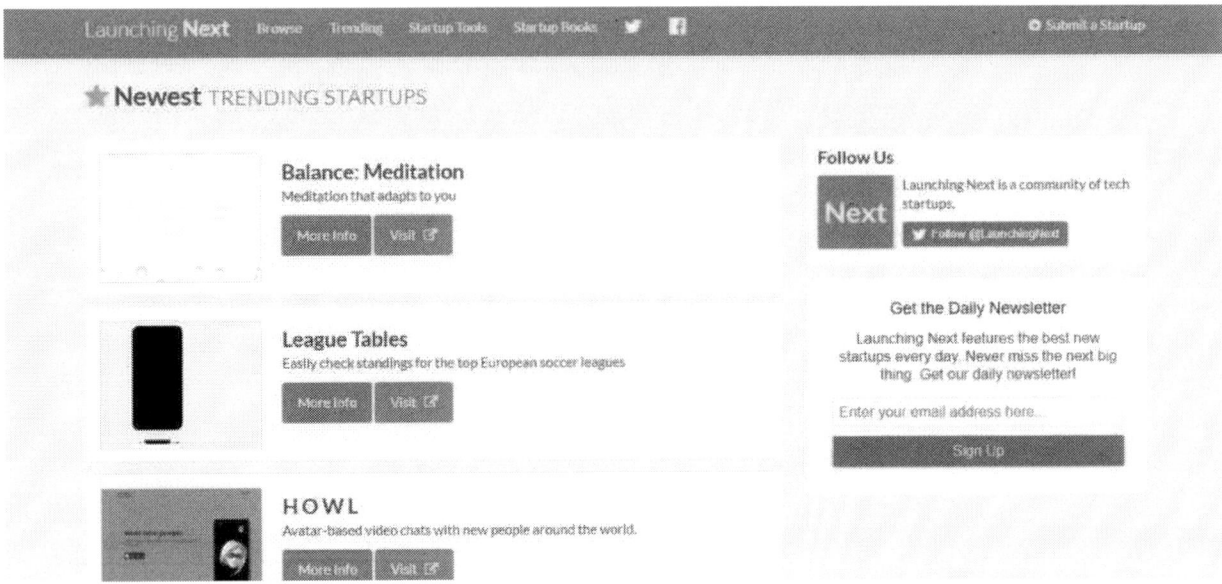

12. Launching Next

Describing itself as 'a community of tech startups', Launching Next has been around since 2013 and features 5,000+ startups. It's free to get your startup included on Launching Next. If you pay a one-off $49 fee, your firm will be up and viewable in one business day. Launching Next also features guides, advice and other resources for startup owners.

13. Springwise

Springwise describes themselves as 'the global source for innovation intelligence'. The site has been sharing 'innovative ideas' with its users since 2002. The site covers all kinds of niches and industries.

It's not easy to get your company or your idea featured on Springwise. They only share four or five new insights a day. If your SaaS offering has a true USP, you might be able to make it happen though. With over 55,000 monthly visits to the site, it's worth a try.

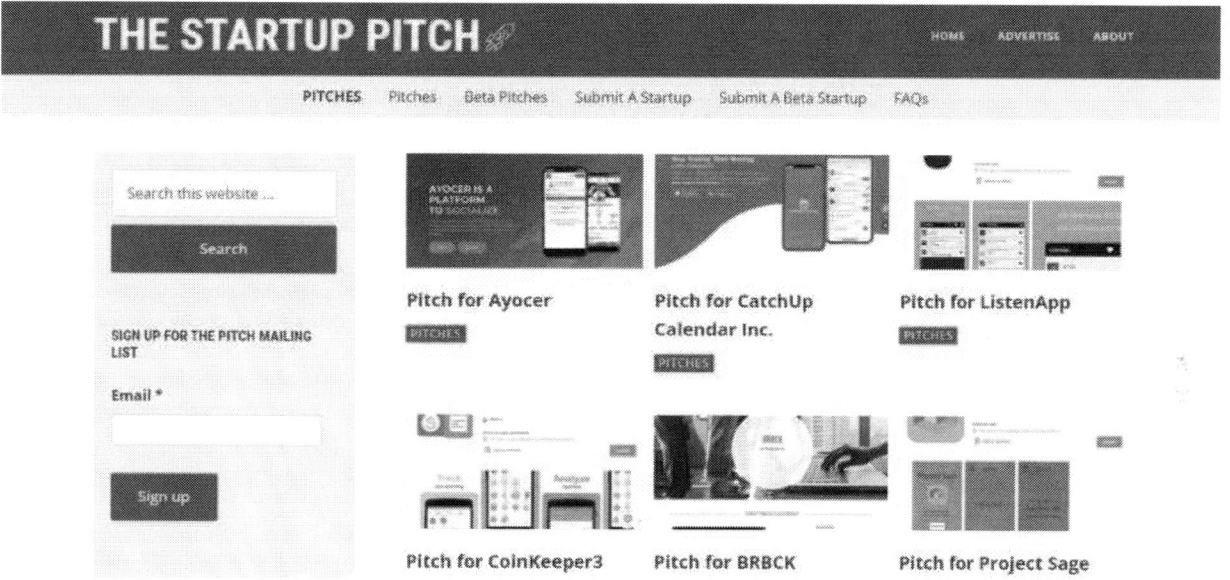

14. The Startup Pitch

The Startup Pitch claims to be the oldest startup directory. It's certainly a little different from other sites on this list. You have to create a business pitch, like you might provide to a print publication, to get featured on the site. Your pitch will be reviewed by the editors and published for visitors to read.

The idea is to give lower budget startups more exposure. In short, it's a great way to promote your startup without denting your bank balance. The site's traffic isn't the highest – it's certainly not in Reddit's league. Users of the site, though, are specifically interested in startups and small businesses.

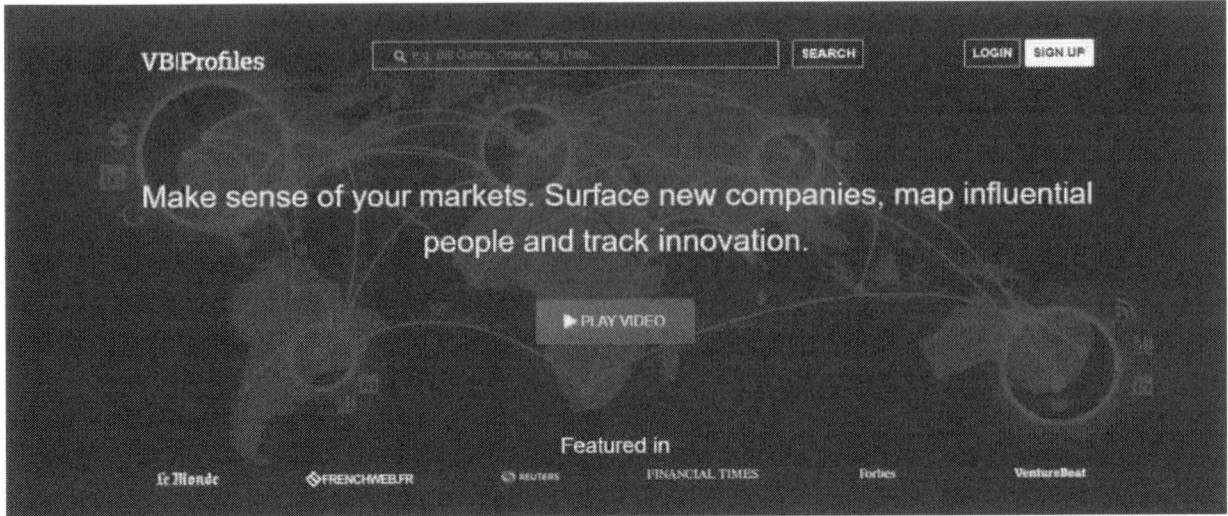

15. VentureBeat Profiles

Our final place to promote your startup is VentureBeat Profiles. VentureBeat is a leading channel for tech news and insights. The company's Profiles service is similar to index.co, which was featured earlier in this rundown.

Once you've signed up, you can create your firm's own VentureBeat profile. The entire service is free of charge. Users are, however, asked to contribute as much interesting information as possible about their company. That information is freely searchable by the site's sizeable and professional user base.

So that's it – 15 websites that have established user bases and substantial traffic where you can advertise your SaaS company (subtly, in some cases) and, at the same time, gather feedback about your software and positioning to help you improve them. Next, we'll expand on the content marketing strategy I mentioned in section 1.1 and discuss defining your customer, keyword and competitor research and give you some copywriting tips.

1.3: How to develop a content marketing strategy

This first chapter in our ebook for SaaS businesses is all about getting traffic to your site. There's hardly a more effective way of boosting the traffic a website receives than with good content marketing. Creating and sharing high-quality content is vital for any business.

Effective content marketing helps establish your brand as an authority in your field. It helps to build trust with those who consume your content and who may then become customers. It also goes hand-in-hand with good SEO. High-quality content will help meet real user intent and so please Google.

To ensure your firm is making the most of this form of marketing, you need a content marketing strategy. That's how you keep producing content that's high quality and useful to readers. Creating content for the sake of it is no good. Your content marketing strategy must be top-notch.

Unlike some aspects of marketing, content marketing planning is easier than it sounds. Below we're going to talk you through four major parts of developing a content marketing strategy.

Defining your ideal customer

We've already touched upon how important it is that the content you create is useful to those who consume it. The way to ensure the utility is by focussing on relevance. Everything you create and share must be relevant to your target audience. To do this, you first need to define your ideal customer.

https://www.goodtoseo.com/what-is-a-buyer-persona-and-why-is-it-important/

A buyer or customer persona is a well-researched representation of your ideal customer. The persona will detail the demographic traits of your customer. It will also reveal their interests, their goals, and the challenges they face. All of those things determine the content they'll want to consume.

Understanding your customer will help you define what content to create and which keywords to target.

Creating a customer persona is an exercise in research. You can build a customer persona through conducting surveys, interviews, and analysing your analytics data. Much of this process will involve focussing on your existing customers. They must be interested in your service, after all, as you want them to pay for it.

You'll probably have a good deal of personal information on your current customers. That should help you pin down the demographics of your target audience. Some of the more complicated Google Analytics tools can help you get a picture of your customer's interests. The platform's Interests reports are most helpful in this regard.

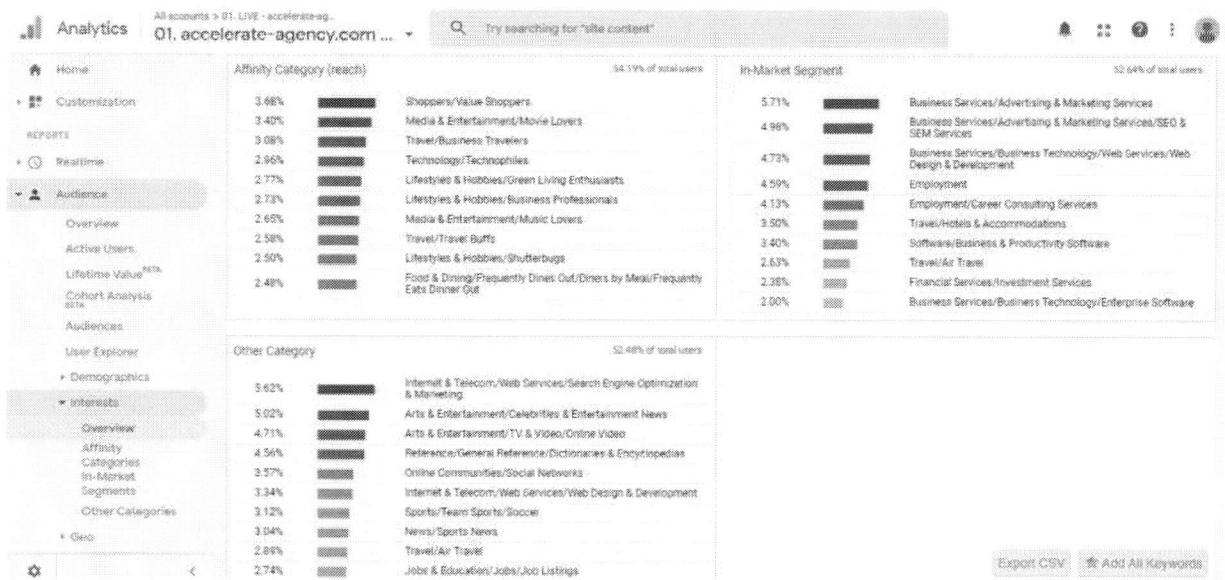

Analytics reports provide you with crucial information on visitors to your website. The reports categorise visitors by their likely lifestyles and list potential interests. You can use this information to bulk up and round out your customer persona.

With a customer persona built, you will know the general interests of your target audience. Now, you need to start finding more specific topics based around keywords people search for that will interest them. These will be the topics that your content can focus on to answer the real intent of your audience. There are many ways to generate these topics.

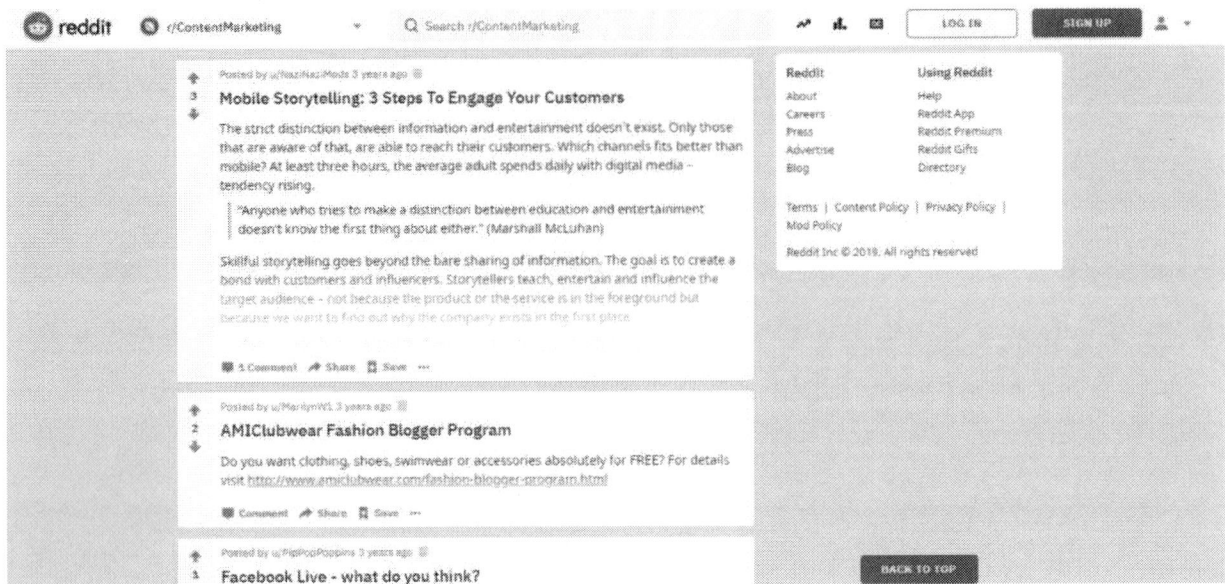

Forums or platforms like Reddit can be a great place to find additional content ideas. Choose a forum or a subreddit related to the interests shared by your target audience. Then, browse discussions to find actual questions that your target audience is asking. These are the things that they're actively looking to find out about online.

Think logically about the info your personas contain and topics should be easy to come by. That's the first significant stage of your content marketing planning.

How to choose your keywords

An understanding of topics your target audience is interested in isn't the same as a content marketing strategy. You need to take those topics and use them to generate keywords to incorporate into your content. If you can choose the right phrases, then with the appropriate SEO strategy, your content will appear on Google.

Keyword research is a crucial part of content marketing and SEO. There's a lot of complexity involved. For the sake of this guide to content marketing planning, we'll give you a whistle-stop tour. First, it's important to understand the different kinds of keywords. There are two main types that you will use in your content.

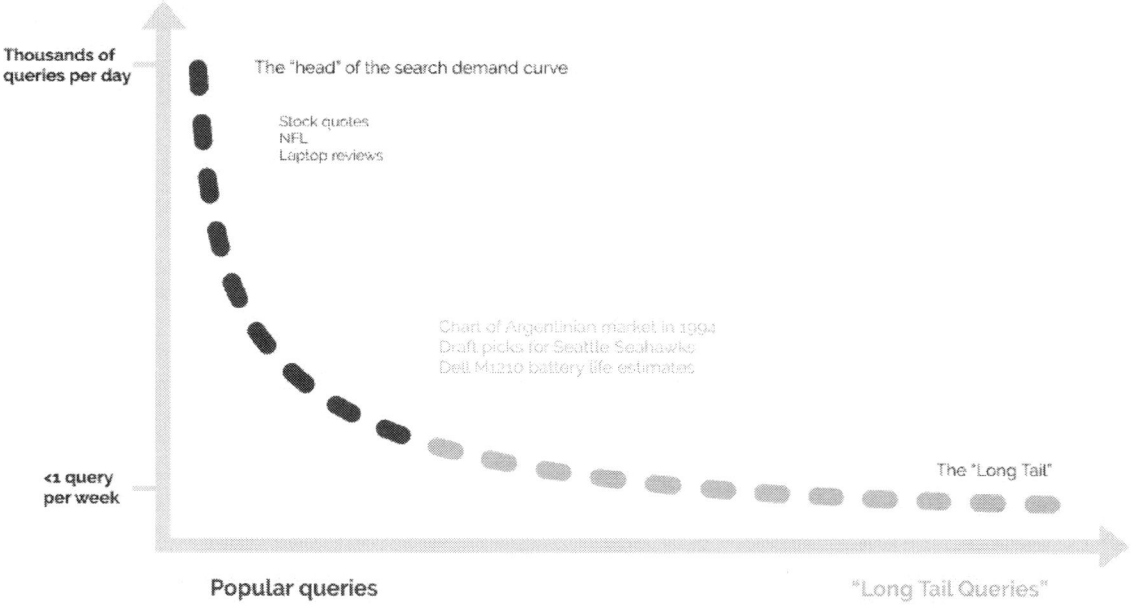

https://www.oreilly.com/library/view/the-art-of/9781449324865/ch05s02.html

Those two types are called 'head' and 'long tail' keywords. They get their names from their position on the search demand curve, as shown above. 'Head' keywords are plotted at the head of the curve. They have a high search volume, and therefore, lots of pages will compete to rank for them.

'Long tail' keywords fit within the long tail of the curve. Each keyword is specific and so searched for less frequently. That also means that competition is lower when it comes to ranking for these keywords.

There are pros and cons to focussing on either type of keyword for your content marketing. You will have to spend more time and money on your SEO to rank for head keywords. If you do rank for them, the boost to your site traffic will be significant.

It's often easier and cheaper to rank for long tail keywords. Each one you rank for will only provide a small bump in traffic. That little bump could still be valuable if your ideal customer is doing that search. To understand what we mean by that, we need to look at the customer journey.

Each customer goes through a particular journey towards buying a product. It starts with awareness of a need or an interest in a topic. At some point, they will decide they need a product. Then, they make a purchase. These are the three most important phases of the journey. At least for content marketing planning.

People searching for long tail keywords, which are buying terms, are often closer to making a purchase decision. They know what they're looking for, so their search phrases are more specific. Traffic from long tail keywords generally converts more readily to sales. Searchers using head keywords are likely to be less far along the customer journey.

Your chosen keywords and the content that you base around them should account for this. Choose a selection of head and long tail keywords. Create content optimised for each. Ensure that the content reflects the stage of the customer journey of its consumers.

Content optimised for head keywords needs to be educational and general. It must appeal to those interested in your overall niche, not only your business or product. Long tail optimised content can be a bit more salesy. It must still meet user intent, but you can pitch this at users close to making a purchase decision.

Your content marketing strategy is now starting to take shape. You know the general subjects and topics your content must address. You've also identified target keywords. Your site doesn't exist in a vacuum, though. What you need to do now is to look at the broader search landscape for your niche.

How to research the competitive landscape

It would be great if your site were the only one trying to rank on Google. That's not the case. Your business competitors will also be your competitors when it comes to ranking for relevant keywords. In many cases, other sites and pages will also be vying for the coveted spots at the top of a SERP.

You need to understand your competition. That way, you can find the best keywords to target for your content marketing strategy.

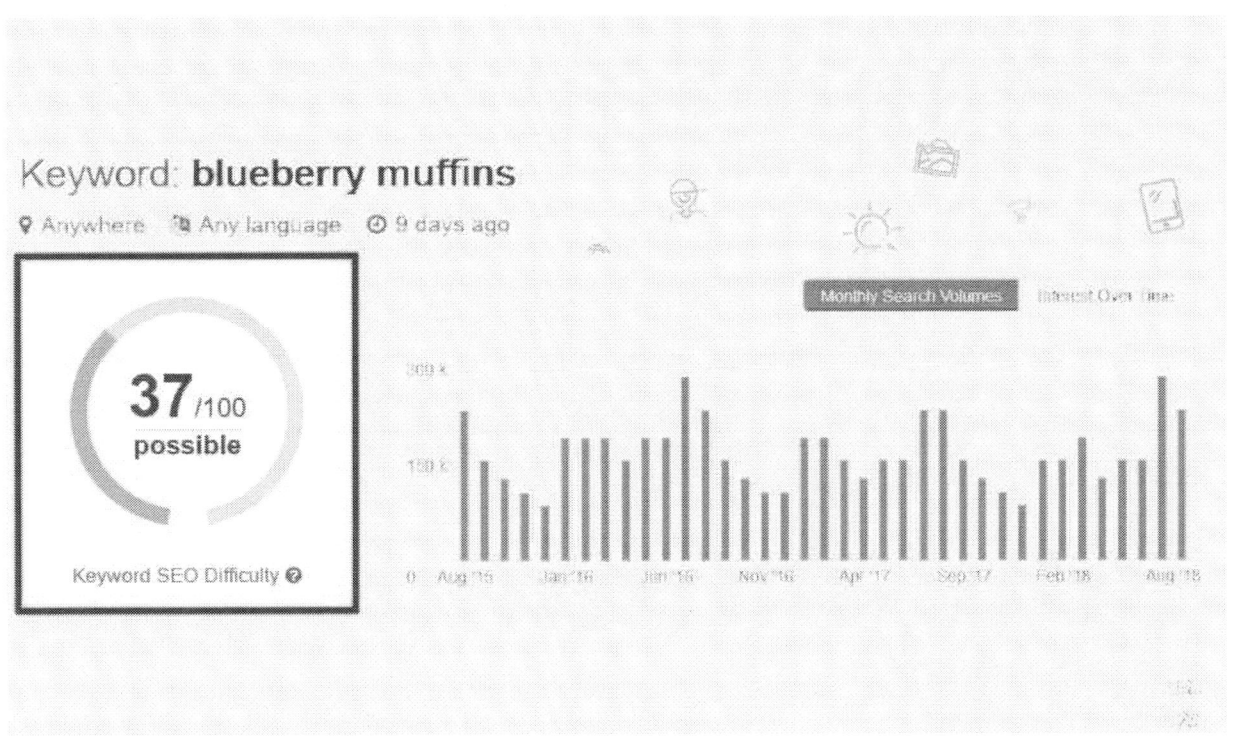

https://mangools.com/blog/what-is-keyword-seo-difficulty/

Your first port of call is to look at the difficulty score for a given keyword. Difficulty or competition is a simple score attached to a keyword. It suggests how tough it will be for you to rank highly for that keyword.

The higher the score, the more difficult it will be. The score will be a percentage from 0-100. You can find keyword difficulty scores using any one of several online tools. SEMrush, for instance, has a keyword difficulty tool.

Focus on keywords with a difficulty score of 75 or less. Any higher and it'll take so long to see a result you might end up bust. Targeting keywords with a lower keyword difficulty is far easier. As long as content optimised for it fits the interests of your audience.

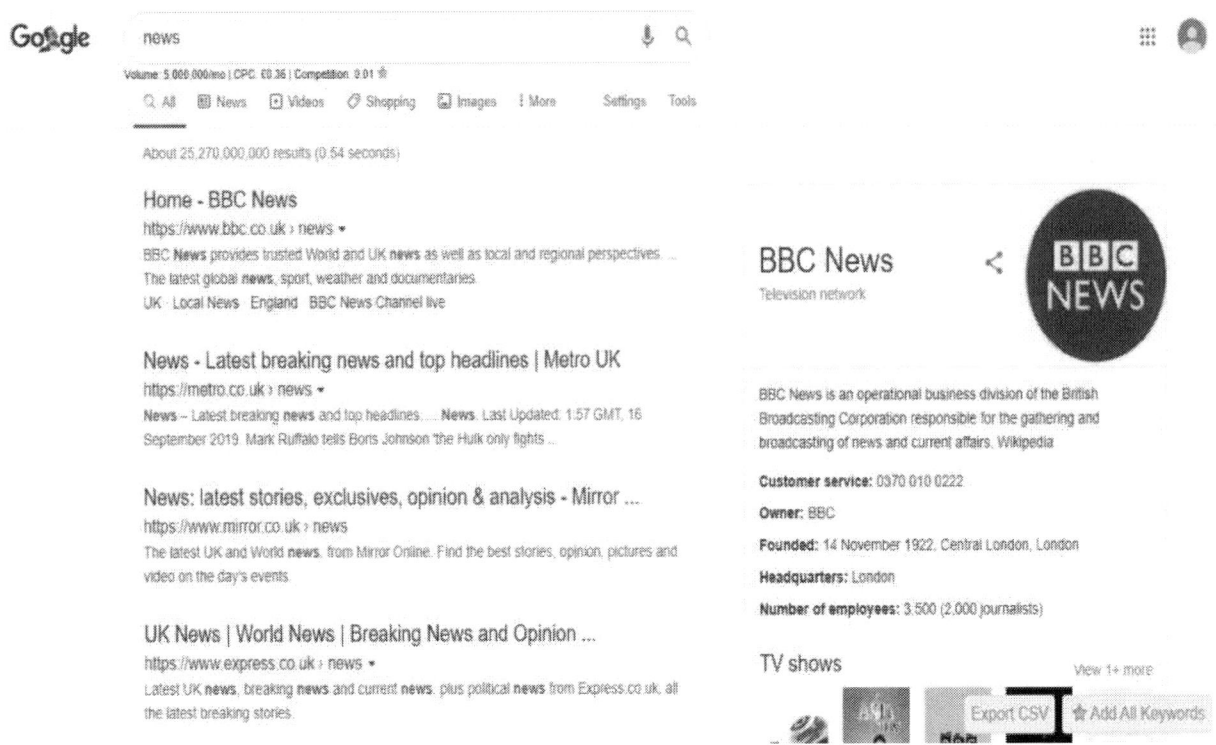

It's also worth looking at the sites already ranking on page one for a particular keyword. They're the sites you'll be competing with. Take, for instance, a SERP packed with sites with high domain authority as in the above example. It will be almost impossible to outrank those sites. You're better served focusing on a different keyword.

Tips for good online copywriting

That's almost it for this section on good content marketing planning. You've built your customer persona and found relevant keywords. That means it's time to start producing your content. Before you do, you might find it helpful to learn a little more about what makes for good online copywriting.

You need your written content to capture and keep readers' attention. There are a few things to keep in mind to ensure this. First of all, your content must be as easy to read as possible. Even if you're discussing complex topics, try to keep both sentences and paragraphs as short as you can.

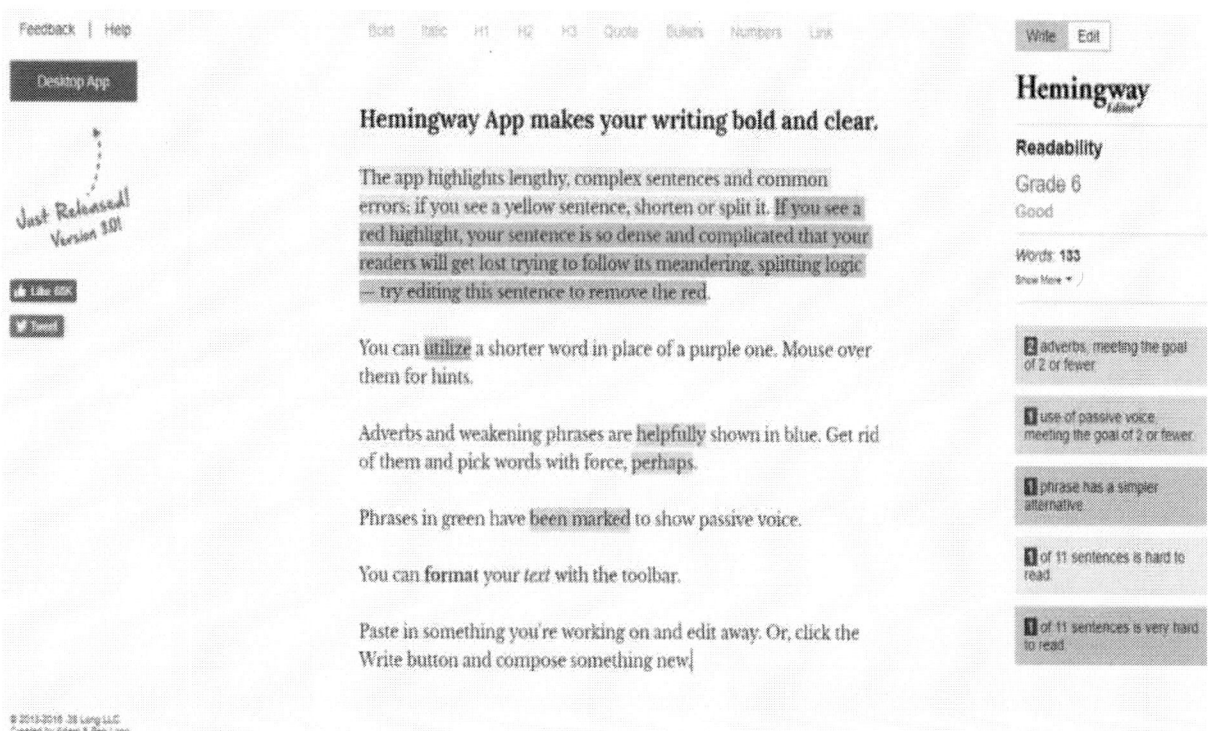

Free tools are also available to assess the readability of your content. The above image is a screenshot from Hemingway. It's a tool that gives your writing a grade based on its Flesch readability score. The Flesch Score shows you how easy something you've written is to read. The tool also offers suggestions to help you improve your content's score.

Aside from readability, the tempo is something else to consider. You can make your content more engaging by mixing up the tempo. Short, choppy sentences can create urgency at the right points. Longer sentences can then be mixed in to keep things interesting.

Conclusion

That's all there is to it. We did say that the content marketing strategy was easier than it sounded. In a nutshell, it involves just three main elements.

First, you identify your target audience. These are the people that you want to target with your content. It's vital to always keep that in mind. Your content is to help them, not your site's SEO. That's a nice bonus.

Once you've defined your audience, you find the topics and keywords to fit — keywords that will help your site to rank and to gain more traffic. More importantly, keywords that fit within the content which is useful to your audience.

Finally, you assess what your competition is doing. That helps you find the keywords worth targeting. With all that info collected, you will have finished your content marketing planning. You're now ready to create top-class content that will get your site more traffic.

Once you have done this, you're going to need to disseminate the content you've created to a wider audience. One way to do this is via social media which we'll cover in the last section of this chapter, another is guest posting. There is a right way and a wrong way to guest posting, but done right, it can provide valuable backlinks to your website while at the same time building your authority as an industry expert. We'll cover finding the right sites and content, adding keyword-rich backlinks and how to pitch to editors successfully in this section.

1.4: Essential guide to guest posting

Building brand authority and getting more traffic are both crucial. They can be the difference between success and failure for any SaaS business. Anything which can help you do both is an absolute godsend. Guest posting is a prime example.

By sharing insights on high authority blogs in your niche, you can do your business a world of good. You'll start to establish yourself as an expert in your field. You'll also get some tasty backlinks and a nice bump in referral traffic.

Those benefits only come if you know how to guest blog the right way. Spamming any and every site with low-quality posts does more harm than good. You need to learn how to get the right content featured in the right places. The following is a guide that will set you on the right path.

How to choose what sites to guest post on

Your first step towards learning how to guest blog is deciding where you want to post. This stage is crucial, as it can make or break the whole guest posting process. You need to find locations for your guest posts that are going to give you the best. Those are the blogs or sites which can offer valuable backlinks. Alongside considerable referral traffic.

There are a few different ways to approach this. One of the best is to take a leaf out of your competitors' books. If you're doing your keyword research right, you'll already know about competitor research. To aid your guest posting, you need to take things a step further.

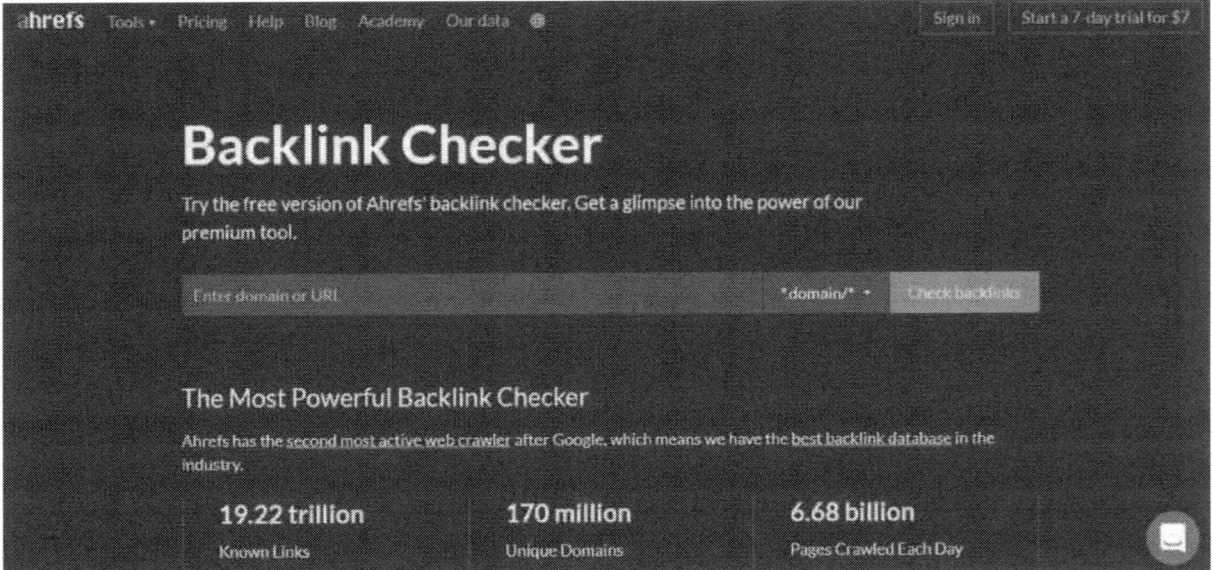

Find one of your top competitors in your niche. Take their domain URL and pop it into the Ahrefs backlink checker. That will give you a full list of the site's backlinks. You'll be able to see every page which links to your competitor's website. This includes any links they may have from blog posts. Just like that, you can identify where your top competitor is guest posting.

Just because your competitor's guest posting with a particular blog, doesn't mean you should. You need to take your list of potential guest blogging locations and check that each of them is worth your time. You can do that by looking at three characteristics of the blog in question.

First, you need to see that the blog or site gets enough traffic to be worth your time. Ahrefs can once again help you with this. What you're ideally looking for is that the blog or site gets at least 5,000 visits per month from organic search. That way, you know that enough people will see a guest post to deliver some meaty referral traffic.

The next metric you need to consider is the Domain Authority (DA). DA is a score developed by Moz for predicting how well a site may rank on Google SERPs. It's essential to know the DA of a website you may guest post to, as it suggests the value to your site of any backlinks you may get.

Google is only interested in links from high authority sites in your niche. DA scores range from 0-100. There are lots of free tools, including the MozBar, which you can use to find a site's DA. If you find it to be less than 50, take it off your list of places to post to and move on to your next option.

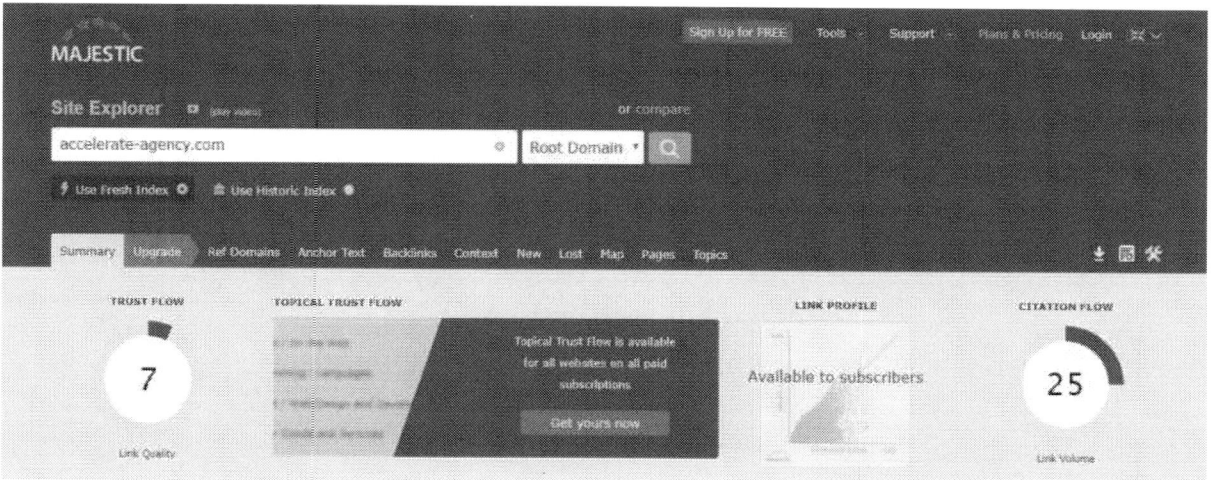

Digital Marketing Agency Bristol | Results Driven Digital Marketing

The DA of a site covers the 'high authority' part for Google, but what about 'in your niche'. That's where Majestic's Trust Flow comes in. This metric shows you the proximity of any page to a particular topic. It can tell you how relevant a site or blog is to your niche.

Head to Majestic and find the Trust Flow score for a prospective guest posting location. You should persevere with any location with a rating of 20+. Now that you've got your shortlist of sites to guest post on, you need to start thinking about what you're going to post.

How to come up with content ideas

What you need first from any guest post is for it to be accepted by your chosen blog or site. That means coming up with an idea for content which the site is going to love. Your first step should be to dig deep into the material already live on the blog. See if you can find any related topics or subjects that aren't well covered.

After that, take a look at some of the blog's competitors. Find posts they have – and which have done well – that your target blog hasn't got a version of. An excellent way to find any blog's most popular posts is by using BuzzSumo.

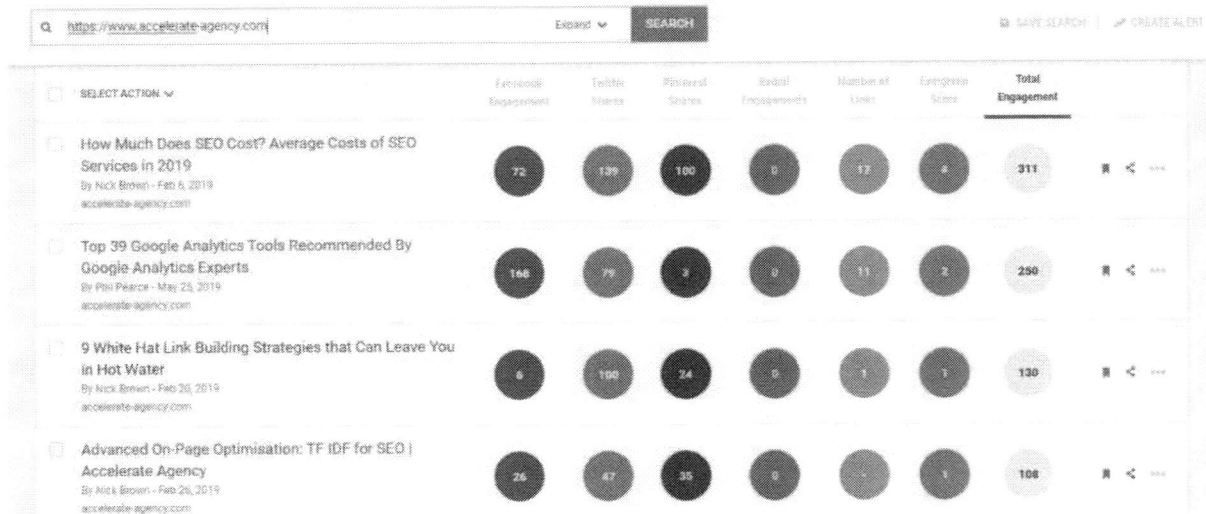

All you need to do is to pop the URL of a site or blog into the tool. It will then show you that domain's most popular content. What you're looking for are the best performing posts your target blog hasn't already got covered. They're the posts you can create a new and improved version of for them.

With content ideas in mind, you can then start thinking about keywords. Use Keywords Everywhere to ID phrases related to the content ideas you've come up with. You'll then be able to use metrics like volume and competition to choose the phrases to target in your content.

Where & how to insert your keywords

You're now nearly ready to start reaching out to the sites where you want to guest post. Before we get to that, it's important to mention how to guest blog in a way to get you the best results. The main benefit of guest posting is to get valuable backlinks to some of your own site's best content.

Backlinks from relevant, high authority sites make a huge difference. They can help the SERP ranking of any piece of content. Plenty of research has shown a direct correlation. Including a major study by Backlinko[1], which has the following results:

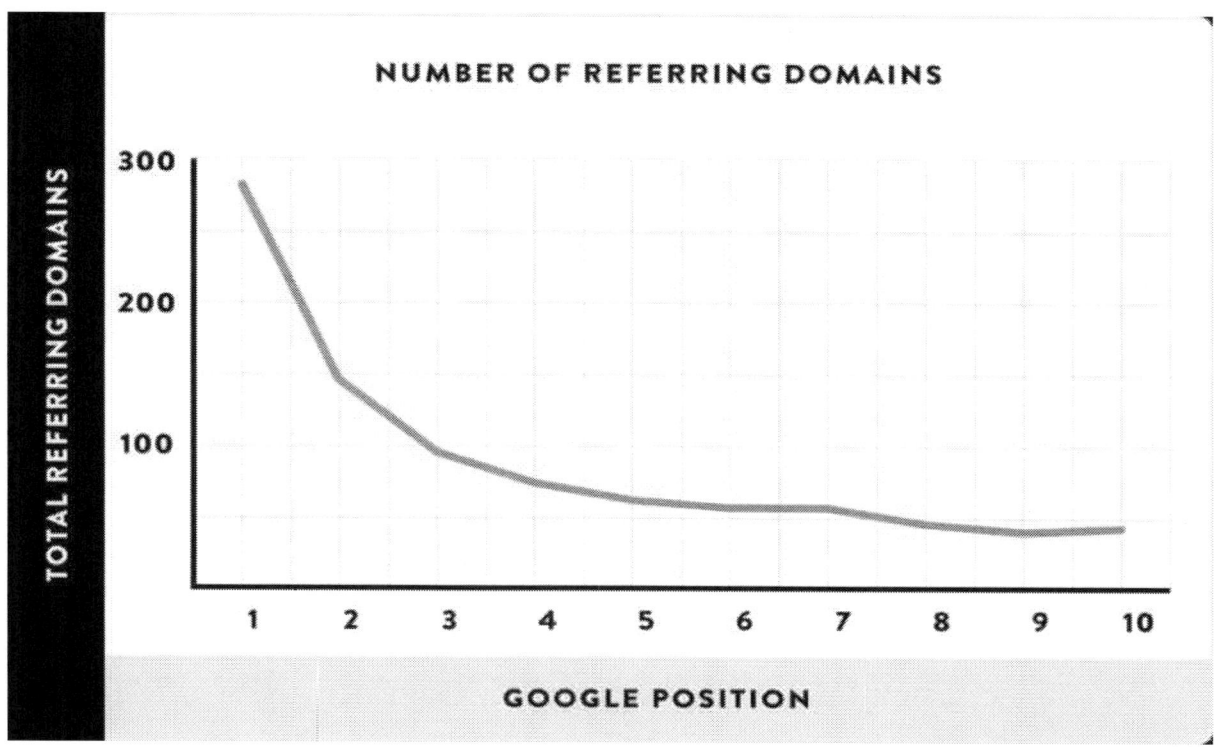

When you write guest posts, include links back to your content. Be careful not to go over the top, however. Most sites will be fine with you including one or two links to relevant content. Try to make sure that the anchor text for those links is helpful to your content.

Google uses anchor text from backlinks as another way to assess what pages are about. As much as possible, the keywords you want your content to rank for should be reflected by the anchor text you use. That way, it helps give Google an extra nudge as to the relevance of your content to that keyword.

Most blogs will also ask you to include a bio at the end of a guest post. You can feature a self-promoting link in that bio. It's the only place where you can use one, so make the most of it. Ensure its anchor text is a real money phrase for the link destination.

How to use Linkedin to connect with people

With target blogs found and content ideas developed, you're ready and raring to go with your guest posts. The only trouble is, you don't have the go-ahead to post to any blog other than your own. You need to start connecting with owners and decision-makers of the sites where you want to guest post.

Some of the biggest blogs have forms or pages on their site for submitting guest post pitches. In most cases, you'll need to do the legwork yourself. One of the best ways of reaching the right people is by using LinkedIn. The social network is great for all kinds of professional outreach. Pitching guest posts to editors is no exception.

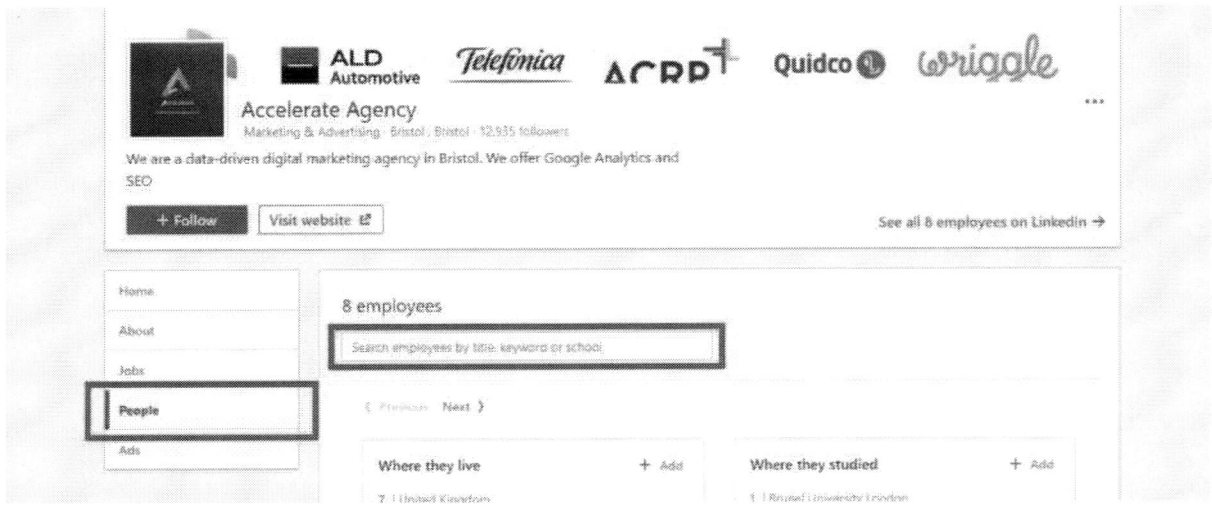

Your first step is to go to LinkedIn and search the name of the relevant company or site. Once you've found the company, head to the 'People' section of their profile. You can then search their employees by job title or another keyword.

Searching for 'editor', 'writer', 'blog' or something similar should reveal the person to whom you need to speak. Send them an invite to connect and then wait for them to respond.

How to pitch to editors

Assuming a blog's editor does agree to connect with you on LinkedIn, you're then ready to pitch. What you want to do is to get the editor's attention without being too pushy. Send them a friendly but formal pitch message, in a similar style to the below:

Hi [Name],

I'm a big admirer of your blog. I've been reading and commenting on your posts for a while. [Example of where you've commented if you have.]

I'm reaching out because I think I could contribute some really interesting guest posts.

From reading your posts, I've noticed that there may be some topics I could cover for you. I think your other readers might find them interesting:

[Possible Title] [Possible Title] [Possible Title]

I've worked with other blogs in the past in a similar capacity, including [Example 1], [Example 2] and [Example 3]. It'd be great if you want to check out my posts there, to see the quality I can deliver.

Many thanks,

[Your Name]

That sort of template is perfect. It doesn't take the editor too long to read but tells them everything they need to know. You're showing them how much you value their blog and your expertise. You've also done lots of the guest posting work yourself, by coming up with possible titles.

Guest posting: share the love & reap the rewards

Follow all the advice outlined above, and you'll have the perfect guest posting strategy. You know where to aim your guest posts and which locations to avoid. You can generate the ideal content ideas and know the best way to get editors to accept them.

That's everything you need when it comes to how to guest blog correctly. All that's left is to put in the work. You'll be happy you did when you start to see those all-important backlinks come in. Not to mention the improvements in ranking and site traffic that they'll help to deliver.

We previously mentioned an obvious way to get your message out to a wider audience is to use social media. Social media has become critical to content marketing strategy. The next section will cover the best social media channels for a SaaS business to use and why.

1.5: Best social media channels

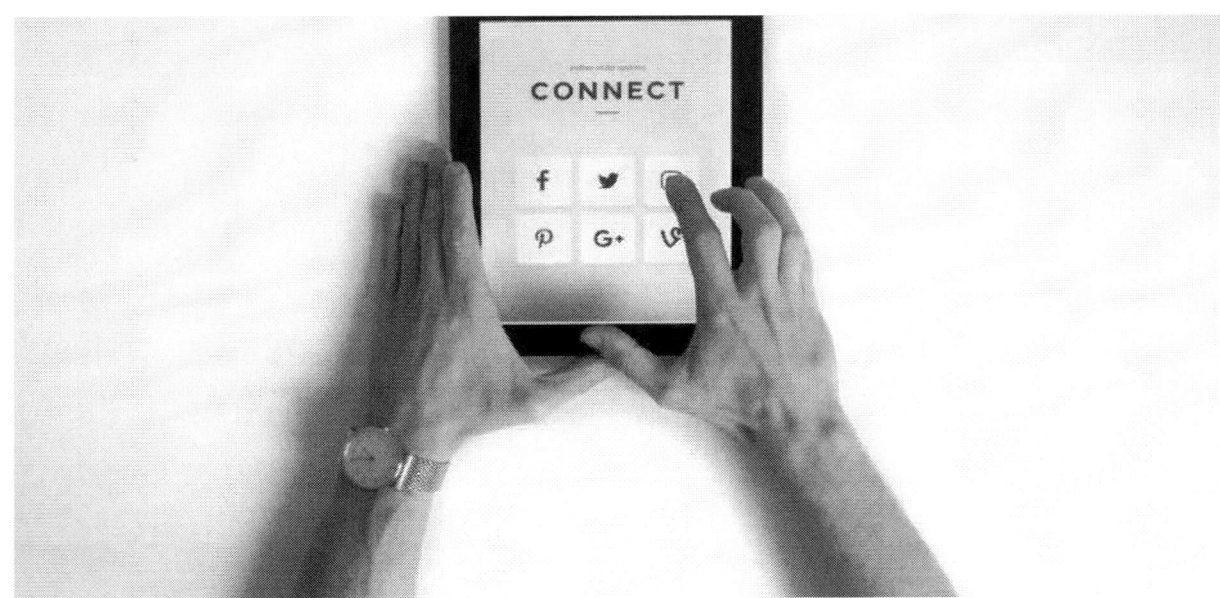

It's critical for any business to get to grips with social media. The reach of social networks in modern society is extraordinary. Worldwide, there were 2.48 billion social network users[1] in 2017, and the number is growing. Firms in all niches simply must make use of a tool that reaches such a broad audience.

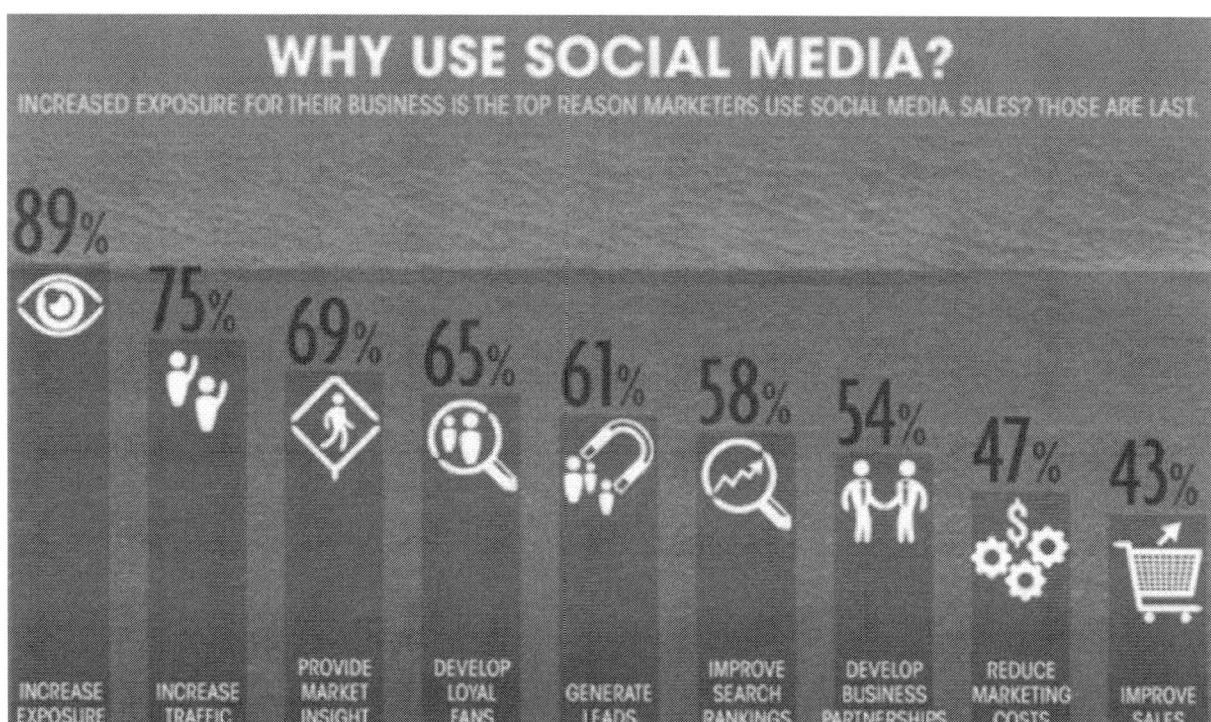

https://creately.com/blog/marketing/social-media-in-brand-building/

Many companies have started to wise up to the potential of social media marketing. Content shared via social networks can do a great job attracting direct traffic to your site. What many people don't understand is that you can also use social media to support your overall SEO. Correct use of the right social networks can also help to build your site's organic traffic.

This section will point you to the four best social media channels to use for SEO. For each, we'll offer some hints and tips regarding social media SEO best practice. Before that, though, it's essential to look at the exact relationship between social media and SEO.

Understanding social media & SEO

Google's algorithms take many things into account when ranking different websites. The various aspects that the search engine considers are called ranking factors. The social media following of a site or the level of social media engagement with the site's content is not one of them. Social media SEO is not as simple as getting more followers and so more organic search traffic.

The judicious use of social media supports your SEO in different ways. Two of the best-understood examples regard backlinks and branded traffic. With a more substantial social media following, sites are better placed to get more backlinks.

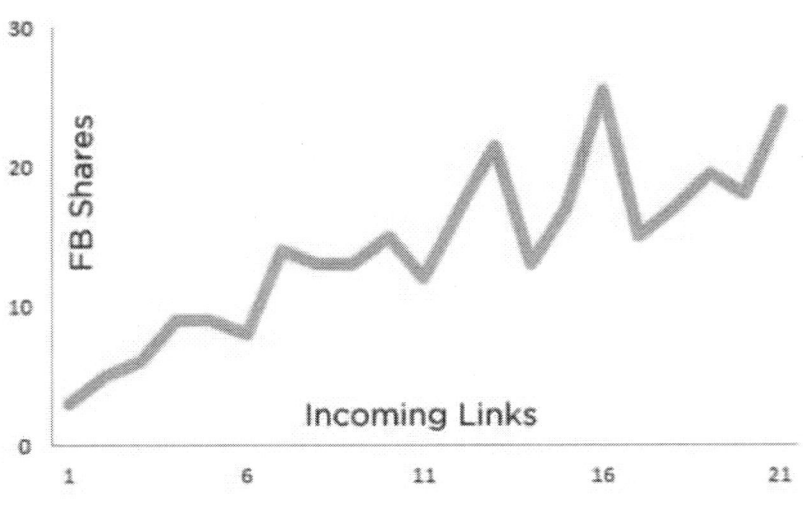

https://monitorbacklinks.com/blog/seo/relation-between-social-media-shares-and-backlinks

The relationship between backlinks and social media following is logical. Brands with more social media followers can share their content with more people. The more people who see a piece of content, the more likely one amongst them will want to link to it from their site. The importance of backlinks as an SEO ranking factor is well-known.

How social media and branded traffic relate is even more straightforward. Branded traffic is traffic to your site from a search that features your brand or company name. Having a more significant social media following means you'll get more branded traffic. Your social channels get your name out to a broader audience, and thus more of them will search for you on Google.

Branded traffic can also have a beneficial impact on your site's ranking for non-branded keywords. Take, for example, a SaaS business that gets a lot of branded traffic from searches for 'brand name SaaS'.

Google will start to notice this traffic. After a while, the search engine will recognise that the site is useful for searchers interested in SaaS. The site's ranking for 'SaaS' as a unique keyword may then start to improve.

Those are just two examples of the general relationship between social media and SEO. There are lots of ways that social media can support your SEO. Which, though, are the best channels for social media SEO, and how can you make the most of them?

The best channels for social media SEO

If you're going to use social media to support your site's SEO, there are a few different avenues to explore. The following are four of the best channels for social media SEO:

1. LinkedIn
2. Facebook
3. Twitter
4. Pinterest

Let's look at how best to use each of them to build backlinks, boost branded traffic, and otherwise bolster your SEO.

Using LinkedIn

You know LinkedIn: it's that social network you signed up to when you were job hunting and then forgot about it. At least, that's how lots of people think of the platform. In reality, it's a convenient tool for connecting with businesses and professionals in your niche. It's also a channel you can use in a few ways to support your SEO.

LinkedIn is particularly useful for getting high authority backlinks to your site. The general process for doing so is pretty straightforward:

- Build up your LinkedIn following
- Share content from your website via LinkedIn
- Encourage further engagement with that content
- Wait for LinkedIn contents to link back to your content from their sites

Building up your LinkedIn following is a slow and steady process. You'll need to use the platform's advanced search feature to find and reach out to professionals in your field.

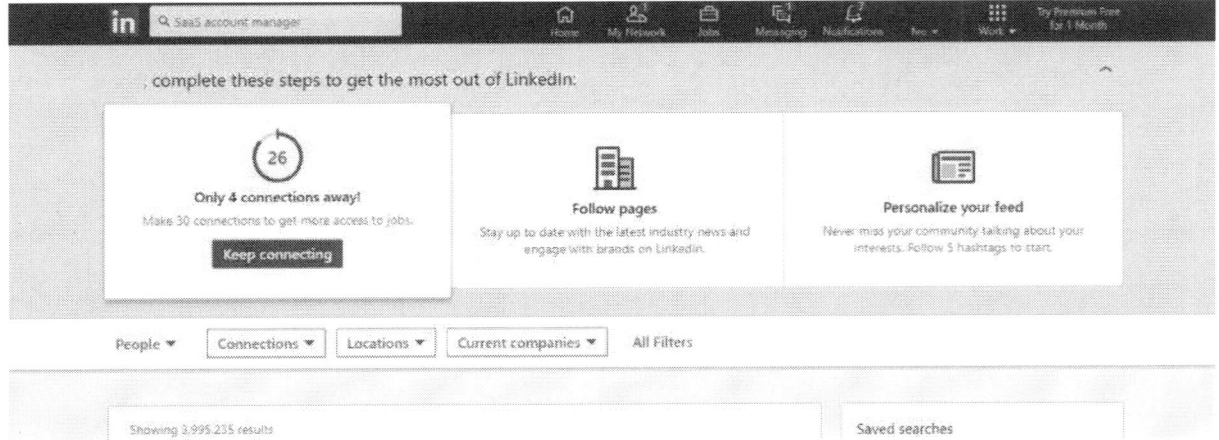

By searching for a job title specific to your niche, you can find loads of likely candidates. Try to send out contact requests to new people regularly to keep growing your following.

Sharing site content via LinkedIn is somewhat idiosyncratic. Those behind LinkedIn don't like people using the platform for direct marketing. As such, they won't share updates with external links in them as widely as other updates.

When you first publish an update pointing followers to a page or post, don't feature a link. Wait a couple of minutes and then edit the post to add the link. That gets around LinkedIn's reticence to share updates, including links.

Once you've shared an update, try to generate some buzz and engagement. Ask followers to comment about your content or even ask them a direct question. That way, they'll get more interested in the content and are more likely to think about linking to it.

Using Facebook

It may seem odd to suggest using Facebook for SEO, or in fact, for business in general. The platform doesn't have the same professional reach as LinkedIn. It is, however, a channel with a vast number of users. At the end of 2018, Facebook still had well over two billion active users.

The best way for modern firms to engage with those Facebook users is via Facebook groups. Groups are now the element of the platform with which users engage most. You can take advantage of this by building a group for your business or brand.

Facebook groups are an excellent way for firms to build a sense of community among followers. They also give you an extra outlet to share content with consumers more likely to find it useful. If you pitch the content right, they then might even share it more widely. That's where you can get the backlinks and the branded traffic that are key to social media SEO.

Using Twitter

Twitter is another channel that's great for sharing your business's content en masse. Getting that content seen far and wide is a great first step to earning those valuable backlinks. It's also an excellent way to get your company's name out there to a broader audience. Using Twitter for social media SEO is a straightforward three-step process:

1. Create great content to share
2. Produce Tweets that are certain to get noticed
3. Use social amplification tools to spread your message further

If you're serious about SEO, you should already be producing great content. Engaging keyword optimised posts and articles are vital to effective content marketing. All you need to make sure of is that what you share with your Twitter followers will interest that particular audience.

Your next step is to think about how you're going to share the content. Any Tweet you put out with a link to a post or page needs to capture the attention. The Tweet has to stop a Twitter follower from scrolling on by.

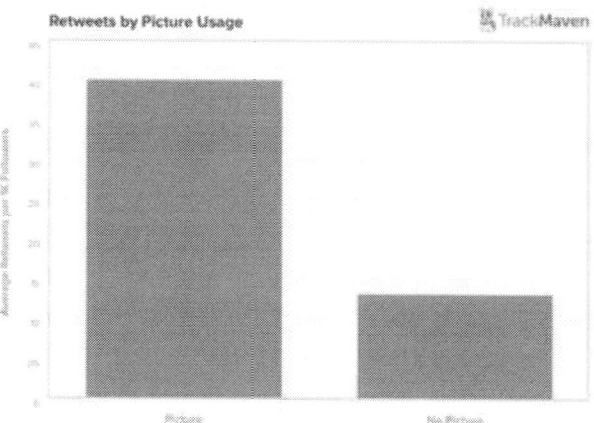

https://www.socialmediaexaminer.com/get-tweets-noticed/

Images and other visuals are great for catching the attention. Tweets with a visual element typically get far more engagement than those with only text. Questions, polls, and other interactive features are also great for getting Tweets noticed.

Once you've got your content and your Tweet, you need to ensure they get seen by as many people as possible. Social amplification channels like Viral Content Bee can help you boost the reach of a Tweet.

Using Pinterest

Pinterest is a final channel to consider for social media SEO. The very visual social network is growing in popularity and can help you reach a different demographic.

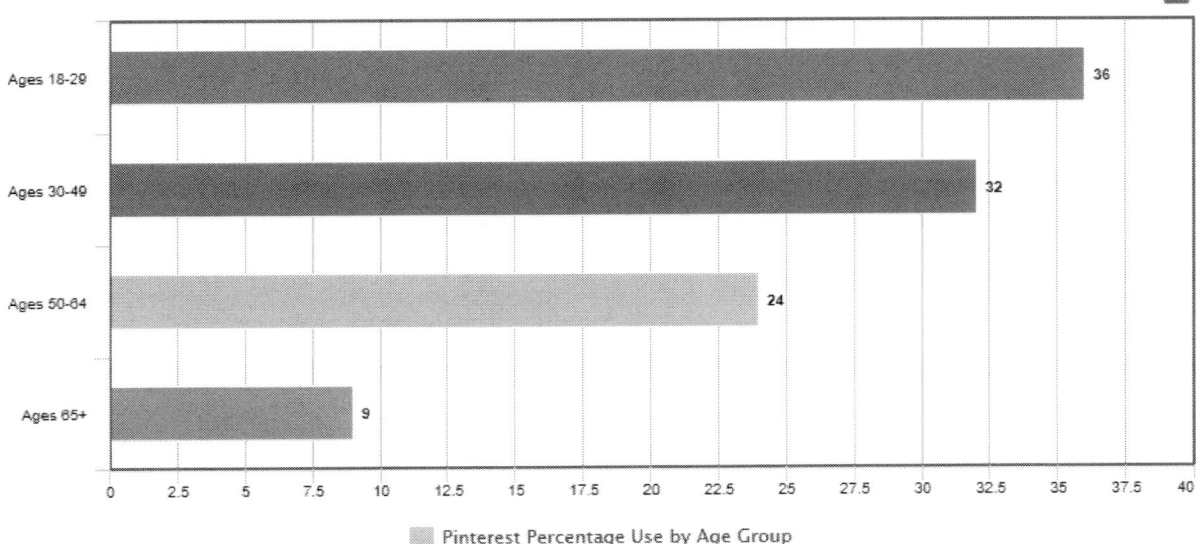

https://www.clearmessagemedia.org/pinterest-bar-graph/

The one downside to using Pinterest to support your SEO is that it takes a good chunk of time and effort. To improve your reach on the platform, you need to be as active as possible. Pinterest rewards active users. The platform makes those users' content visible to a wider variety of other users.

You also need to produce a steady stream of engaging content. It's your content that you want users to notice and 'repin' to get your name out there. An excellent way to improve your chances of getting your Pinterest content noticed is by being experimental. Try sharing content with different images and pins to see what works best for you.

Boost traffic via smart social media SEO

Google doesn't measure your social media following. Nor does the search engine assess how engaged those followers are. Social media presence isn't an SEO ranking factor. You can use social media, though, to support your wider SEO efforts. Sharing content and engaging with audiences on social networks is undoubtedly worthwhile. It can help you gain valuable backlinks and branded traffic, both of which will help boost your SEO.

Social media SEO is similar, regardless of the channel you use. You aim to connect with as many people as possible, and to share your content with them. You're then hoping they may share the content with their contacts and help you reach a broader audience. The guidance included here should help you do that for four of the best SEO social media channels.

Driving traffic to your website is only one part of your marketing strategy. Once they are on the website, you'll want to convert them into paying customers. The next chapter will cover ways to engage your website visitors and encourage them to sign up for free resources like email or webinars which will give them a chance to get to know and trust you. We'll start with the basics of the customer journey to show how retargeting can help your business convert customers that already know something about you, or in other words, are 'warm' prospects.

Chapter 2: How to get paying customers

At the start of this ebook, we talked about how getting customers to your website is critical to your business success in a competitive landscape. That's why we dedicated two chapters to building traffic and getting paying customers.

This chapter continues with two other methods to drive traffic and engage customers: retargeting adverts and affiliate marketing. Once you have made customers aware of your expertise and driven traffic to the website, you will want to encourage visitors to the site to sign up for email campaigns and take part in webinars, converting them into prospects.

In the next section, we will start with retargeting adverts. Retargeting can be a valuable method of advertising. The potential customer has already shown some interest in your service by visiting your website or liking & following you on social media. This makes them a warmer prospect than someone who has never heard of you before but views your PPC advert on a search engine.

2.1: How to run retargeting ads

Ever visited a website, started to fill out a form, or added a product to your cart, but then left? Chances are, you have. The average web form or eCommerce shopping cart abandonment rate is estimated at close to 70%. That means seven in ten people leave sites before doing what site owners want them to.

When you have abandoned a site, have you ever noticed how often you start seeing ads for that site? They might pop up on the banners of pages you visit or in your social media. It's no coincidence. It's a marketing tactic called retargeting, which the site you visited is running.

Ask a digital marketer, and they'll tell you that retargeting is one of the most effective ways for a website to improve conversions. That's why it's one of the first avenues a SaaS company should explore when looking to get more paying customers.

This brief guide to retargeting ads will help you get started. It will explain why social retargeting is so important and so effective. It will then explain when you might choose to use social media retargeting. Finally, we'll talk you step-by-step through the perfect Facebook retargeting strategy.

What is retargeting?

Before we get into why retargeting matters and how to do it, it's worth looking at the basics; starting with what retargeting is. At the basic level, retargeting is when you try to re-engage with someone who visited your site. Somebody who's shown an interest in what you offer but hasn't yet converted into a customer.

The process of retargeting lets you focus your marketing efforts on a warm audience. An audience that you know has at least some interest in your products or services. This guide is going to focus on social retargeting, specifically using Facebook.

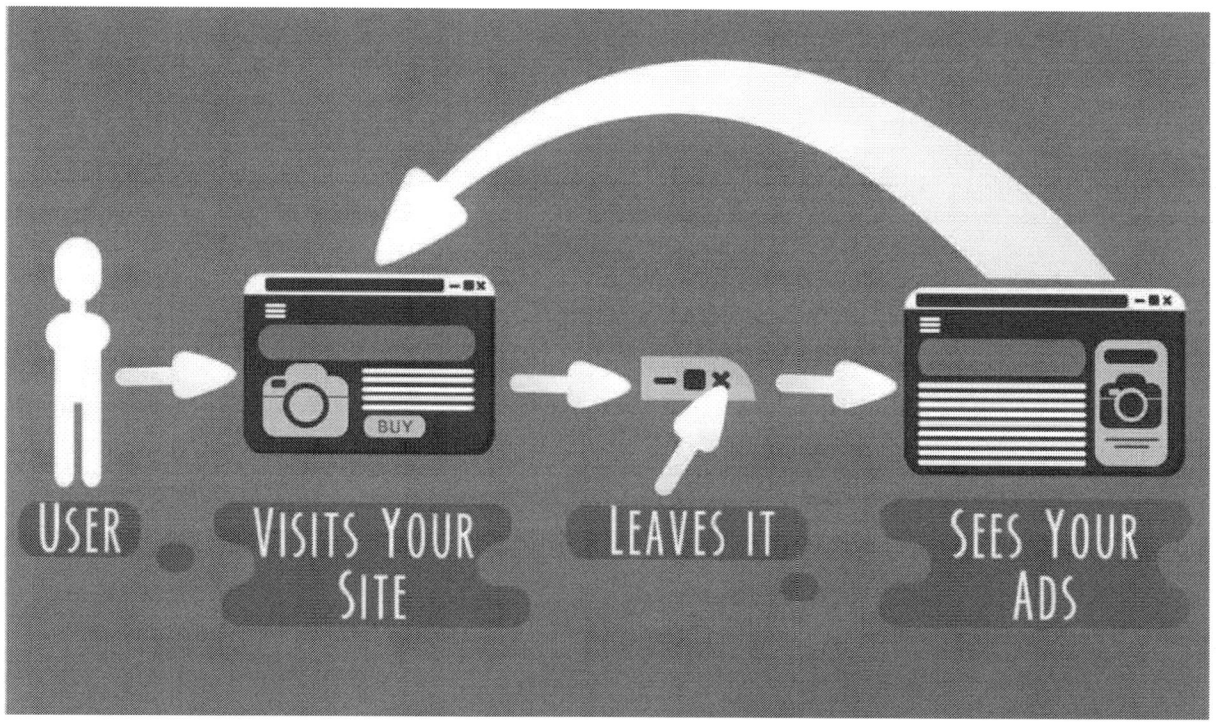

https://www.singlegrain.com/marketing-funnels/why-retargeting-is-absolutely-essential-for-any-marketing-funnel/

Later, we'll talk you through the simple steps you can take to set up your Facebook retargeting strategy. First, let's look at the basics of how Facebook retargeting works. A short snippet of code installed on your site is all that's needed to get the ball rolling. That code places a cookie in the browser of your site visitors.

Information is then sent back to Facebook about pages that website users visit. You can use this information to set up specific retargeting ads designed to convert different people. You can tailor the ads according to what individuals did when they visited your site. Before we get to how you can do it, though, let's talk about why you want to.

Why social retargeting is important

As we mentioned at the outset, website abandonment rates are very high. Most visitors to your pages will leave without completing the action you want from them. Whether that action is to buy a product, register for a service, or join your email list.

Social retargeting gives you a way to target those people. Not only does it provide a method of targeting those people, but it's also proven to be effective. Connectio shared some compelling stats[1] about how effective retargeting can be:
- Three of four customers notice retargeted ads
- On Facebook, retargeted ads are 76% more likely to be clicked than regular ads
- Retargeting ads lead to a 1046% increase in branded search

There are a few reasons why social retargeting does deliver such good results. Firstly, it's a channel where you know the target audience is at least somewhat interested. The people you aim the ads at have already visited your site. It might be that they only need a slight nudge or reminder to come back.

Even if those you retarget are farther from buying, you still aren't starting from scratch. It's not like content marketing targeting long tail keywords for organic search traffic. They know something about your company and what you offer. That means a much better ROI for retargeting than many marketing alternatives.

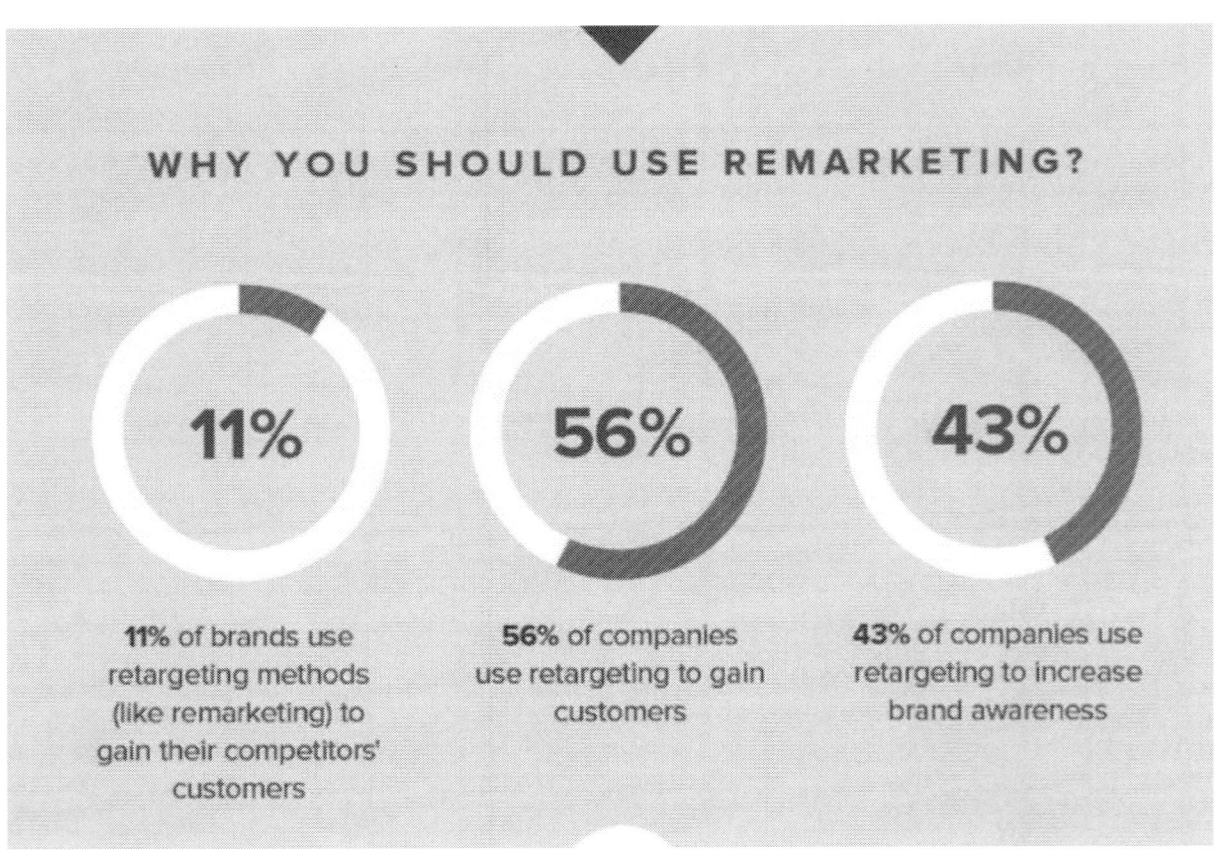

https://neilpatel.com/blog/a-simple-yet-effective-guide-to-generating-sales-from-remarketing/

Another reason to think about retargeting is because of the different options it can open up. A good Facebook retargeting strategy is more than hitting site visitors with generic ads. You can tailor what people see according to what they did on your site. We'll talk at length about the applications of this below.

One other thing that Facebook retargeting can lead to is the creation of lookalike audiences. A lookalike audience is a group of Facebook users who share key characteristics. Not only with each other but also with your existing customers or site visitors. If you create it correctly, a lookalike audience will be a long list of your ideal customers.

Assuming you have a Facebook business account, it's easy to create lookalike audiences:
1. Head to 'Audiences' in your account
2. Click 'Create Audience' and choose the 'Lookalike Audience' alternative
3. Choose your source. It makes sense for this to be the custom audience you create for your retargeting
4. Choose the nation or nations from which you want to draw your lookalike audience
5. Select the desired audience size using the slider
6. Click 'Create Audience', and your list of prospective customers will be ready in a matter of hours

You might by now be convinced of the importance of a good Facebook retargeting strategy. If not, perhaps looking at some real-world examples of when retargeting can work will win you over.

When would you use social media retargeting?

Social media is an increasingly useful tool for marketing. There are lots of ways that businesses in all different niches can use it. Many firms now use social networks for things as varied as sales prospecting and SEO. Retargeting is a great way to use social media to improve your website's conversions.

As a SaaS business, there are many examples of times retargeting may prove invaluable. Take, for instance, if you're looking to promote a particular piece of content on your site. You may have produced a fantastic blog post that you know will wow anyone who sees it. Social media retargeting can help you to get your post seen by a wider audience.

By following the instructions you'll find below, you can set up a retargeting campaign with that aim in mind. You might choose to target any site visitors who've previously viewed one of your blog posts. Your ad can then tell them that you've produced some juicy new content for them to read.

https://swiped.co/file/frankkern-facebook-retargeting/

Retargeting is also great for persuading people to join a webinar or sign up for something else you offer. The above example shows how this can work in practice. By knowing that someone has been on your site, you can address them more directly. You can thank them for checking out your content and then sell them on what else you offer.

Whatever the exact aim of your retargeting, it often pays to include an incentive in your ads. Some of the best retargeting ads tempt their targets with a specific reward. You might, for instance, run a special offer only for those who see the ads. Alternatively, you could offer the targets of the ads a special content upgrade.

How to set up a Facebook retargeting campaign

To get started with Facebook retargeting, you need a Facebook Ads Manager account. If you're active in promoting your firm through social media, you should already have this up and running.

Log in to your account and then head on over to Facebook Ads Manager. From there, you can take the first step toward retargeting. That first step is to create a custom audience made up of visitors to your website. They're the Facebook users who will be going to see your retargeting ads.

Creating a custom audience

Once you've accessed your Ads Manager account, you need to go to the 'Audiences' section. If it's your first time creating an audience, you'll see the following page:

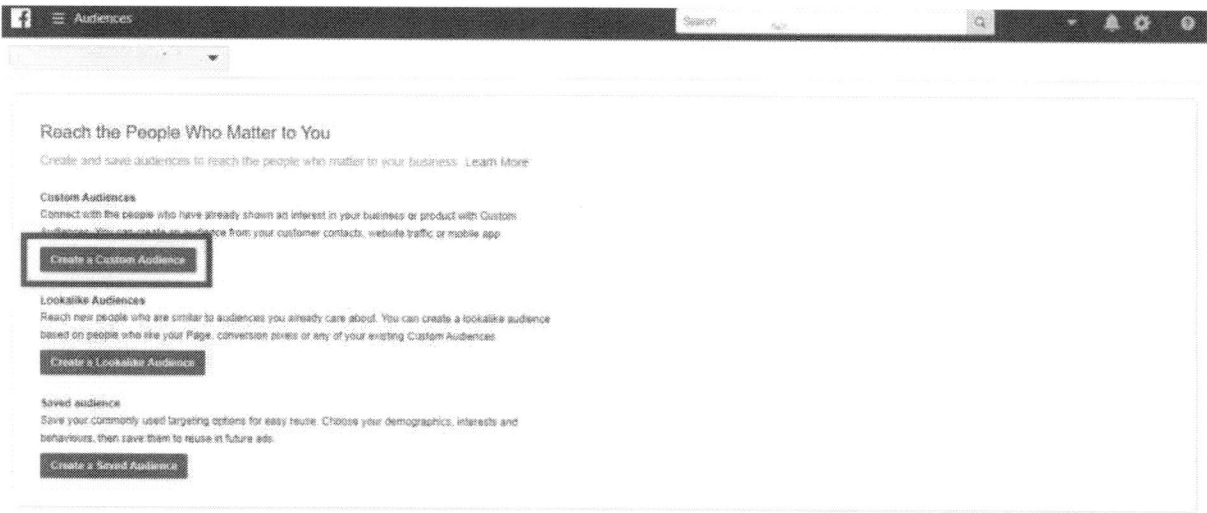

From that page, click the 'Create Custom Audience' button. If you've already created audiences, the same option can be found on the 'Create Audience' drop-down menu.

On the next page, choose the 'Website Traffic' option, as shown below:

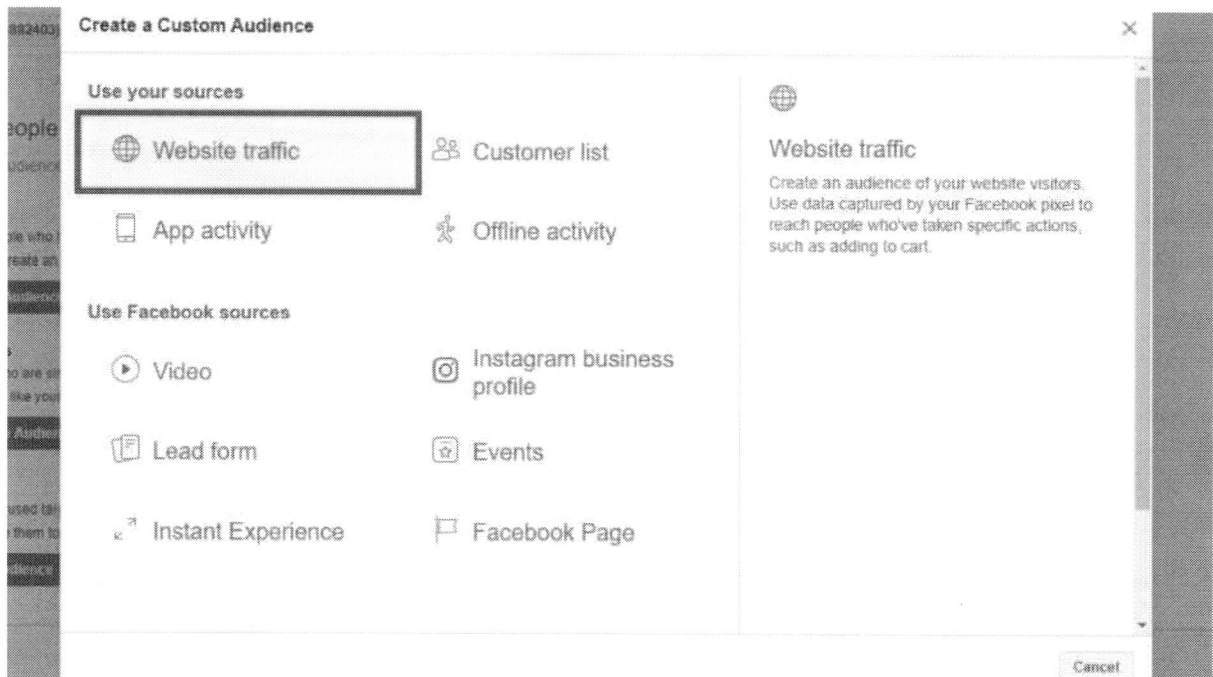

If you don't already have a Facebook Pixel, you'll then be prompted to create one. The Facebook Pixel is the snippet of code that puts a cookie in the browser of your site visitors. You need to have the pixel set up for Custom Audiences and retargeting ads to work. In the same way, as you need to add a Google Analytics tracking code to your site for that platform to work.

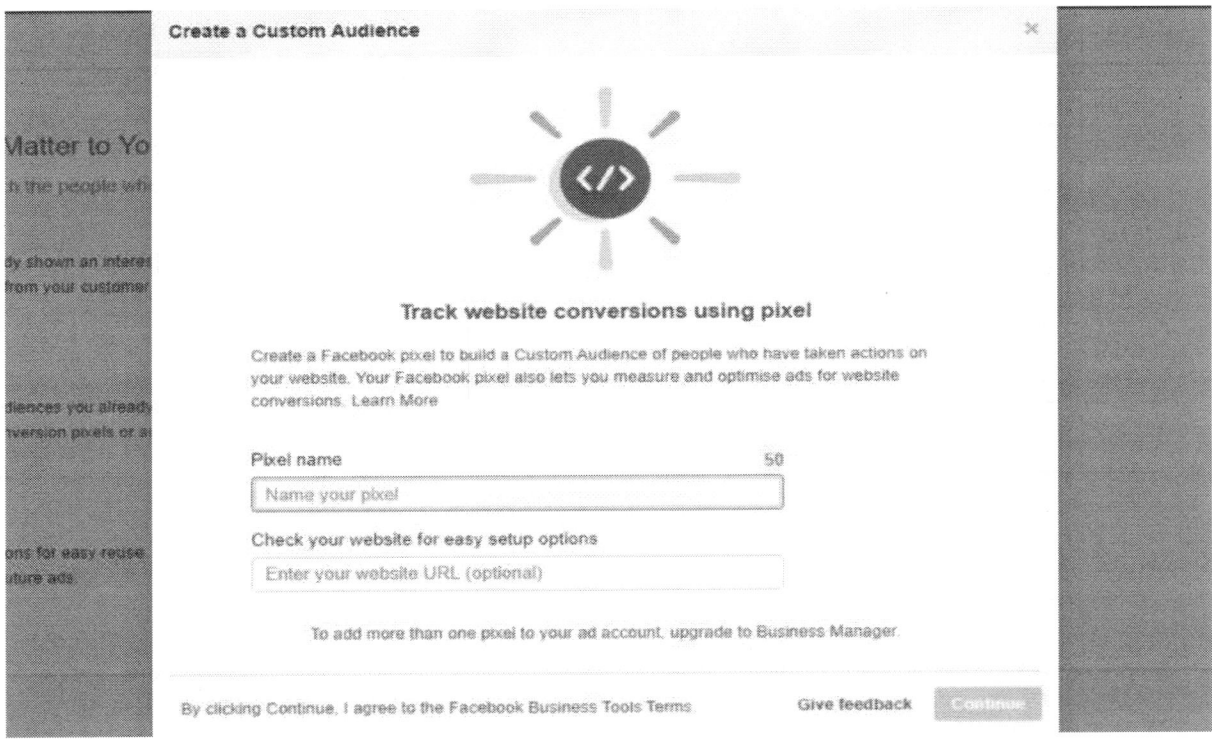

Once you've created your Facebook Pixel, or if you had one already, you can then move on to the next step. That's setting up the rules for your Custom Audience. These are what determine who falls within the audience and who doesn't.

You have several options when it comes to those rules. Different alternatives let you create audiences of people who fulfil certain criteria. Criteria such as the following:
- Anyone who has visited your website
- Only people who have visited a particular page or pages on the site
- Visitors who go to one page but not another
- Former visitors to your site who haven't been back in a certain amount of time

Those are just a few examples. You can tailor your Custom Audience to suit your circumstances. The last thing you need to do is to name your audience. You can also give it a description if desired. Then, click 'Create Audience,' and you're done. You'll be able to select this audience for any future Facebook Ad you create.

How to create Facebook ads

Setting up Custom Audiences is the lion's share of the work involved in Facebook retargeting. All you have to do now is create the ads you want your audience to see. You can create these ads through Ad Manager in precisely the same way as any others.

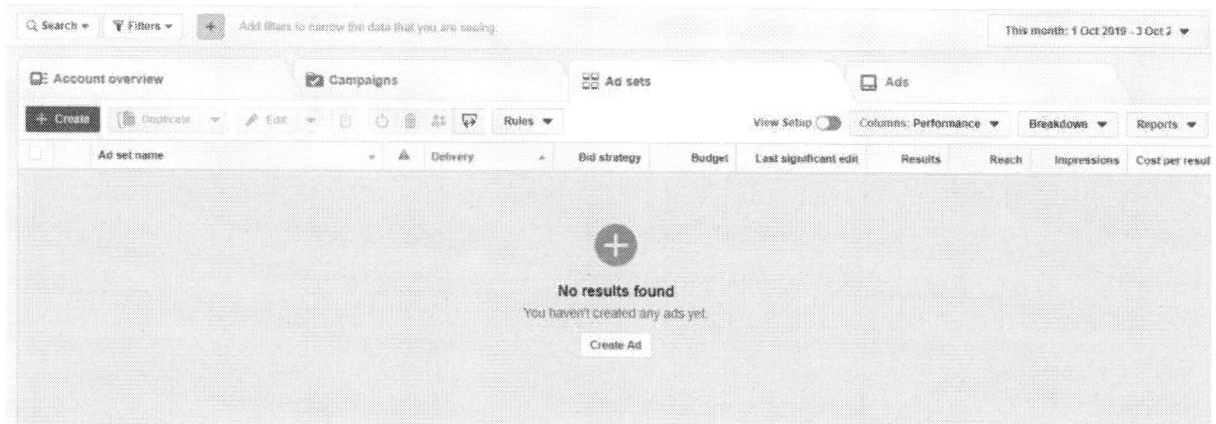

The only difference comes when you choose the audience for the relevant ad set. For your retargeting campaign, you need to select the Custom Audience you've just created. Of course, you will also want to tailor the ad's creative and text to the specific aims of your campaign.

Your Facebook retargeting strategy may aim to turn one-time visitors into customers. Your ad's creative and copy, in that case, will want to sell them the benefits of doing so. It's like tailoring your website's content to its target market.

Retarget to rekindle the interest of your audience

As the owner of a SaaS business, you'll spend a lot of time trying to get more traffic to your website. It's unavoidable, however, that most of the people who do visit will leave sooner than you'd like. Many will abandon your pages without buying from you or filling in a contact form. Those visitors don't have to be lost to you forever.

Social retargeting is a way for you to rekindle the interest those visitors have shown in you. It allows you to target them directly in a way that's proven to deliver results. Facebook retargeting ads are far more impactful than standard ads. Such ads also help to boost your site's branded search traffic. That's why an excellent Facebook retargeting strategy is so valuable.

Setting up retargeting campaigns could hardly be more straightforward. All you need to do is to create Custom Audiences and related ads on Facebook. It's a good idea to create as many different versions of each as you can. That way, you can be sure you're getting the most out of your retargeting. If you do implement the perfect strategy, you might be surprised at how good your results are.

In this section we've talked about how to retarget visitors who have been on your website but not taken any action, whether that is signing for your email newsletters or registering for a webinar or, for that matter, purchasing your service. In the next section, we will cover setting up email marketing campaigns, one of the most effective marketing methods available for SaaS startups to use.

2.2: How to set up email marketing campaigns

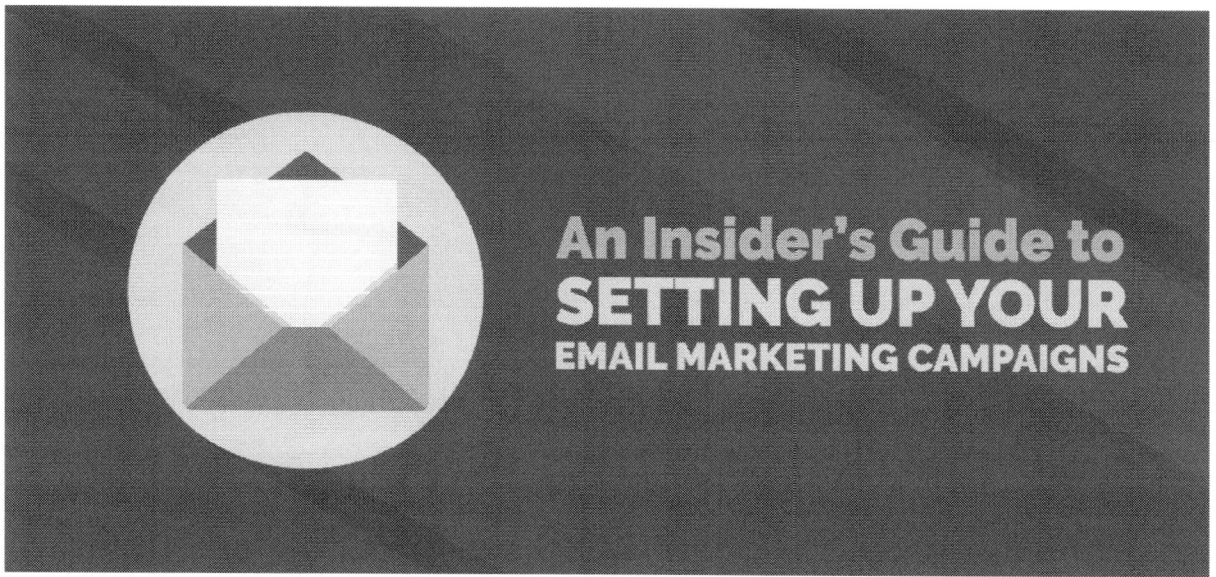

Modern businesses have a lot of choices when it comes to digital marketing. There are many varied channels you can explore to reach new audiences and convert new leads. Options like influencer and other social media marketing have recently come into vogue. One of the most effective marketing channels, though, is still one of the more traditional. That channel is email.

Email marketing campaigns can and do deliver outstanding results for companies across niches. A report[1] estimated that the average ROI for email marketing was a whopping $38 for each $1 spent. What that tells you is that done right, email campaigns can bring your company a considerable amount of business.

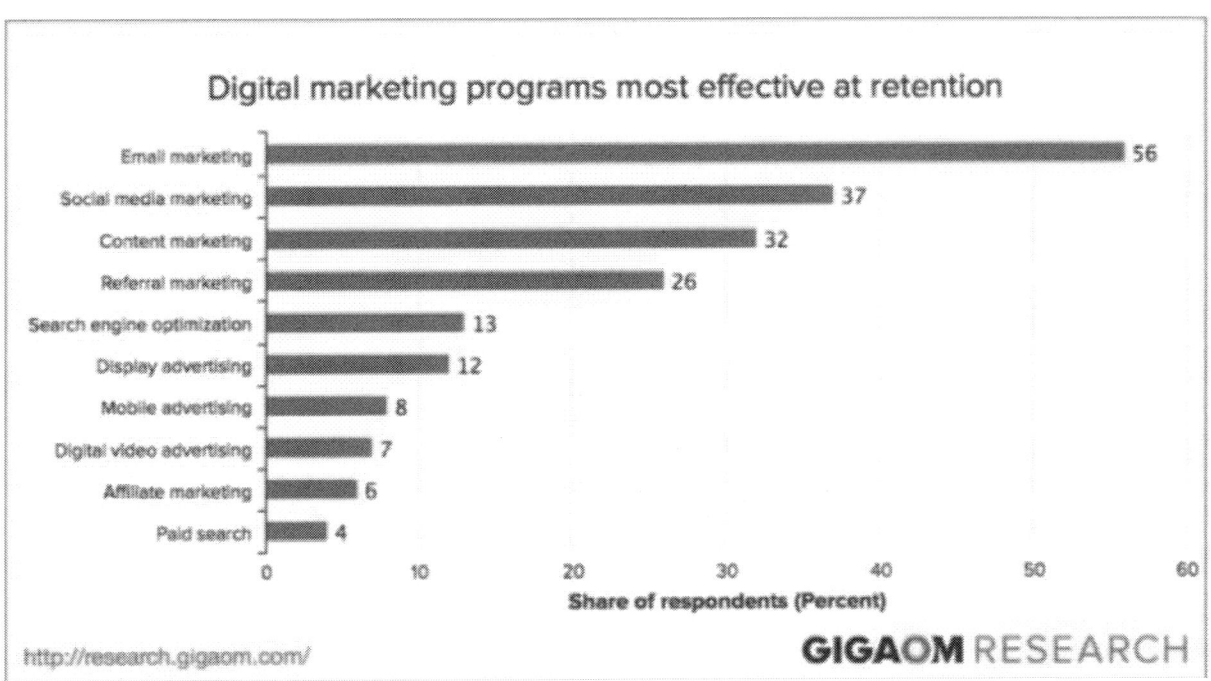

Source: Skyword

What you need to know, then, is how to set up email marketing campaigns that will get you those kinds of results. It takes more than one section of an ebook to share all the ins and outs of excellent email marketing. Fortunately, though, getting to grips with the basics is pretty straightforward. It's also enough to help you build your first high-converting campaigns.

Read on, and you'll learn;

- What a drip email campaign is
- Why they're the campaigns that you want to run
- Which campaigns to focus on and how to get them right

What is a drip email campaign?

A drip email campaign is a sequence of emails sent by a company to a recipient. It's also sometimes called an 'autoresponder cycle'. You can set up these campaigns through an email marketing platform and then allow them to run. You don't need to send each message yourself; it's an automated process. In the email marketing field, that's called a 'set and forget' campaign.

Emails within a drip campaign get sent at specified times and intervals. Exactly how many emails there are in a sequence and how closely spaced those emails are, can differ. A traditional welcome email campaign – more on this later – can have as few as three messages. Those messages often cover only a couple of days.

More complex campaigns can include many more messages. They can also extend over several weeks. In some cases, the more involved campaigns will also incorporate 'action-based tracking'. They track what recipients do with the messages they get and send different emails as a result. For example, if someone doesn't open the first message, they'll get a different series of emails to someone who does.

The best drip campaigns target a specific issue or opportunity. Brands use them to resolve a particular pain point or to achieve a defined goal. Common examples include the following:

- To win back site visitors who abandoned their cart
- To turn one-time visitors into returning ones, and ideally customers
- To improve engagement of your current subscribers
- To persuade adopters of a free trial to become a paying service user
- To upsell an extra service or add-on to existing customers

Now you know what a drip email campaign is, you'll want to see why it's the type of campaign you want to run. Many factors combine to make drip campaigns effective.

Why should you run drip email campaigns?

The main feature of drip campaigns is that they include a sequence of messages, rather than one. That multi-message nature is also one of the reasons this type of campaign is so effective.

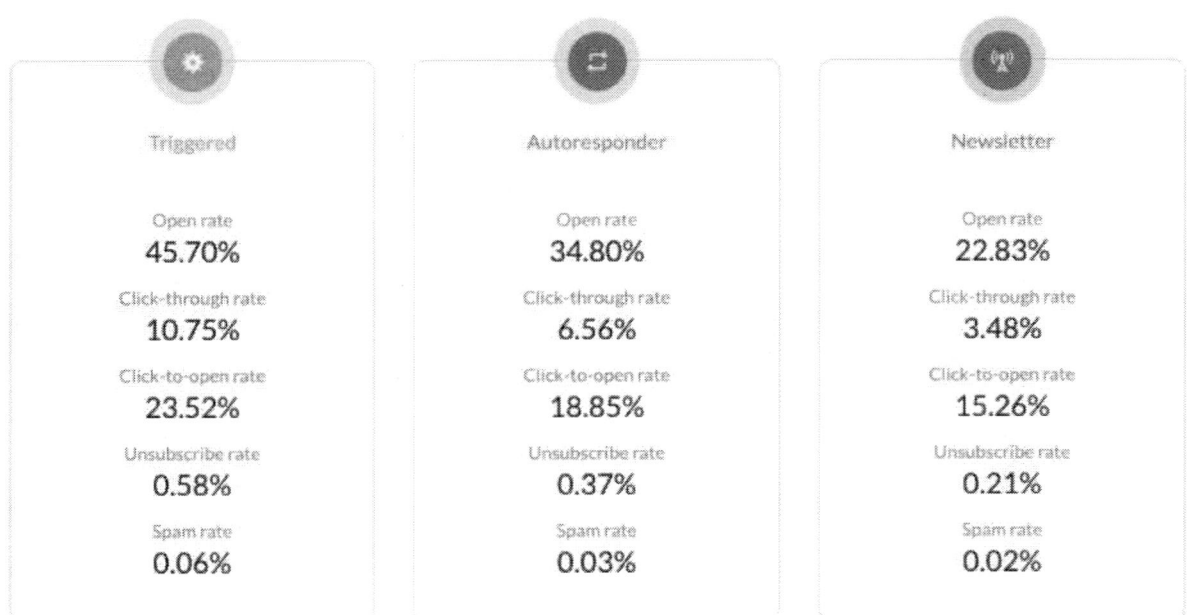

Source: SmartInsights

A useful way to think about it is to focus on the 'drip' part of the name. Imagine you're in your kitchen, and the tap drips once. You might notice it, but you're not going to stop what you're doing and give it your full attention. If it keeps dripping, though, you'll eventually decide you need to do something about it.

In the same way, people who receive more than one email from a sender are more likely to react. Depending on the ultimate aim of the campaign, that reaction may be a reply, a new subscription, or a sale. Drip campaigns can have a positive impact on any company's bottom line.

The effectiveness of these campaigns isn't all about volume. It's not a case that the more messages a campaign includes, the more success it will have. At a certain point, recipients will start to view your emails as spam if you send them too many. You need to strike a balance between getting their attention and causing a nuisance.

Your campaigns also need to stay focused on the issue you designed them to resolve. Each message should move you one step closer to your campaign's ultimate goal. Take, for instance, a cart abandonment campaign. It aims to persuade a customer who added a product to their cart but didn't buy it, to come back to your site and do so. Each message in the campaign must try to address one reason they may have abandoned the purchase. That way, it's more likely to hit the specific pain point of each recipient.

Five key email marketing campaigns & how to get them right

By talking about what makes drip campaigns effective, we've already given some general hints on setting them up. You should understand the exact issue you want a campaign to address before you start. Then, you need to assess the length of the message sequence you need to get the best possible response rate.

Now, it's time to get a bit more focussed. The following are five key email campaigns that you'll want to consider for your business:

- Welcome campaigns
- Upselling campaigns
- Cart abandonment campaigns
- Promotion-specific campaigns
- Special date campaigns

Each of those campaigns can bring significant benefits to your company. To get the most out of them, you need to know what they are and how best to set them up. By looking at them in turn, we'll tell you everything you need to know.

Welcome email campaign

A crucial drip campaign for any business to utilise is a traditional welcome sequence. That sequence is a short series of emails that you send when a new subscriber joins your email list. It's best to keep these campaigns short and sweet. You should shoot for a trio of messages spread across a few days.

There are a handful of simple things you're trying to achieve with your welcome sequence:

- To introduce your company and yourself if you tend to work directly with customers or clients.
- To get subscribers interested in the firm and its services.
- To gently explain what the products or services your service might do for a subscriber.
- To provide links to useful and engaging content that a recipient will appreciate.
- To get the recipient to follow you on social media or otherwise signal further interest in your firm.

The first email in the sequence is where you introduce yourself or your firm. It's looking to make a good impression, but not be too salesy. Make it an informal welcome message that might make a recipient smile. The below email from Virgin America is a great example:

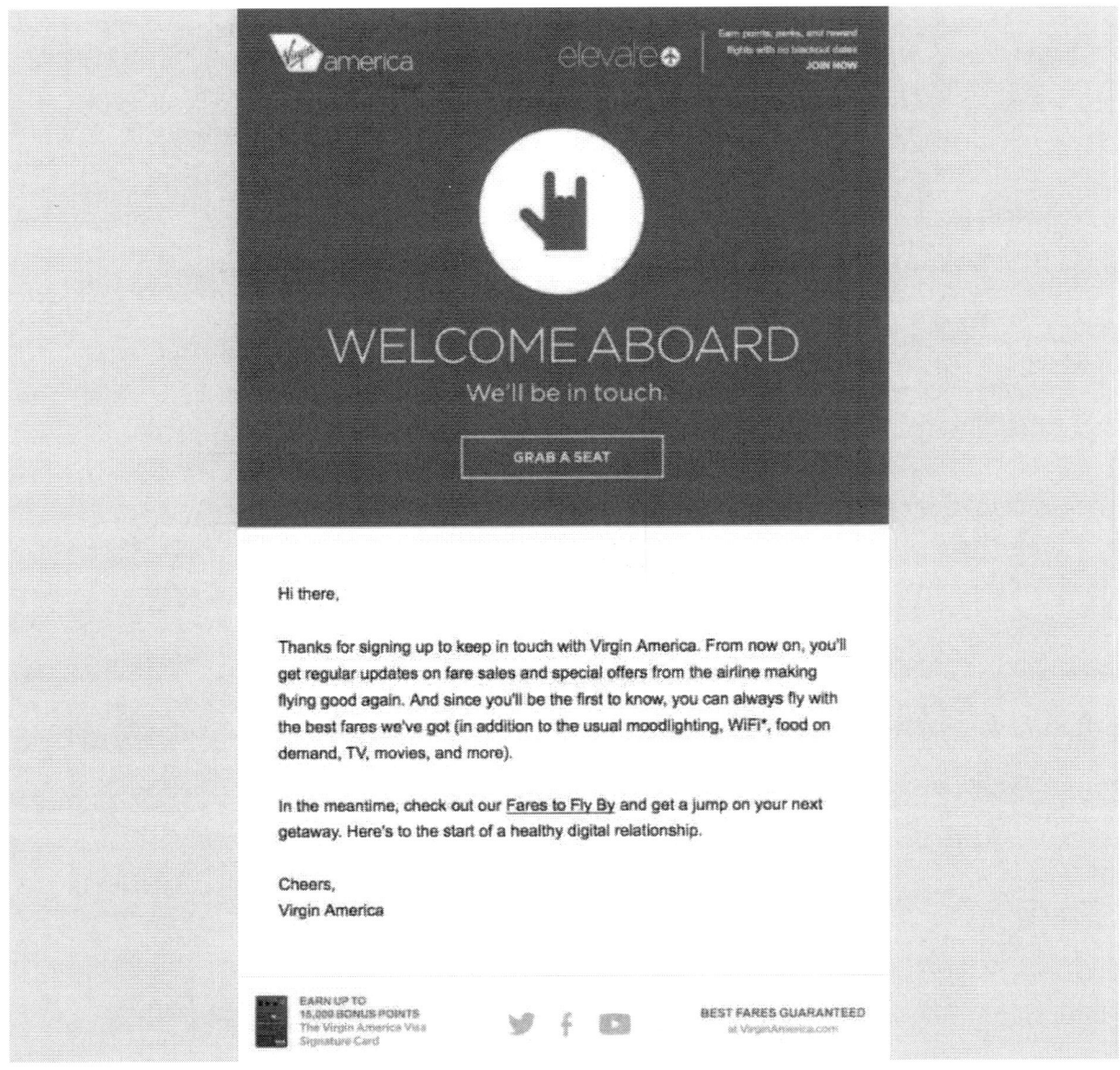

Source: Hubspot

You can then follow up that first email with a second, a day or two later. The email should point the recipient to a blog post, video, or another piece of content that they'd find useful. Try to convey the fact that the material is only available to those you email, or it would otherwise be difficult to access.

You should send your final welcome message a couple of days later. Pop in another link to a different piece of content or perhaps even to a freebie or offer. Don't go over the top selling a recipient on your service or products. That's not the purpose of this campaign.

Upselling campaign

An upselling drip email campaign is where you can be more sales focussed. It's a campaign you can use to persuade an existing customer to spend more with you. When someone has purchased a product or service, they're more likely to be willing to buy more. They've decided your offerings are for them and have taken their purchase decision. You can strike while the iron's hot.

Once again, it's best to keep this email sequence nice and short. A simple pair of messages should suffice. The first needs to come quite soon after the recipient's initial purchase. Try to make sure they get the email within two weeks at the most. The message should reference their purchase and point them to related possibilities.

Take, for example, a SaaS firm offering several service alternatives. Two or more of those services may work well in combination. The company should make that point in the initial email of the upsell drip email campaign. They should then offer their email recipients a discount or offer on the related product.

The second and final message of the sequence is about creating urgency. You should send it a few days to a week after the first. The second message must tell the recipient that their offer will soon expire. That will help to spur them on and make them more likely to take up the offer.

Cart abandonment campaign

Whatever your niche, if you sell products or services online, you'll have an issue with cart abandonment. That's when people get as far as adding a product to their shopping cart, but don't go through with buying it. You can use a platform like Google Analytics to track your site's exact cart abandonment rate. Rates, though, are high for every industry and sector:

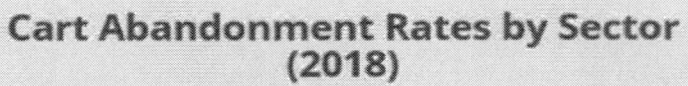
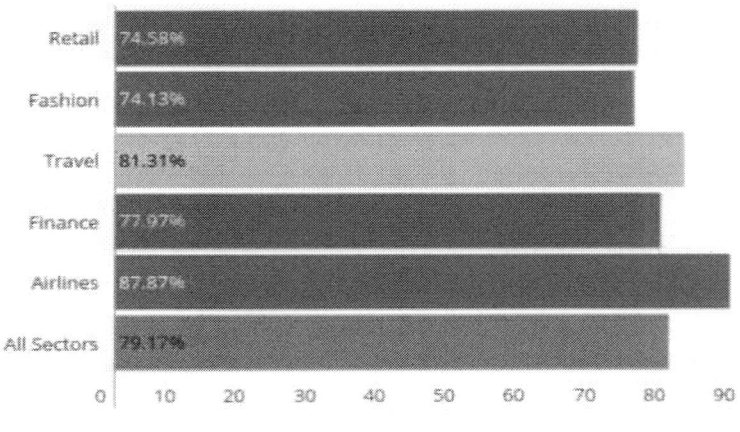

Source: Sale Cycle

A cart abandonment drip email campaign is a way to get some of those potential customers back. It's a sequence – often of around three messages – to persuade those near-customers to complete their purchases. The chain can aim to address specific reasons why you think a lead may have abandoned their cart.

Alternatively, a more straightforward option is to use scarcity and promotion to win back business. In that case, you should use a campaign which looks something like this:

1. **First Message** – sent a few hours after cart abandonment. Be friendly and mention the stock is running out, or the item often sells out. When selling a service, highlight the benefits the recipient is losing out on all the while they haven't signed up.

2. **The Second Message** – sent 24 hours after the first email. Offer a time-sensitive discount on the product or service a recipient added to their cart. Give them 48 hours before the promotion expires.

3. **Final Message** – sent 48 hours after the second email. Tell the recipient they have one last chance to buy and offer an even more significant discount or promotion. Explain that this is a one-of-a-kind promotion.

Promotion-specific campaign

It's not only those who abandon their carts at your site who you can offer promotions to via email. A promotion-specific drip campaign is a great way to turn a contact or lead into a customer. To make this sequence as effective as you can, you need to think about why a recipient may want to take up your offer.

Often, customers take up an offer for a combination of reasons. Put simply; they first desire the product or service on offer. Then, they get convinced of the logic behind buying it through the specific promotion. You should build your email campaign to account for this. In three simple emails, you can create desire, appeal to a recipient's rational side, and create urgency. Like this:

- Send an initial message extolling the virtues of the product or service on offer. Make sure the recipient knows how beneficial or enjoyable it will be for them. Appeal to their emotional side.

- Follow up with an email laying out the savings or benefits of the promotion you're running on the product. Show them they'd be a fool not to take up the offer. Appeal to their rational side.

- Finish the sequence with a message that creates urgency. Explain that the promotion will end soon, and anyone who doesn't take part won't get another chance. Exploit the recipient's fear of missing out.

Special date campaign

You have lots of information on your customers and visitors to your site. You get that info when they fill in forms and thanks to the data collected by Google Analytics and other tools. A special date campaign is a way to make clever use of some of the information. You send this kind of sequence on or around a specific date. Often, that will be on the recipient's birthday or the anniversary of when they became your customer.

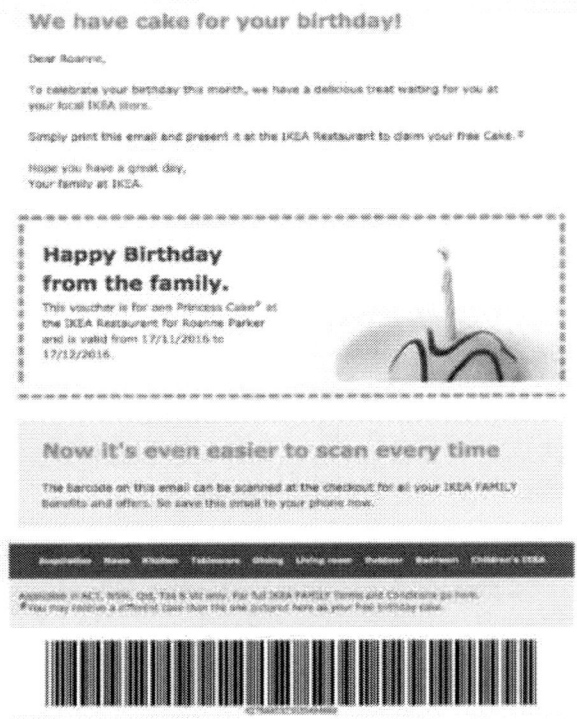

Source: Calibrate

You need only send two messages as part of this campaign. Send the first during the day in question. Congratulate the recipient on the special occasion and offer a promotion or bonus as a gift. Then, send a follow-up email the next day, telling them that their offer will soon expire. These campaigns are great for two reasons. They drum up additional business and build a more personal relationship with customers.

Drip your way to the forefront of a contact's mind

Drip email campaigns are a vital part of any firm's marketing strategy. They're proven to be effective in warming up cold leads and turning prospects into customers. Used right, they can also get more business from your existing customers. What's more, thanks to their 'set and forget' nature, the campaigns are far easier to manage than most.

The above hints and tips should set you on your way toward building effective drip campaigns. By following our simple guide and tweaking campaigns to suit you, you'll soon start to see the results. As part of a well-rounded marketing strategy, the email sequences can play a crucial role in the success of your business.

In addition to signing up for email newsletters, potential customers can be encouraged to take part in webinars. Webinars can be educational or provide the opportunity to answer any questions the buyers might have about the service before purchasing. The next section will cover how to run webinars that convert.

2.3: How to run webinars

There are a couple of simple things that are fundamental to running a SaaS website. You need to get as much traffic to your site as possible. You then need to convert as many of those site visitors into actual customers. You must then get them to sign up for and buy what you're selling.

The earlier sections of this ebook for SaaS businesses broadly focussed on getting more site traffic. Once you've got to grips with that, you need to start thinking sales. There are lots of different avenues to explore. We've been offering our advice and guidance on navigating the main options.

One excellent way to boost conversions on your site is by running webinars. Webinars give you a platform to both build your credibility and sell your service. They take time and effort to get right but are well worth it. Read on, and you'll learn how to run a webinar that will convert.

Why you need to think about webinars

A webinar is a seminar held online. They're a tried and tested sales and marketing technique. How you use webinars can differ depending on the target audience and the nature of your company. The online seminars work throughout the customer journey. You can use a webinar to educate general prospects or to sell to warm and qualified leads. They work as effectively in each case.

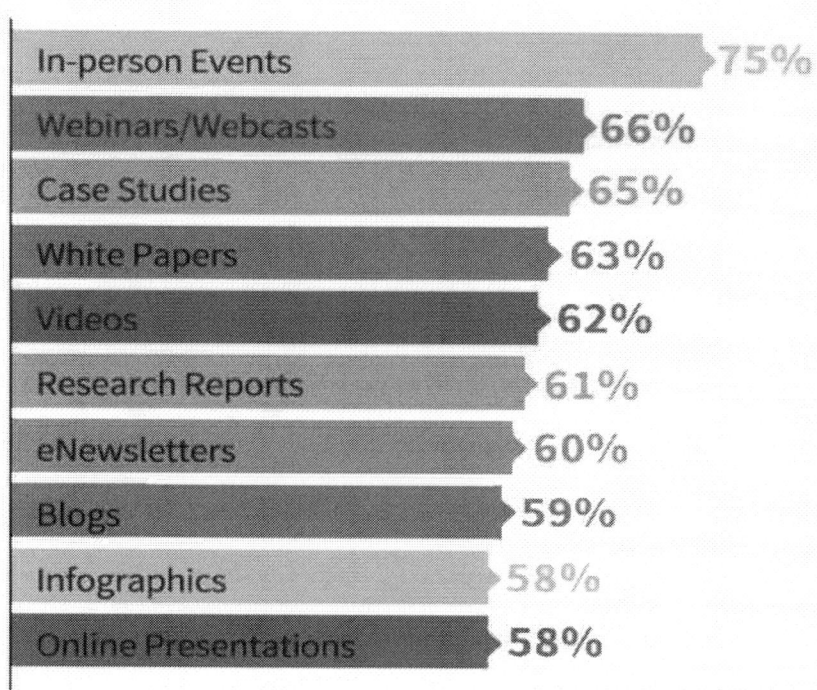

Source: Leadbridges

One of the best things about webinars is that they're highly engaging. According to GoToWebinar, the average attendee viewing time is 61 minutes[1]. That means you have the attention of prospects or leads for over an hour. The amount of information you can convey and the impression you can make in that time is vast.

In an hour-long webinar, you can establish yourself as an authority. You can also deliver a broad range of useful information to attendees. That creates a much more stable platform from which to sell your service.

Whether you sell directly through a webinar or use it for lead generation, the dynamic seminars get results. All you need to know is how to run a webinar that will work for your firm.

How to run a webinar

Running a webinar can help your business in three main ways. You can use webinars to:

1. Build your email list of prospects within a target audience

2. Create engagement with and trust from your existing contacts
3. Promote and sell your products, packages, and services

Those three facets combine to boost your site's conversions. Whichever way you use them, getting webinars up and running isn't as complicated or foreboding as it may sound. Four main steps go toward running a successful sales webinar. Follow our advice at each stage, and you'll soon be a dab hand at offering must-see webinars.

Understand & define your goal

Deciding to run a webinar 'to make more sales' isn't a good enough starting point. You want your webinar to be as effective and engaging as possible. For that, you need to understand its purpose wholly. Your first step is to think about exactly how you want the webinar to support your sales efforts. Do you want it to:

1. Be a tool for lead generation?
2. Work to warm up your existing contacts and get them generally more engaged with your firm?
3. Definitively sell your service or one of your service packages?

Which of the above options you opt for informs the rest of your preparation for running the webinar. If you're shooting for lead generation, your primary focus needs to be promoting to new audiences. For warming up an audience, you must make the webinar educational and informative. To use a webinar to sell directly, you have a whole extra level of questions to ask yourself.

Source: Brafton

One fundamental question is what products or services you want to sell on your webinar. You can't take a scattergun approach. A sales webinar should focus on the virtues of one product option and how it can help your customers.

When choosing the service to sell, you need to think about each option's characteristics. Is the service evergreen? Or is there an end-date after which potential customers will no longer be able to buy it? How much does a specific package cost? How many sales would you need to achieve to make running a webinar worthwhile?

You're best off choosing an evergreen service to promote via a webinar. That takes some of the pressure off when it comes to how quickly you need to secure conversions. If you're just getting started with webinars, you should also keep sales goals realistic.

Once you've addressed all those questions, you should have a defined goal for your webinar. You'll know what you want from it and what will constitute success when all's said and done. That means you're ready to start shaping the webinar itself. You can now make decisions about the content, tone, and style of your webinar. All those decisions need to work toward the goal you've defined.

Plan your webinar content

For a webinar to be successful, you need people to register, attend, and get value from what they hear. As such, the topic and content of each presentation are vital. They need to appeal to the right target audience to get them to register and attend. The webinar then needs to deliver insight that the audience will find useful.

Creating this content may seem like a tough ask, but in truth, it can be pretty straightforward. You've defined your webinar's goal. That means you know the audience. Your job then is to put yourself in the shoes of that audience. Think about a significant challenge they face, which you can help them to solve. As a digital marketing agency in Bristol, for example, we might look to help people use social media for SEO.

Each webinar you run should look to solve a single problem. If you try to cover too much ground, attendees may feel overwhelmed. You want them engaged, interested, and able to follow the advice you're giving. Otherwise, they might abandon your presentation before it gets going. Webinars with the right focus can achieve impressive levels of engagements, as shown by a recent study[2]:

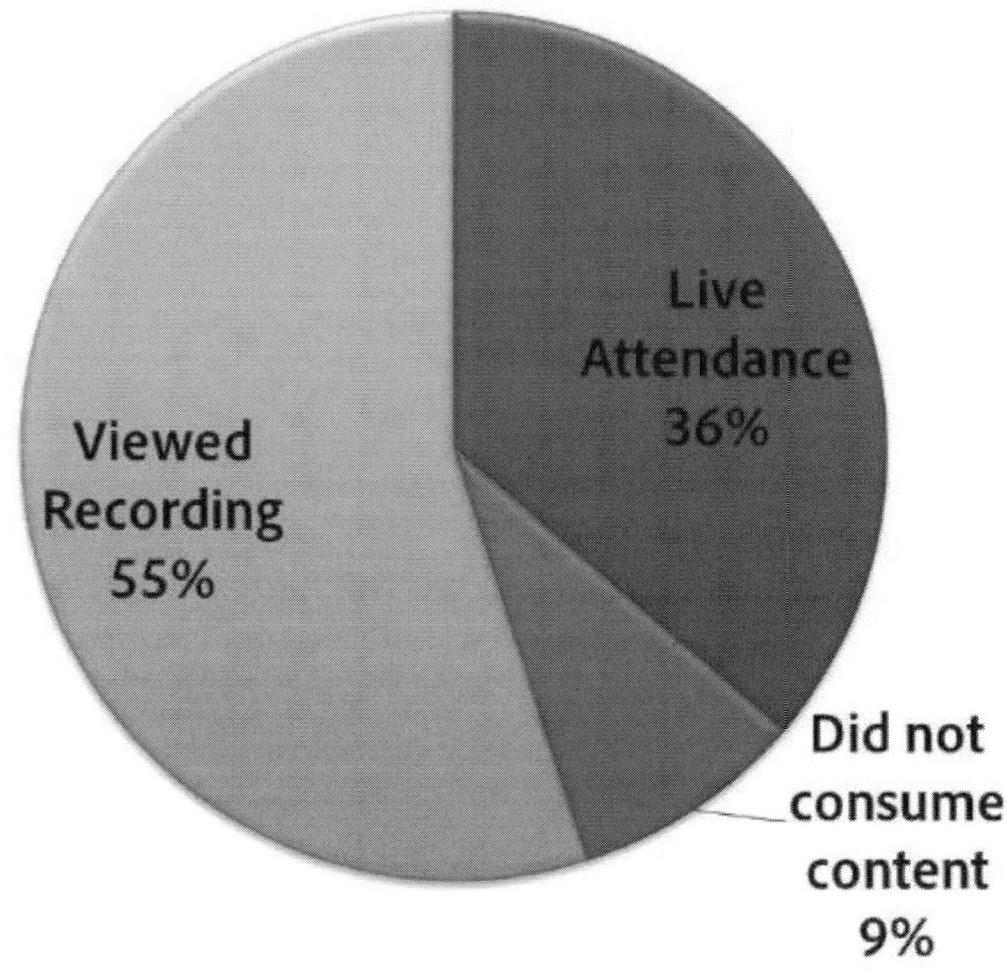

Source: Adobe

If you're thinking of how to run a webinar for direct sales, this approach makes it easier to pivot to your product. Your target audience for a webinar should be prospective customers. Their challenges, then, will be ones that your service can help them solve. You can then run a webinar on this pain point and weave in how your product can be part of the solution.

If you find yourself struggling to develop topics, your sales team might be able to help. They identify customer pain points and use them to sell every day. Get your staff together and ask them about the challenges they discuss with leads. Ask them what it is that persuades prospects to become customers in their experience. That can help you find the best webinar topics in short order.

Promote & prepare in advance

Promotion is a crucial part of many aspects of business operations. In the same way that you need to promote your SaaS website, you also need to get the word out about a webinar you're running. That's how you persuade people to register for the presentation and attend.

Exactly how to promote a webinar depends on the nature of the webinar you're running. If the aim you defined was to warm up existing contacts, you need to promote the webinar. You can send out email invites. You may even want to contact those people by phone to tell them all about your presentation.

If you want the webinar to reach new leads, you need to promote it more widely. There are several promotional avenues open to you:

- Share the sign-up link for the webinar across all your active social media channels. Get the link out there on multiple Tweets, Facebook statuses, and LinkedIn updates.
- Promote the webinar in niche-specific Facebook groups, if the group rules allow it.
- Reach out to other businesses, sites, or blogs that may be able to help you with promotion.
- Run targeted Facebook, other social media, or PPC adverts.

Getting the word out is only the first step of the webinar promotion process. You then need to get the people you've reached to register for your webinar. Your registration page is the tool to help with this. The best webinar registration pages feature a handful of essential elements:

- **A compelling title** – tell people what the webinar is about and why it will help them.
- **Teasers** – include a few bullets or short sentences to tease the webinar's main insights.
- **Credentials** – explain why you're qualified to cover the topic in question and how you can help attendees. Include a good photo to make the presentation seem more inviting.
- **Testimonial or quote** – try to incorporate a review or other testimonial. The quote should talk up your expertise on the topic.
- **Details & call to action** – make sure the time and date of the webinar features prominently. Twin those details with a clear call to action, asking people to register.

We're almost ready to start talking about your actual presentation. Before that, though, you'll need to do a bit more preparation in the week before your webinar. During those seven days, you need to prepare yourself and ensure registrants do attend the webinar.

Familiarise yourself with the equipment and software you're going to use for the webinar. If you can, run through your presentation once or twice to iron out any kinks. You're looking to make sure it's as polished as possible on the day.

You need to remind registrants of the webinar a few times in the days leading up to it. You can set up an automatic series of emails to do so using your email CRM. Try to nudge each person who signed up at least two or three times in the days leading up to the webinar.

Present confidently & follow up

The preparatory steps above make giving your webinar presentation much more straightforward. You can be confident that the topic you're speaking on will engage your audience. You also must get to grips with the tech you're using. That way, you can guard against any frustrating glitches on the day.

All you need to keep in mind is to be clear and confident. Keep the presentation's central topic and overall aim at the forefront of your thoughts. Ensure that the information you're imparting is relevant to both of those things. Impart as much info as possible yourself. Don't rely too much on slides or visual aids. They should support what you're saying; they shouldn't be something attendees have to read.

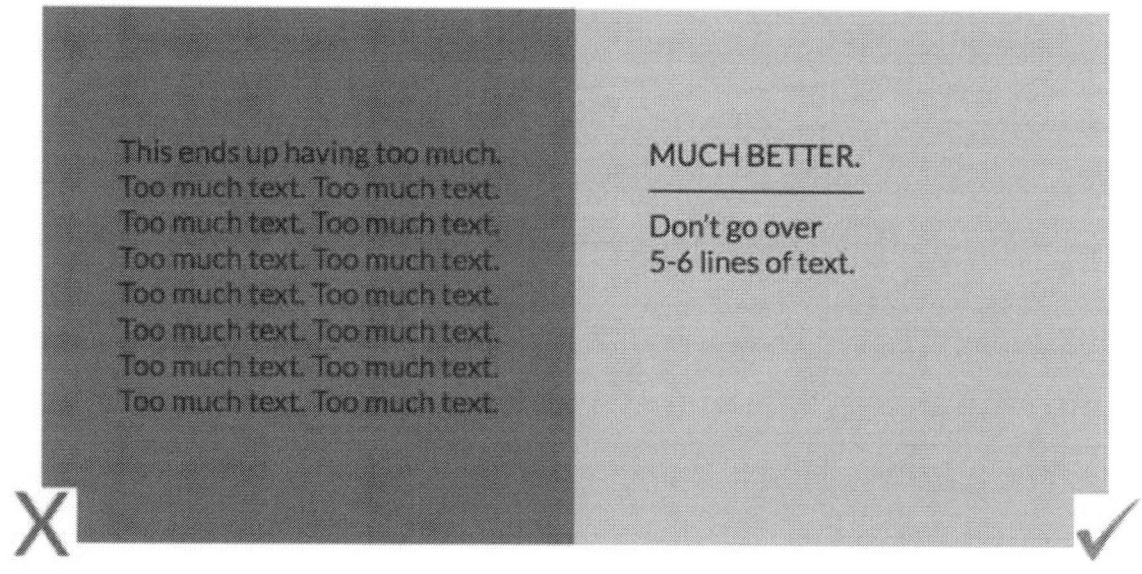

Source: Telspan

It's also important to remember that a webinar is a real, interactive process. You're speaking live to actual people, albeit remotely. Introduce yourself at the beginning of your presentation as you would in person. Invite questions and interactions from your audience. If you're giving your first ever webinar, you can even tell your audience so. Being honest and genuine is never a bad way to go when you're looking to build trust.

When it comes to direct selling via webinar, balance is crucial. Going for a hard sell won't endear you to many attendees. Speak passionately about your service. Highlight how it can solve the problem that is the focus of your webinar. If you're sincere and your service really can address their issues, leads will recognise that.

Selling to webinar attendees doesn't finish at the end of your presentation. Following up with attendees in the days after a webinar can be very lucrative. Try to send them at least three or four different follow-up emails. Ideas for those follow up emails may include any of the following:

- A recording of the webinar so that attendees can re-watch it
- A link to a blog post you've written to support the webinar
- Promotional emails with an offer on the product or package offered on the webinar

Plan, prepare & present your way to a successful sales webinar

You now know how to run a webinar that sells. Planning and preparation are what you need to make any webinar successful. If you put in the hours to devise and tailor a top-notch presentation, you'll see the results in your conversions.

Be sure to understand what you're trying to achieve with an online seminar. That way, you can plan content and promotion with your overall goal in mind. Speaking of promotion, try to explore as many avenues as you can to reach your webinar's target audience.

As a result of this work, you should be in a position to deliver a confident and genuine presentation. Presenting in such a way is sure to endear you to attendees. Some may buy your product or service then and there. Focussed follow-up can then get you plenty more sales. As with all good marketing, if you put in the work at each stage, you'll reap the rewards.

We said at the beginning of this section that webinars work effectively to drive sales and now you know the basics to set up, run and promote one for your SaaS business. Webinars feature in the next section too, which covers a proven five-step online strategy to help your SaaS business reach a six-figure payday. Interested? Read on.

2.4: 6-figure payday: a proven 5-step online sales strategy

Launching a SaaS product isn't easy for any business, whether you're just starting or have been around for years. Getting a brand-new offering off the ground is a tricky proposition. Get it right, though, and the results can be spectacular.

The best online sales strategy can help your product launch bear fruit in only a matter of days. There are examples of well-handled product launches netting six-figure sales returns. Sometimes in 48 hours or less.

You're probably wondering how you can get a piece of that action. No product launch is ever guaranteed to pay off big time. The following online sales strategy, though, is one that's proven itself in the past. Follow its simple five steps, and you'll give yourself the best possible chance of speedy success.

Developing your product

Before we get to the nuts and bolts of a product launch, it's worth talking about building your product in the first place. It's quite easy to create a great product within the SaaS niche. With the right funding and tech support, you can produce a powerful piece of software.

Most services offered through the SaaS business model exist to do one of two things. They either save people time or they make people money. How they do either job depends on the individual product. If you can come up with an idea which is either time or cost-efficient, you've got a product you'll be able to launch effectively.

Developing a product to launch from scratch gives you an additional chance to help your online sales strategy succeed. You can keep a couple of things about your eventual launch in mind from the get-go. The most successful software launches, for instance, involve an inherent upsell.

You'll want, then, to design your product in such a way to accommodate that upsell. The nature of the upsell depends on your product. You might offer a whole new range of more complex features. It could be that you extend the standard capabilities of the product. Dropbox, for example, provides a 'business' version of its service. That premium offering allows extra storage and enhanced collaboration.

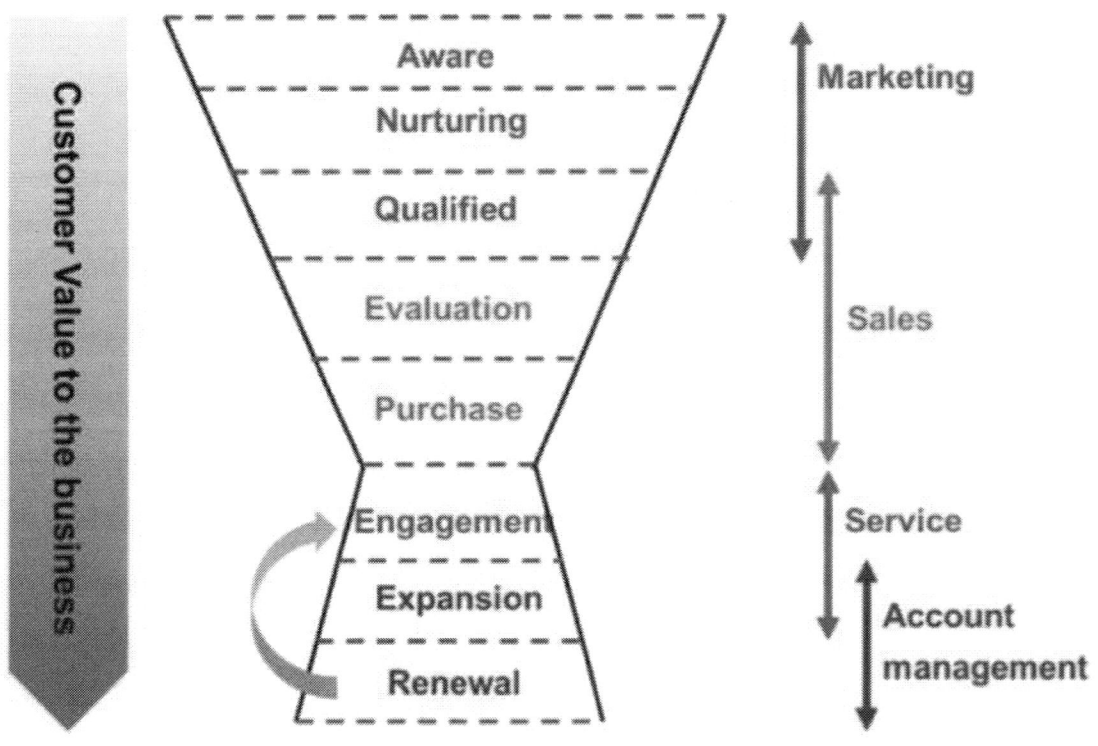

Source: VC With Me

You're aiming to produce the perfect SaaS sales funnel. Where an eCommerce funnel would end with a purchase, the SaaS version has more scope. You can expand the offering you provide each customer. That's the upsell we mentioned earlier. You then also look to get more from each customer by securing renewals.

With a compelling product ready to roll, you can start thinking of your launch. First, set a date for the launch. It's often helpful to go with a day in the middle of the week. Make sure that the date you pick is at the very least a month away. You'll need all that prep time to work through these five vital steps of your online sales strategy:

- Reach out to & secure affiliates
- Produce a high converting sales page
- Run a compelling email promotion
- Setup & deliver a sales webinar
- Closing sales & providing customer support

Finding & working with affiliates

Affiliate marketing isn't a new idea. Businesses of all shapes and sizes have been working with affiliates for decades. The idea behind the process is quite straightforward. You reach out to people and ask them to promote your SaaS product. They use their website, blog, social media, or other channels to get the word out to as broad an audience as possible. You then pay each affiliate a commission for the value of sales their promo efforts net you.

Source: Absorbed Online

Building up a network of affiliates is an excellent way to promote any product launch. Creating that kind of system takes time and effort. You need to build a Joint Venture (JV) page for your affiliates. You then need to explore different avenues to find marketers with whom to work.

You need to build your JV page before you start searching for affiliates. It needs to be up and running before you start your outreach. The JV page must provide an affiliate with everything they need to know about your product. It should also provide details on just what you're looking for from the relationship. Outline what you expect from them and what you're offering in return.

Key things to put on your JV page include:

- The date of your product launch
- An in-depth description of your product and its benefits
- Promotional copy or exact sales phrases you want affiliates to use
- Graphics for banner ads, sales videos or email swipes
- Bonuses, incentives or prizes on offer for affiliates who generate the most sales

The last of those JV page elements is worth dwelling on for a moment. You'll be paying your affiliates a commission. Its value depends on the subscriptions they deliver for your product. That's what makes them want to promote your launch. A prize or bonus, however, can incentivise them to go the extra mile. That can only be good for your product launch. Having a good reward, what's more, makes it easier to attract affiliates in the first place.

Speaking of attracting affiliates, that's your next step after building your JV page. There are a few different places to look to find marketers to promote your product launch:

- Launch calendar websites
- Affiliate marketing forums and communities
- Affiliate marketing related Facebook groups
- Your existing professional network

If you've never worked with affiliates before, you aren't going to have many existing contacts to help you. Things change once you've run a few campaigns or product launches. Then, your professional network becomes an outstanding source for affiliates. For a first affiliate-supported launch, you'll need to rely more on the first trio of sources above.

Reaching out to affiliates

Launch calendar websites are places where you can list your launch. You put your event on the calendar and include details affiliates need to start working with you. Affiliates visit the sites to learn what opportunities there are out there for them. Any interested marketer can then contact you or visit your JV page. A couple of good examples of launch calendar sites for SaaS companies are Warrior JV and Muncheye.

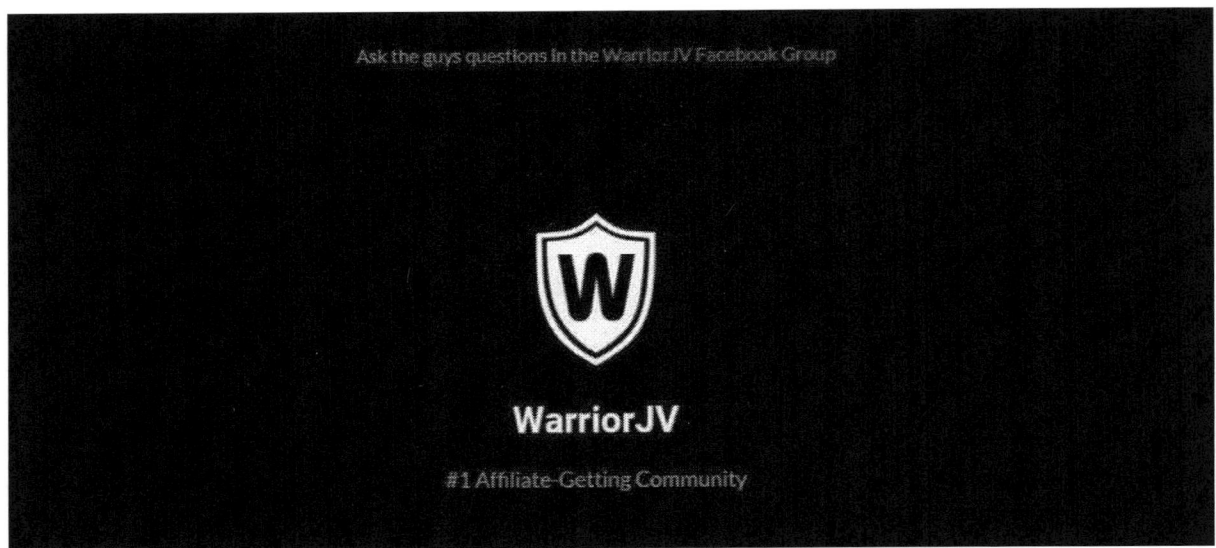

As well as listing on those calendars, you can reach out to potential affiliates directly. There are affiliate marketing communities on many social networks and channels. Warrior JV, for instance, has a forum. There, marketers discuss all things affiliate related. There is also a diverse selection of Facebook groups for affiliate marketers.

Finding and building a good network of marketers is key to your product launch. It's an efficient way of promoting the launch to a broader audience than you'd be able to reach yourself. To make it and your other promotional efforts worthwhile, you now need a top-class sales page.

Making a sales page that converts

Your sales page is critical to a launch. In some ways, it's more important than the product itself. It has the power to make or break all of your promotion efforts. The page, after all, is where you funnel all the leads you generate by marketing the launch. It's the page that must turn a visitor into a customer. With qualified traffic, you're looking for a minimum conversion rate of 5%.

Unfortunately, there's no shortcut or simple trick to crafting perfect sales copy. Copywriting is a skilled trade that takes lots of time and practice to hone. If you've not put in the hours practising the skill, you may want to hire a pro copywriter to handle your sales page for you. Good copywriting isn't cheap, but it's worth it for something as crucial as your product launch.

If you're going to write your copy yourself, try to get as clued up as you can before you start. Find examples of sales pages other firms have used to launch their products. Those examples are particularly helpful if they relate to launches that you know proved successful.

You'll also want to refresh your memory on some of the intricacies of sales copywriting. A site like Copy Blogger is an excellent place to find invaluable insights. If you're going to try to get organic traffic to your sales page, you will also need to think about the page's SEO. Do your keyword research and make sure Google will like your page as much as any visitors do.

Running a short-term email promo

Your online sales strategy to support your product launch is now taking shape. You've got an active affiliate program set up. That network of marketers will send prospects to your top-class sales page. The page will then work to convert them into customers. What you must do now is tell as many leads as you can about your product launch. A short email promo campaign leading up to launch is one excellent way to do so.

A lot goes into building a good email campaign. The main thing to keep in mind, though, is your target audience. Put yourself in the shoes of your potential customer. Think about the challenges they face and how your new product can solve those for them. How your product answers their pain points should make up the content of the campaign.

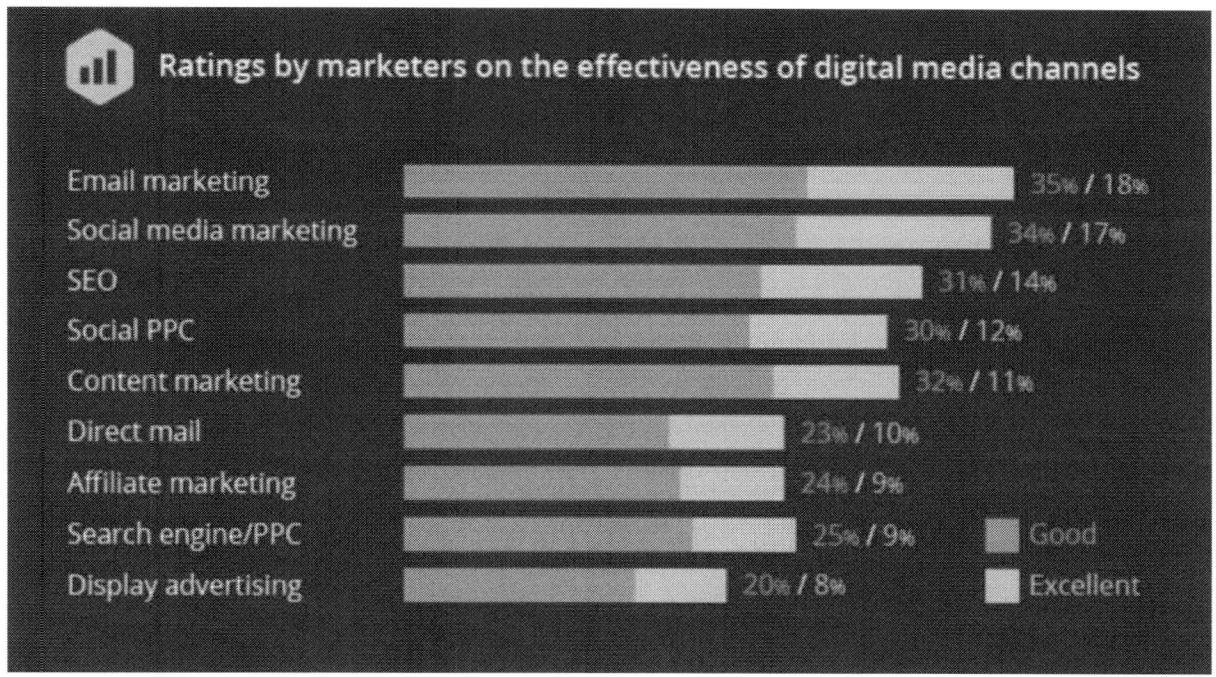

Source: SmartInsights

The exact assets featured in the emails should reflect the target audience. Build a customer persona for the typical prospect you're targeting. Use that to choose the elements that will work best in your emails. Some viewers will respond better to sales videos, and others may prefer an infographic. Get the shape of your emails right, and your conversions are sure to improve.

Having a launch date to focus on will be a crucial part of your email campaign. Using multiple emails to count down to the launch creates a sense of urgency that can help generate interest. A countdown to a big event is sure to produce an element of FOMO in any email recipient. They won't want to miss out on a special promotion or offer.

Setting up & delivering a sales webinar

A sales webinar is another useful way to promote your new product and its launch. Webinars engage an audience in a way that other marketing channels can't. You can speak directly to prospects and build a rapport. That helps to create trust with your audience that can translate into a sale. A webinar is also an opportunity to demonstrate your product and address pain points.

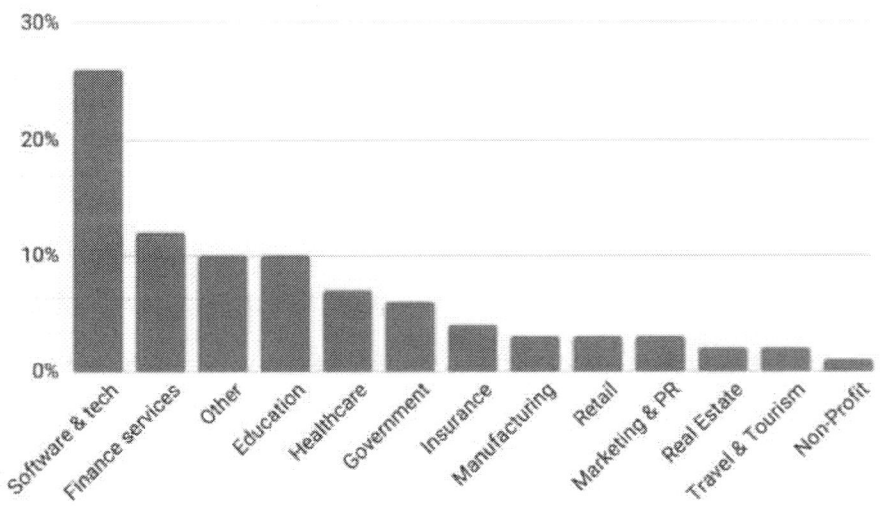

Source: G2

Demonstrating your new product ahead of launch is a superb topic for a webinar. With the right promotion, you can convince attendees of the value of your product. You can market the webinar as an exclusive, behind-the-scenes look at the new product. That's sure to grab the attention of your leads.

The exact content of the webinar, though, shouldn't be too practical or technical. It needs to show off the product you're launching but in a particular way. Ensure that you always demo the product with half a mind on the problems it can solve. Especially problems that you know the attendees and their firms are most keen to address.

Closing sales & post-launch support

The preparation for and promotion of your product launch is now complete. What's left is handling the launch itself. It's an obvious point, but you need to have the human resources in place to cope with the process. If your online sales strategy is a success, there may be a lot of calls on your staff's time in the days after the launch.

You need agents on hand to close sales with uncertain prospects. Someone may get as far as your sales page only for a final objection to come to mind. If they contact your staff directly, those staff must be able to overcome the lead's opposition. Make sure you train and educate all agents well on your new product before it launches.

No matter how good your product or your online sales strategy, there will be issues as your launch progresses. After any launch, there will be a high proportion of early adopters who decide they want a refund. Top-class customer support is a way to address problems, thereby reducing refund requests.

Implementing a proven online sales strategy

For any SaaS business, launching a new product is vital to its commercial success. The best product launches bring astounding results in terms of overall sales. Some firms have achieved turnovers of six-figure sums in a matter of days. To get your business a piece of that action, you need a superb online sales strategy to support your launch.

The simple five-step strategy outlined above is one that's proven to deliver. Via affiliate marketing, an email campaign, and a webinar, you can reach a broad audience. Your top-class sales page and practical customer support will then woo that audience. We can't guarantee you'll get that six-figure payout, but you'll be giving yourself the best chance of success.

Great landing pages convert visitors into customers and are key to the success of your product launch. In chapters one and two, we touched on the importance of sales copy and user experience once you have driven traffic to your website. In the next chapter, we will be covering those topics in more detail including AB testing and website analytics that can inform improvements to your landing pages.

Chapter 3: How to keep visitors on your website

The introduction to this ebook talked about how getting traffic to a SaaS website or app is only half the work that is required. Once you have visitors arriving on your website you need to ensure that what they find there is attractive and informative enough to convert visitors into subscribers.

Chapter three will look at landing page examples with notes about what works well. We'll also look at management and analytical tools that can help identify how visitors are using your website and which elements and copy work (or not).

First, let's look at some examples of landing pages that we believe work well, with a specific focus on design that works for SaaS businesses.

3.1: 11 SaaS landing page examples & why they work

Well-designed landing pages are a must for any SaaS business. They play a massive role in increasing conversions. That can be for email campaigns, PPC advertising, or any of your other marketing efforts. A landing page lets you guide traffic in precisely the direction you wish. That keeps them engaged with your site and helps limit your bounce rate. What, though, makes for a well-designed landing page?

There's no cut and dried template for SaaS businesses to use. Different firms can and do explore different routes to find the right page design for them. To help you make your decision, we've picked out some of the best SaaS landing page examples on the web. Scroll down through the 11 excellent examples, and you're sure to find plenty of inspiration.

Landing pages – the basics

Landing pages are used to persuade a visitor to take a specific action. That action depends on what your conversion goal is for the page. Some landing pages add leads to your email list, download an eBook or guide, sign up to a webinar, and more.

The beauty of landing pages is that you can tailor them to any goal. There's plenty of room to be creative with landing page design. To flex your creative muscle fully, you need to know what options are open to you.

The best way to learn how to build your perfect landing page is via research into what works. Looking at some existing SaaS landing page examples is sure to get you inspired. In just the same way as competitor research is vital to content marketing.

SaaS landing page examples

The following eleven landing pages provide a snapshot of various effective designs. These pages are used by SaaS companies to generate conversions of one kind or another.

What makes each of these SaaS landing examples compelling differs from one to the next. We're going to look at them in turn and explain why they work brilliantly to meet the site's needs. We'll explain the major elements of each page.

What we can't do is provide Analytics data for any of the pages – they're not ours, after all. By taking a microscope to the page's features, though, it should be clear why aspects of them are worth imitating. Let's get to it, then, and give you that all-important inspiration for your landing pages.

Shopify

The Shopify landing page for the company's free trial is an excellent example to start with. The beauty of this page is the way that it manages to be both detail-oriented and straightforward.

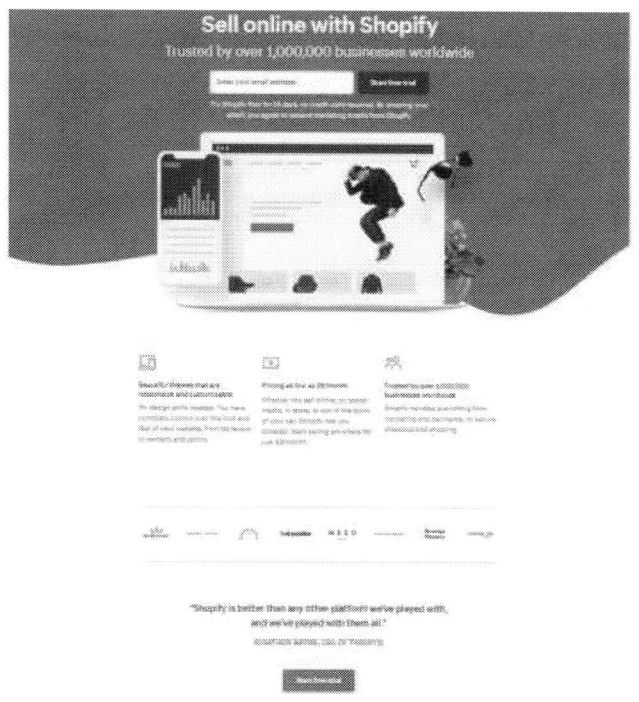

Toward the top of the page, there's plenty of white space and no clutter. That gives the page a clean and attractive look. It also means there's little getting in the way of a visitor who wants to 'Get Started' straight away.

The page does still manage to sell the trial to those visitors who are less convinced. The informative yet straightforward selling points of Shopify's platform appear below the image. They explain why people should go ahead with the trial. They do so without turning the page into an unappealing factsheet.

Shopify's subheading copy is also worth dwelling upon. The company is globally popular and they make sure to tell people as much. By citing the volume of businesses they already work with, they immediately build trust with new visitors to the page.

Muzzle

If your landing page aims to sell your service, there are a few basic things it needs to impart to visitors. It must tell them what the product does and explain why it might benefit them. Many pages use text or perhaps a video to do that. This landing page from Muzzle takes a different approach.

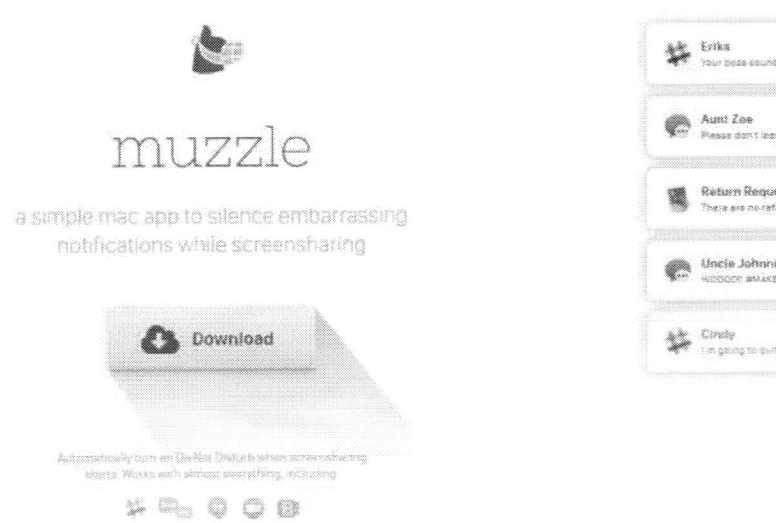

Muzzle is an app to silence notifications when you take screenshots or share your screen. The landing page instantly shows visitors when and why that's a good thing to have. As soon as you hit the page, potentially embarrassing notifications appear.

The notifications fill the right of the screen, and you would not be keen to share any of them. The innovative page makes you laugh, and it sells the benefits of Muzzle's product right off the bat. It also allows Muzzle to keep copy to a minimum and retain the clean, sharp look of the page. The simple copy they do use does a great job summarising their product in one sentence.

Teambit

Where Muzzle uses humour for their landing page, Teambit goes down the route of making theirs cute. The firm sells HR software. They use fun illustrations of animals to make their landing page more interesting.

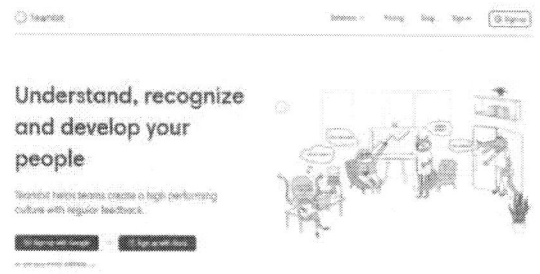

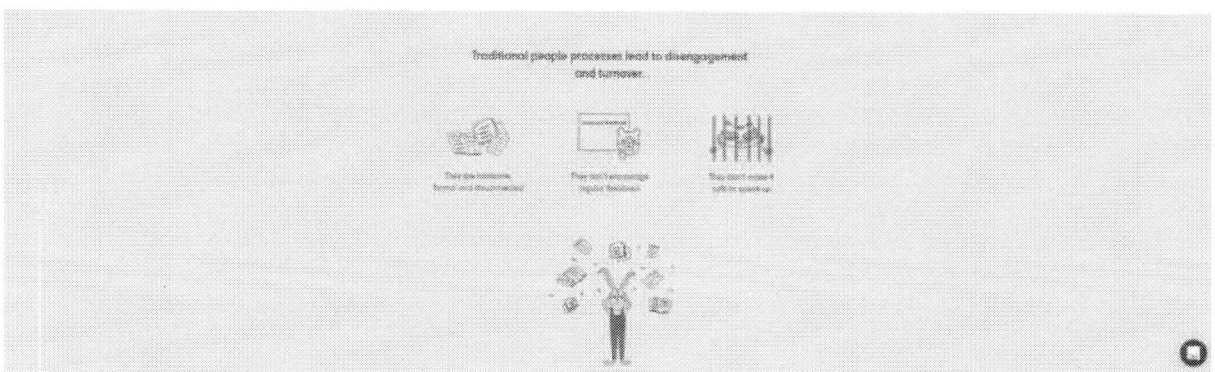

The illustrations are tailor-made for the page. They all relate to HR and office environments where the software applies. The regular employees have been turned into critters.

A different image appears next to each distinct section of what is a long landing page. Once you've seen the first one, you can't help but keep scrolling to check out the rest. That means you also see all the features and benefits of the Teambit software.

That's one major strength of this quirky yet straightforward page design. Another is the actual shape of the content in its top section. If you look at the text to the right of the page's first image, it looks like a capital 'F'. That's not by accident. Research has proven that people scan content in an F-shaped pattern[1]. By steering into that, Teambit is ensuring visitors to their page take in the information they want them to.

Wistia

The landing page Wistia uses to get visitors to create a free account is like the Shopify page from earlier. Keeping things simple and using white space are the two most notable design choices the firm has made.

A form field and a button to 'create a free account' are all you see when you first hit the page. That makes it almost frictionless for pre-qualified leads to get started straight away.

Like Shopify, Wistia has then added more info 'below the fold.' By which we mean, it's only visible once you scroll down. In this example, the extra content is in the form of a set of FAQs. They're there to help overcome any objections visitors may have to sign up for a free account.

The page is an ideal combination of clean design and high-converting content. The 'above the fold' view is clean and simple. The copy featured below gets down to business answering any queries a more cautious lead may have.

Webflow

Webflow is a design tool for web developers. It stands to reason that their landing pages ought to be slick, stylish, and sure to convert. Fortunately for the company, that's just what they are. The below landing page shows off Webflow's product impressively.

There's a comparatively small amount of text on the long(ish) page. Instead of laying out their platform's features in prose, Webflow relies on animations. Throughout the page, graphics and gifs show the tool in action. Notice once again, however, the definite 'F' shape of the copy which is included.

That has a dual benefit. It makes the page more attractive and much easier to grasp the tool's main elements. This page's CTA buttons are also a notable feature. They all feature the same text; 'Get started – it's free.' This removes a major pain point for potential customers.

Industrial Strength Marketing

This landing page from Industrial Strength Marketing starts strong. Its headline text is punchy, intriguing, and relatable for visitors. It immediately gets to the crux of the issue that the company's product exists to address. That product helps businesses build mobile-friendly websites. The kind of websites that work on all devices, without site visitors having to zoom.

The overall design of this page is also compelling. The use of a black background serves to make the contact form appear more appealing. Intelligent application of red at the head of the form and for the button works well. It shows off the simplicity of the sign-up process. All of that attracts a visitor to complete the site's desired conversion. In this case, that conversion is the download of a guide.

Inbound Emotion

It may seem odd to include a foreign-language page among our SaaS Landing page examples. The dynamic design of this page from Inbound Emotion, though, is well worth highlighting. It's so good that even if you don't speak Spanish, it's easy to appreciate the page's appeal. "eBook gratis," too, is pretty self-explanatory even to the most lingually challenged.

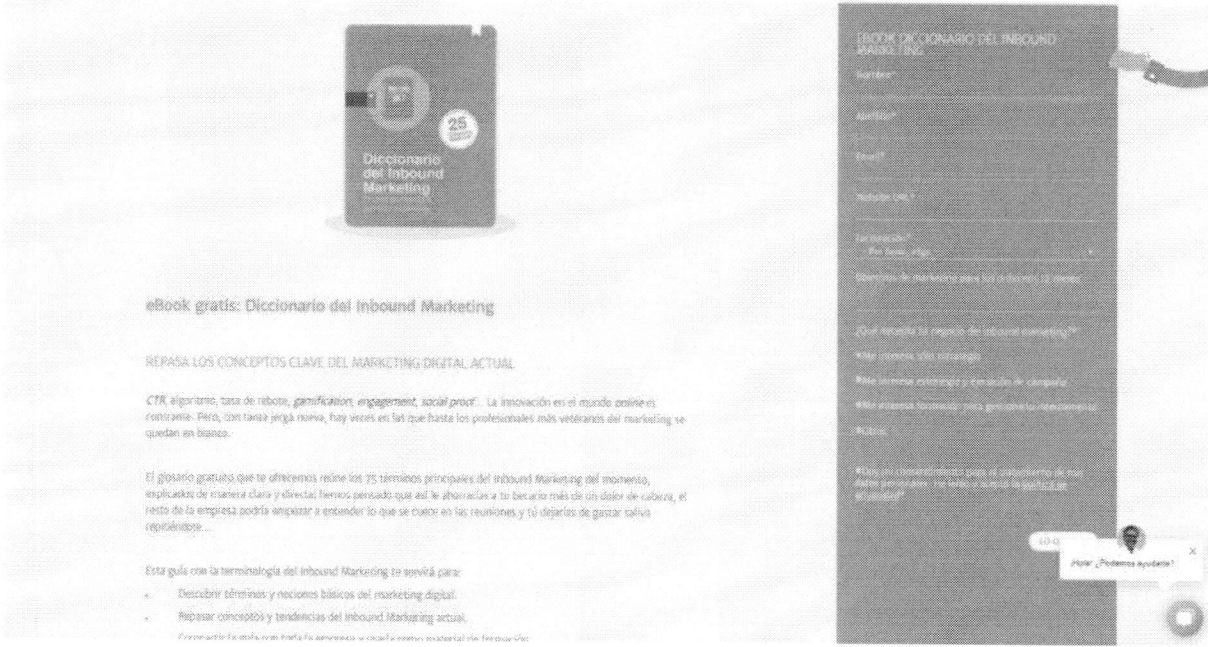

The most innovative part of this page's design is its contact form. That simple form features at the right-hand side and stays bolted in place as you scroll. That means it's always there, reminding you how easy it is to sign up for your free eBook.

The form, too, includes an eye-catching hand design, which points you toward the signup form. A matching hand also points to the page's sharing options, and similar images appear within the firm's eBook. That kind of consistent branding is excellent for building trust with leads.

Velaro

Velaro offers "out of the box" live chat and customer engagement software solutions. eBooks, guides, and other free downloads are a big part of their marketing strategy. Each different download they offer has a landing page like the one below.

>> **For online retailers, the busy season is a time that shines a spotlight on issues with customer service, the website and the ordering process.**

One of the great things about those landing pages is their consistent format. Each one looks similar and aids consistent branding across the firm's site. The design that the pages do follow also includes a couple of small but impressive features.

Green double chevron designs feature prominently on the pages. They always point to the most pertinent copy on the page. They also appear next to CTAs, to subconsciously suggest how important they are.

When it comes to the copy itself, it works to tease the content of the eBooks and guides themselves. That helps to build excitement with visitors to download the content and find out more. The most important copy sections, too, are always at the top and/or left of each page. That, once again, takes account of the F-shaped pattern of reading we've mentioned a few times before.

Other small design flourishes help make each page more user-friendly. The inclusion of the PDF icon at the corner of images of different downloads is a prime example. That shows users how they'll get those downloads.

Unbounce

Unbounce specialise in helping clients build landing pages. Taking a look at the pages that they use can give you some excellent inspiration. Below is the top section of an Unbounce landing page for one of their online informational courses:

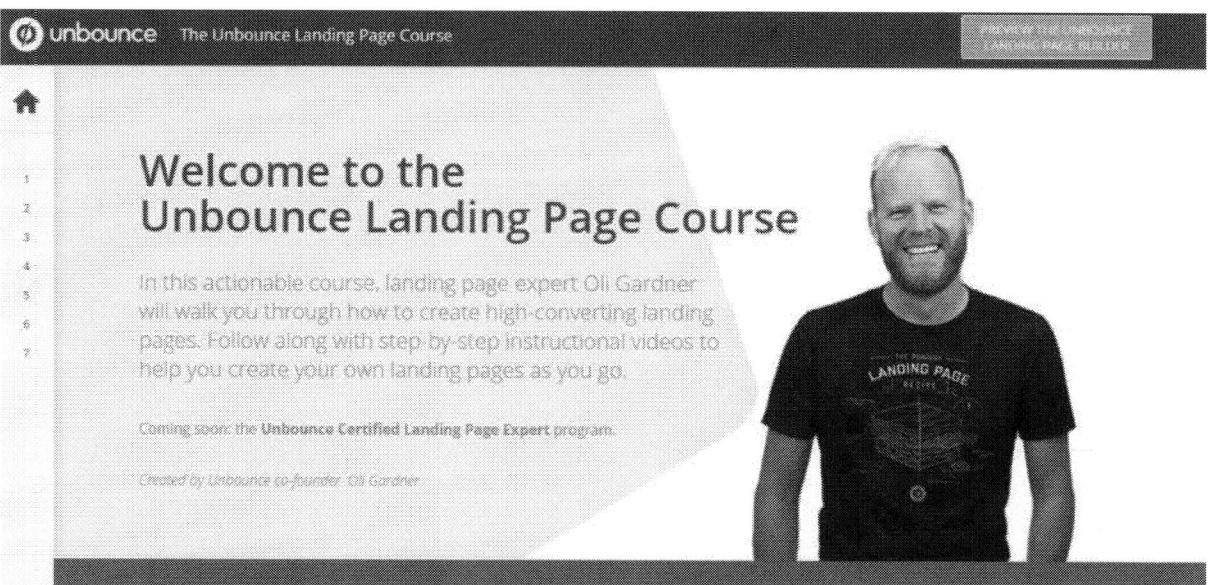

There are a couple of essential things to note about the page. First, is the prominent picture of the firm's co-founder, who also wrote the course the page promotes. That photo puts a human face to the company. It helps to build trust and rapport with the site's users. That makes those users more likely to progress with the course.

The amount of content packed onto the page is the other notable feature. Links to industry-specific stats, as well as menus to navigate through the course, are all included. FAQs also appear toward the bottom of the page, and yet the overall design is never compromised.

Landbot

Landbot is another firm that puts its product front and centre on their landing pages. Landbot creates chatbot-style landing pages, and they're what you'll see when you first hit their site.

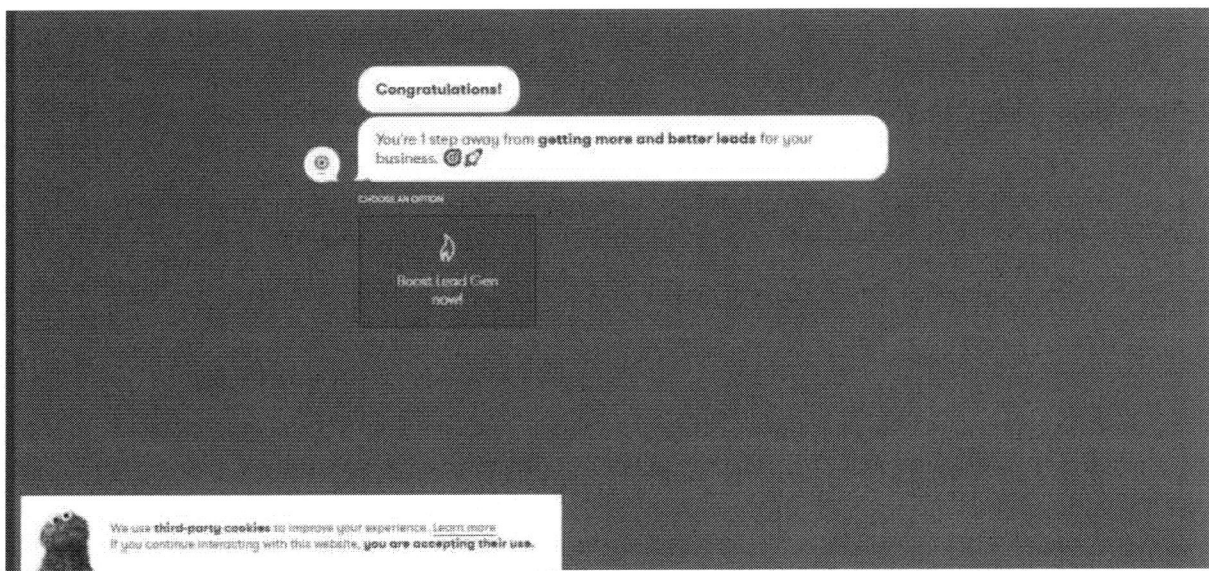

The landing page looks every inch like an IM chat. It talks to you like a friend would, and even sends emojis and gifs along the way. You're immediately engaged by being asked to choose reply options to keep the chat going. You then fill in your contact details as part of the chat, rather than in a separate form. It's an ingenious way to ask site visitors for their information. They'll give it, without feeling like it's a chore or an imposition.

Bills.com

The last of our SaaS landing page examples is the debt relief company, Bills.com. They don't feature their main form fields on the initial page you see when visiting their site. Instead, they present a question pertinent to every member of their target audience:

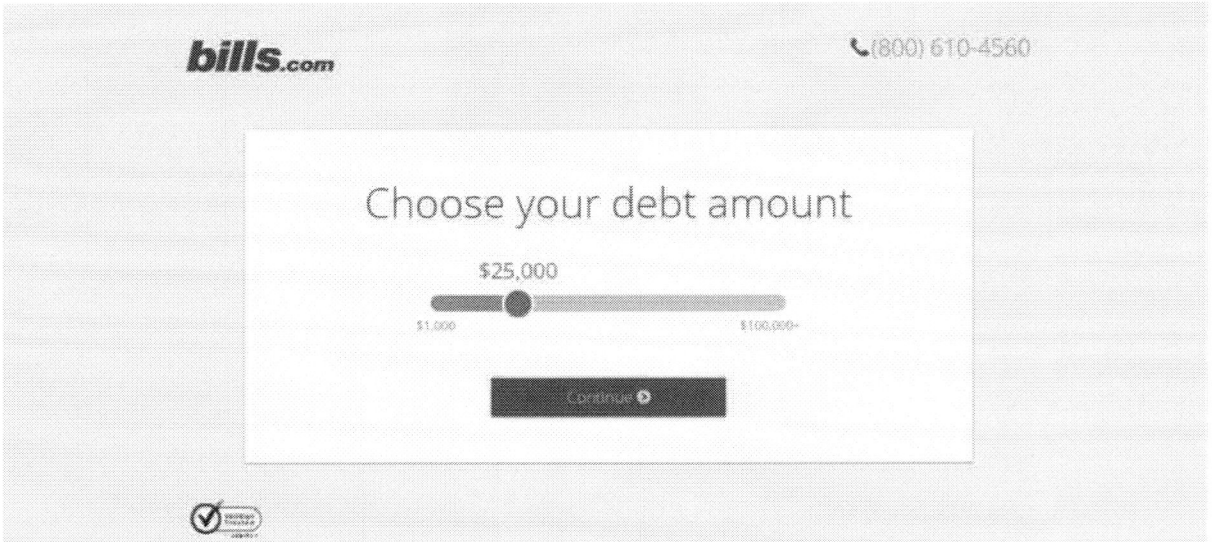

As soon as you hit the Bills.com landing page, you're invited to interact with the web form. This multi-stage form assesses your eligibility for the service. It's clever in the sense that the action required by the user is clear.

Landing pages aren't one-size-fits-all

Browsing our SaaS landing page examples should have shown you one thing, above all else, pages don't have to follow one prescribed template to be successful. The examples we've highlighted above could hardly be more different. Some prize simplicity and directness, others leverage innovation and humour. They all have their styles and tones.

What all the examples have in common is that they're engaging and fit their target audiences. Hopefully, the case studies have given you lots of inspiration for your site's landing pages. By twinning some of the elements you like with your creative twists, you're sure to produce pages that will boost your conversions.

If you have built a landing page, and it doesn't work as well as you had hoped, how can you tell what you need to change? The last thing you want to do is change the one element that is working or change the copy and see even less conversions. In the next two sections, we will cover analytics and heat-mapping software and AB testing. Both these methods can help you get to the bottom of why a landing page isn't working and how to improve it.

3.2: 4 free website management tools you can use to generate more sales

As a SaaS business, your website is the lifeblood of your company. It's as essential to you as a shopfront is to any traditional retailer. The modern website is far more than words and images on a screen. There are lots of aspects of site design, operation, and performance that you must keep an eye on. To name just a few, you need to track and manage:

- How your site looks across different devices
- How your website performs and the user experience it delivers
- What users like about your pages and what isn't working as well
- How your pages rank on Google
- The effectiveness of different marketing efforts in bringing visitors to your website
- The rate at which site visitors convert into customers

Running a SaaS business and its website is no easy task. To keep all of those plates spinning, you're going to need a little help. Fortunately, there are different website management tools out there to make life easier. There are even a few great ones that are free to use. The following are four examples of tools or types of tools that you're going to want to check out:

1. Landing page builders
2. Heatmap tools
3. Google Analytics
4. Google Search Console

Let's take a look at each in turn. Along the way, we'll explain why they're so handy and what you should look out for when choosing and using them.

Landing page builders

When you're looking to generate more sales and grow your business, lead generation is essential. You can prospect and qualify leads in a variety of ways. Good options include email marketing, guest posting, and promotion via social media. When it comes to converting leads, you can't do without a well-designed landing page.

> Landing pages are effective for 94% of B2B and B2C companies.
> marketingsherpa.com

> 650 targeted landing pages get an average visitor-to-lead conversion rate of 35.62%.
> hubspot.com

Source: Neil Patel

Your landing pages are what convince prospects to become customers. They're the first point of contact that people have with your website. A landing page is where visitors end up after moving through one of your marketing funnels. As such, it's vital you design and optimise your landing pages effectively.

You need to tailor each page to the target audience that's going to see it. You also need each page to be set up just right to achieve the high conversion rates you need.

It's never been easier to build that kind of high-converting landing page. You can do it with ease and without ever having even to see a line of code. That's thanks to the availability of landing page builder tools. Those tools let you produce perfect pages, all via an easy to understand drag-and-drop interface.

There is a wide variety of landing page builder options. Many of them are available to use for free. Each different option will have particular strengths and weaknesses. There are four primary features, though, that you'll want any landing page builder to have:

1. A/B testing features
2. User-friendly interface
3. CRM integration
4. Specialised analytics

A/B testing features

You probably won't get the optimisation of your landing page right straight away. A/B testing features are crucial to find out what converts and what doesn't. The facility for testing allows you to tweak and change your pages as needed.

Some landing page builders have built-in A/B testing. Other tools allow integration with third-party testing platforms. Either way, you want this facility to be a part of your chosen page builder. Unless you can 100% guarantee that you'll get all your pages spot-on first time around.

User-friendly interface

One of the primary benefits of using a landing page builder is that it's much easier than building a page from scratch. With the right tool, you can get a page designed and created without having to know anything about coding. The best tools have a user-friendly interface that makes the whole process intuitive.

 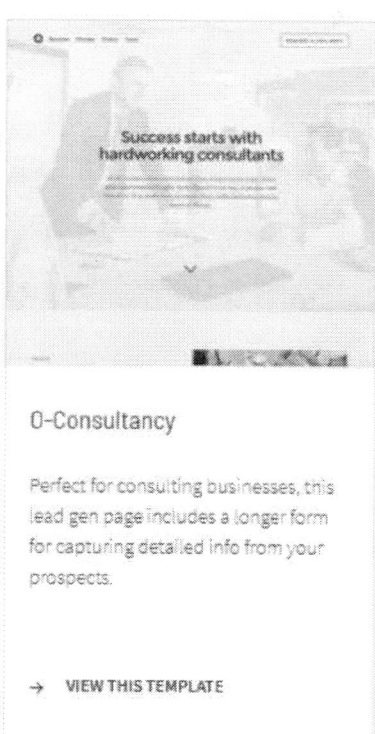 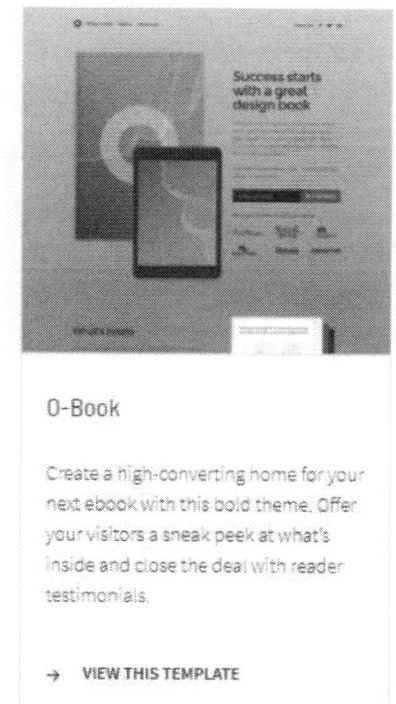

You can often create a whole page purely by dragging and dropping elements within the interface. Some of the tools, such as that offered by Unbounce, even provide you templates from which to work. The image above shows some examples of the niche-specific templates the Unbounce provides.

CRM Integration

Modern business is all about joined-up thinking. Your company's different departments and operations must all work seamlessly together. It's helpful if the various tools and software solutions they use can integrate.

The point of the landing pages you create is to convert leads and generate more sales. It's useful if your builder tool can interact with the CRM software you use to log and track leads and sales.

Specialised analytics

To keep your landing pages working to their best, you need to get to grips with their user data. You must be able to see the traffic they get and how they're converting at the very least. When you choose a landing page builder, check out the kind of analytics that the tool offers.

Some of the best tools will deliver detailed reports on landing page performance. Those are great for informing your testing and tweaking pages over time. With free tools, you may have to make do with more basic analytics options.

Heatmap tools

The conversions your website achieves are all down to how users interact with your pages. You need to engage those users and get them to consume your content. You need them to take the actions required to move down your sales funnel. If conversions aren't as high as you'd like them, it's because you've got problems somewhere along the way.

How, though, are you supposed to know what's putting site visitors off? How can you find out where along the process of viewing your pages, you're losing them? The answer might be by using heatmap tools. Heatmap tools are handy for analysing what people are up to on your site. They can help you answer crucial questions, like:

- Are users reaching your most important content, or failing to see it?
- Which links, buttons, and CTAs on your site get the most use?
- Are unnecessary site elements distracting visitors or putting them off?
- Do visitors interact with your site differently depending on the device they're using?

There are four main types of heatmaps. Some tools let you generate all four, while others focus on only one or two. It's worth looking at the full quartet that is around. Each enables you to assess different aspects of your site's performance.

Scroll maps

A scroll map is the simplest of the four heatmap varieties. It shows you how often each area of a page gets viewed by visitors. Areas shown in red on these maps are what most users see. Areas shown in blue get seen the least. You can use scroll maps to think about and tweak the placement of different elements on your pages.

Source: Hotjar

Click maps

Things get a bit more in-depth when it comes to click maps. They show you an aggregate number of clicks that different parts of a page get. Or taps in the case of pages viewed on mobile devices. The most-clicked elements show up in red, and the least clicked appear blue. These maps help show you the links, buttons, or CTAS on your pages that are and aren't working.

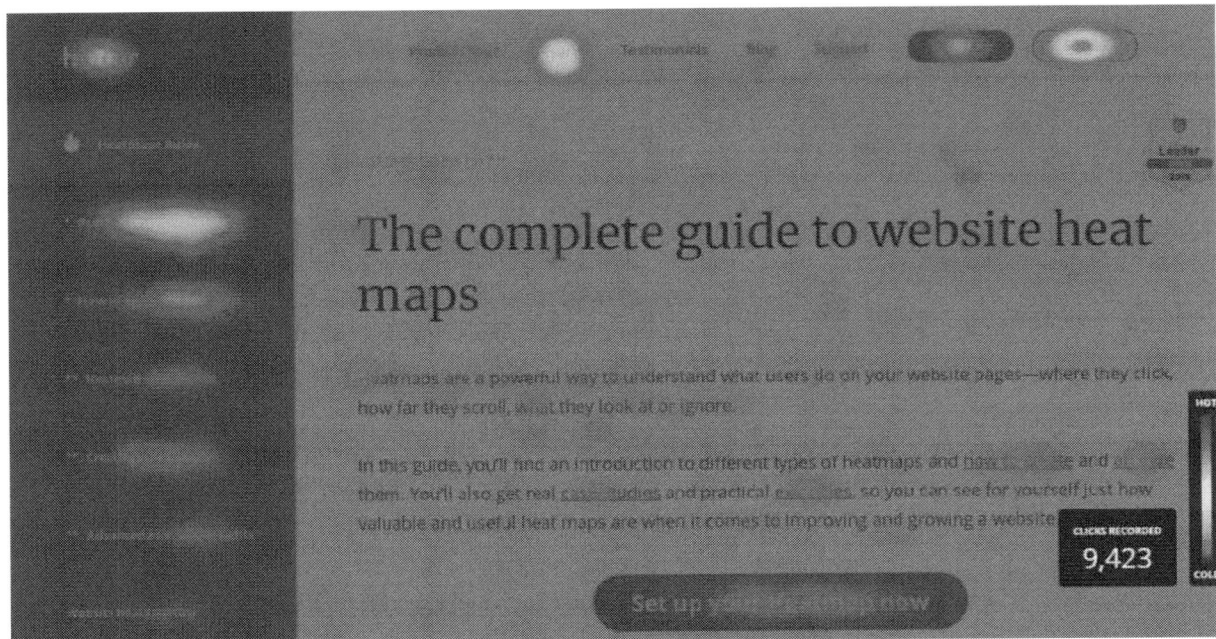

Source: Hotjar

Move maps

The utility of move maps is a little more questionable. These maps track where site visitors move and pause their cursor as they view a page. The so-called 'hot-spots' shown on these maps in red are where users leave their cursors for the longest.

There's some thought that where a site user puts their cursor correlates with where they're looking. As such, these maps may give you an idea of the elements or areas of text most interesting to your visitors.

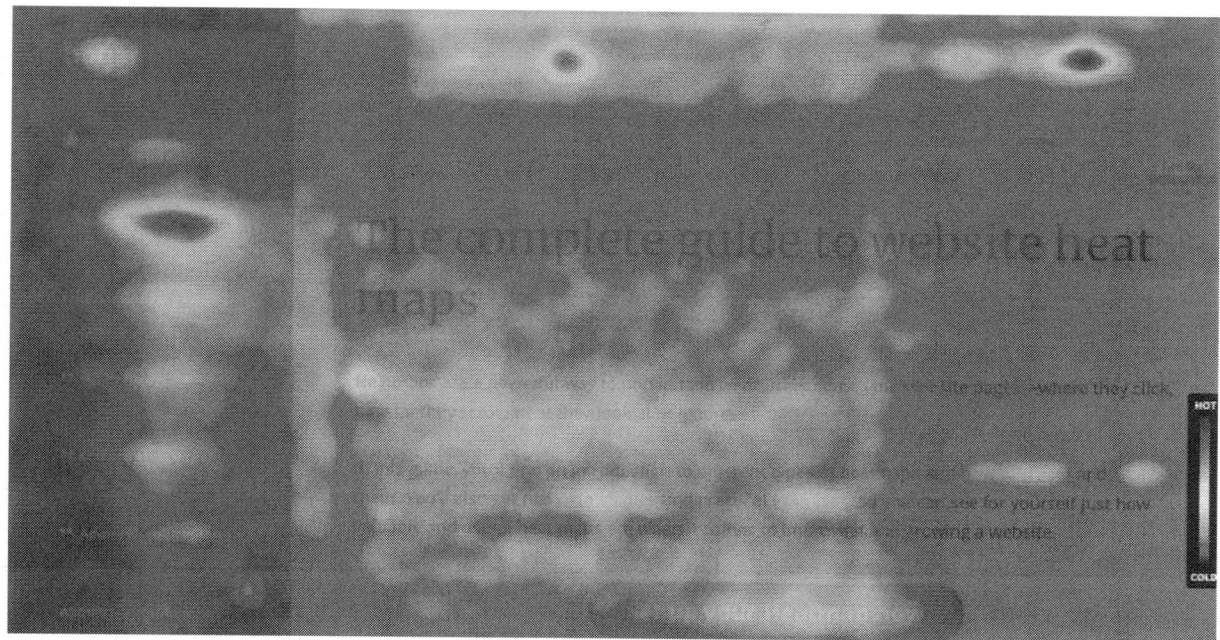

Source: Hotjar

Device comparison maps

Some website management tools let you create heatmaps for your pages as they appear on different devices. You can see if some elements or pieces of content are more popular on one type of device than another. Such insights help you judge how mobile-friendly your site is. They can also tell you if you should create separate mobile pages.

Google Analytics

Taking a customer-centric, data-driven approach will help you track sales. What that means is to focus on your customer's needs and desires and tailor your service accordingly. As a SaaS business, your customers are also your site visitors.

To learn their needs and what they do or don't like about your firm, you must know how they interact with your pages. Google Analytics is the perfect platform for gaining just those kinds of insights. The free platform from Google collects data and generates reports. Those reports tell you a wide range of things about your site and its users.

Analytics is a platform that can support many different arms of your business. The insights the platform gives will help you tailor your efforts in those various areas. Those changes, as a result, will have a significant knock-on effect on your bottom line. The following are the three primary areas where Analytics can prove invaluable:

- Marketing

- Site performance
- SEO

Improving marketing with Analytics

With Google Analytics, you can view a range of reports to inform your marketing efforts. Insights from the reports will show you marketing channels to focus on or to avoid. They'll also provide you with demographic information about your typical site visitors.

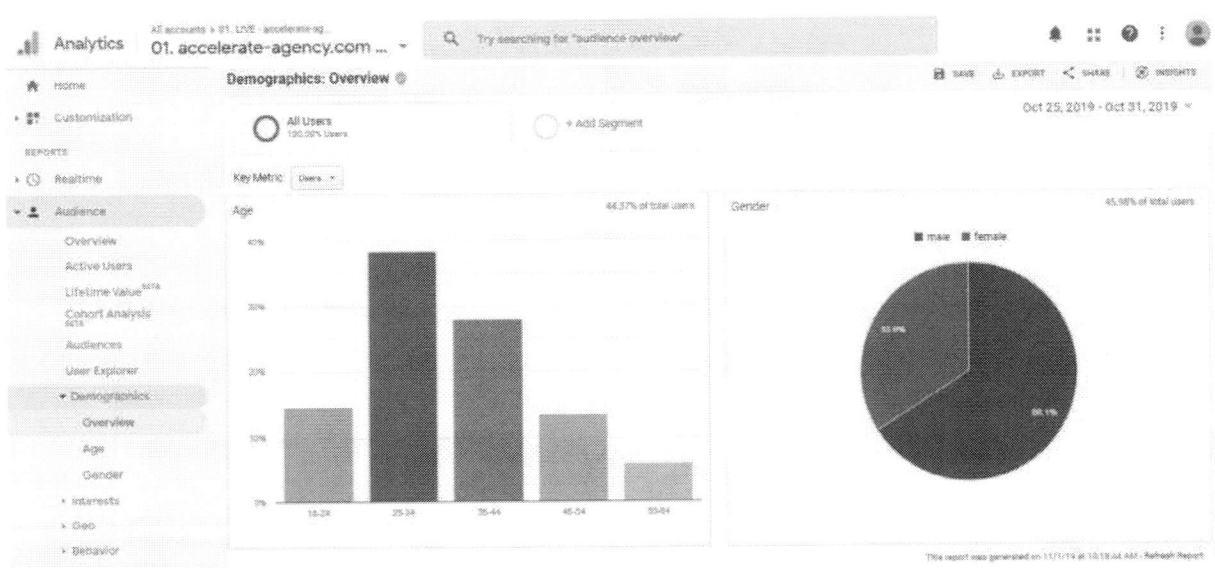

This information makes it much easier to tailor content or communications to suit those visitors. In short, Analytics helps you answer a range of questions vital to the marketing of your site. They include:

- How well does traffic convert from different marketing channels?
- Which channels deliver the most traffic to your pages?
- Where do your typical site users live, and what's their demographic make-up?
- How do visitors from different channels interact with your website?

Improving site performance with Analytics

The Google Analytics platform also helps you better understand your site. That understanding comes via insights into how people use your website. Those insights help you identify any issues with content, elements, or pages. They also show you what's working well with your target audience. Through Analytics reports, you can get answers to vital questions like those below:

- Which pages do site visitors most often abandon?
- How much traffic do various pages and posts get?
- Is the page load time quick enough?
- Does the site perform better on some devices than others?

Improving SEO with Analytics

Get more organic traffic to your site, and you'll generate more sales. The fundamental aim of SEO is to boost your organic traffic. Analytics is an excellent source of data to assess the value you're getting from your SEO efforts. The platforms reports will help you find out all of the following, and more besides:

- How much organic traffic do your pages get?
- Which landing pages convert most effectively?
- Which content gets viewed most by visitors gained via organic search?
- Are the bounce rates of your different pages within an acceptable range?

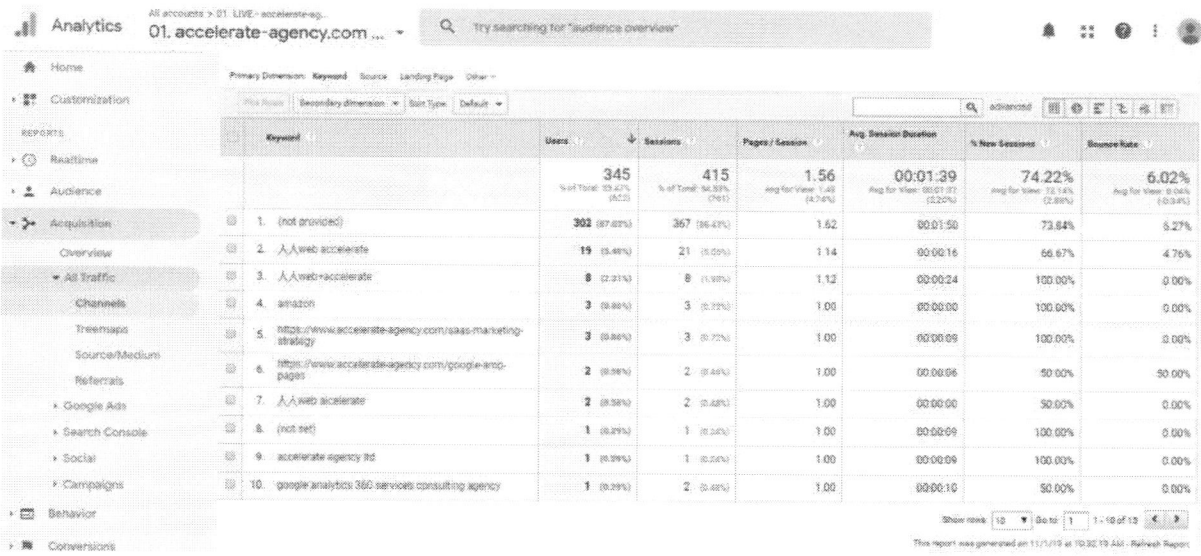

Speaking of helping SEO, our last website management tool is also invaluable in that area.

Google Search Console

Google Search Console is another of Google's free website management tools. It helps you to find out how Google views your website. Via the tool, you can better understand your pages' places in Google search results. By gaining that knowledge, it's much easier to improve the rankings of your pages. Pages that rank high in a search will get more traffic.

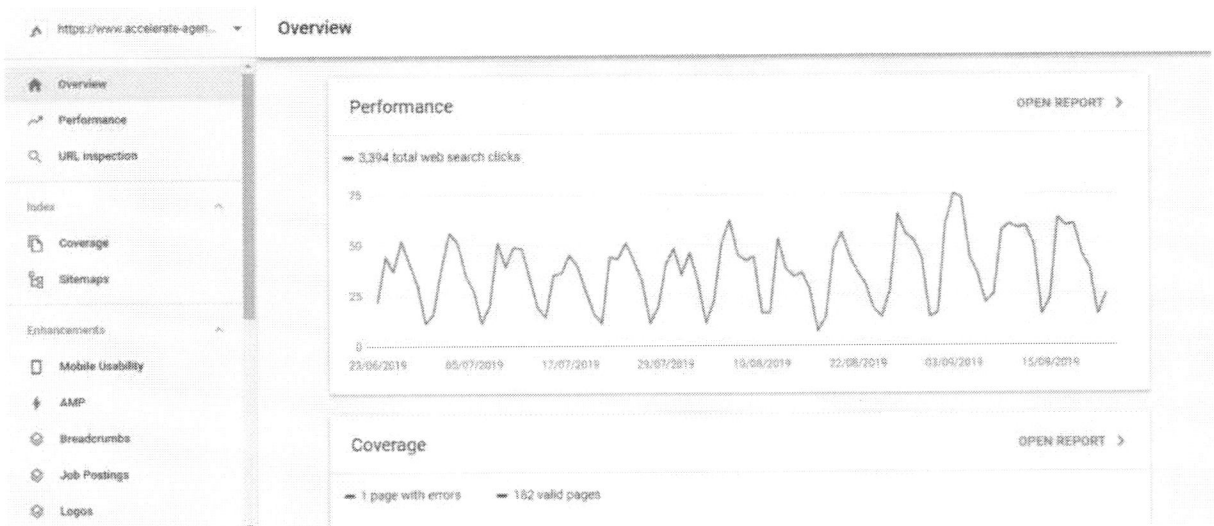

You can perform effective SEO without Search Console. Using the tool, though, makes several processes much easier:

- **Tracking search data** – Search Console is a one-stop-shop for assessing your site's performance in Google searches. You can see how often and where your pages appear on Google SERPs. You're also able to view the different search queries people use to find your website.

- **Optimising content** – the platform shows you quickly and clearly when there are issues with your site's content. It identifies issues, explains them, and suggests how you can solve them. You can then ask Google to re-index offending pages or posts, all in the same place.

- **Troubleshooting indexing issues** – one of the most beneficial features of Search Console is the alerts it provides. It notifies you about issues with duplicate content. It also flags up other issues that are hampering indexing. You can then get those issues straightened out before they have a more pronounced impact.

- **Site enhancements** – new elements or features of your site can be tricky to get right the first time around. Introducing things like structured data or AMP pages isn't straightforward. Search Console makes life much easier. It tracks your site enhancements and reports back if they're not working as they should. Or if Google doesn't recognise them at all.

Tool up to generate more sales

Your website is your most important sales tool as a SaaS business. The success of your business model depends on the site working well. You need it to get as much traffic as possible and to convert traffic into custom at a high rate. Optimising your website to achieve those goals is a vital part of business operations.

Anything that can make that crucial process more manageable is a godsend. The four free website management tools listed here, all do exactly that. By leveraging those tools, you can get all aspects of your site running smoothly. From marketing and promotion to SEO and user experience, the tools help you keep your site ship-shape.

In this section, we mentioned AB testing as an essential feature for landing page tools. In the next section, we will look at some testing examples that will help you decide what might need testing or tweaking on your landing pages and how to go about AB testing.

3.3: 10 AB testing examples that will help you improve your website

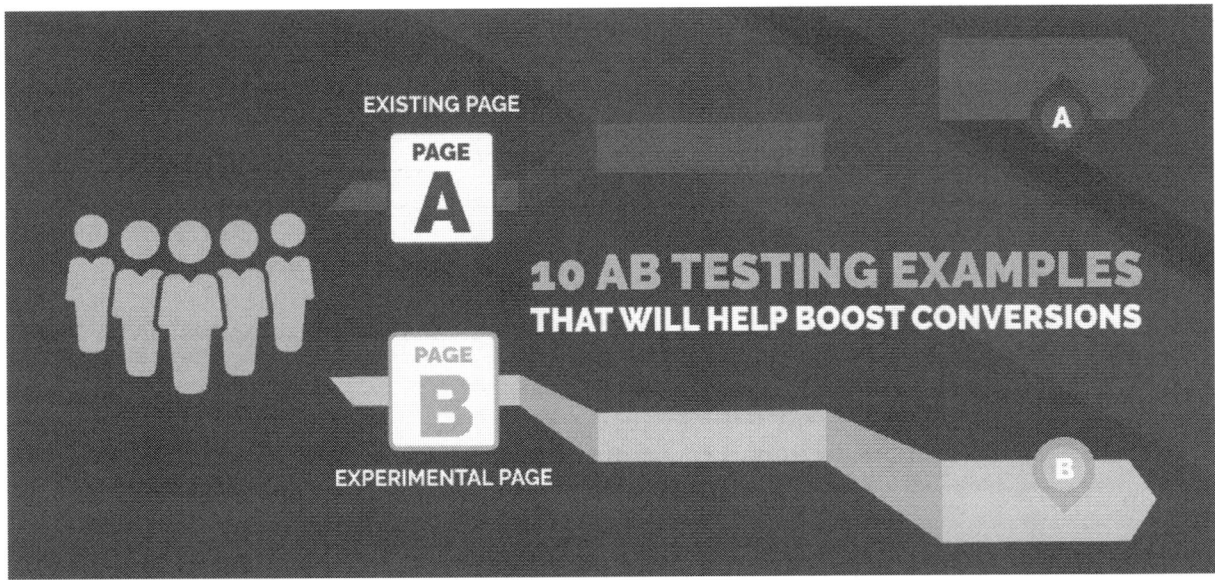

If you thought tests were something you'd got away from when you left school, we've got bad news for you. Testing is a crucial part of owning and running a successful SaaS website. At least in this case, though, you're the one setting and not sitting the tests.

What we're talking about is AB testing. You need to test everything you present to the public, as a business owner. You should scrutinise all elements of your website and your marketing materials. It's only through testing that you can be sure what you're showing to the public converts.

In the previous section, we mentioned that even the best web designers and marketers can't expect to get everything right the first time. AB testing gives you the data you need to tweak and update your site content and marketing assets as you go along. It allows you to test conversion rates.

If you're not sure what AB testing's about or how to do it, you're in the right place. We're going to give you a quick refresher on what AB tests are. Then, we'll run you through 10 real-world AB testing examples. All of them made a real difference for the firms involved. They should give you plenty of inspiration for tests of your own.

What is AB testing?

An AB test is where you compare two different versions of something. You're essentially testing 'option A' against 'option B.' This is where AB testing gets its name. For web developers, site owners, and marketers, what they need to test are versions of web content or marketing materials.

For example, you might look to test one version of a landing page against another. You'd create the two pages, and then expose them to equal-sized audiences. Using a platform like Google Analytics, or a split-testing tool, you can then get data on the effectiveness of each page. By analysing metrics like bounce rate and goal conversion, you can see which page is better.

Source: Invesp CRO

The most effective AB tests are those that allow you to draw definitive conclusions. You want to know why one page is better than the other, not just that it is. When testing, you might, for example, change only the style of

CTAs on your two pages. If one page has a higher conversion rate, you know which the better CTA is to use moving forward.

AB testing is an ongoing process. You need to keep tweaking and testing. That might sound like an arduous task, but it's well worth it. The gains you can make by properly optimising a page for conversions can be significant. That's borne out by the following ten AB testing examples. Each of them delivered stunning results for the businesses concerned.

AB testing examples

Whatever your niche or business model, AB testing is vital. It's what ensures you always put out the right marketing materials. The following are ten examples of how such testing has helped firms of all shapes and sizes.

HubSpot CTA test

HubSpot is a recognisable name in the marketing and SEO field. They have a massive online presence and a popular blog. The first of our AB testing examples regards how they attached a lead generation magnet to their blog posts.

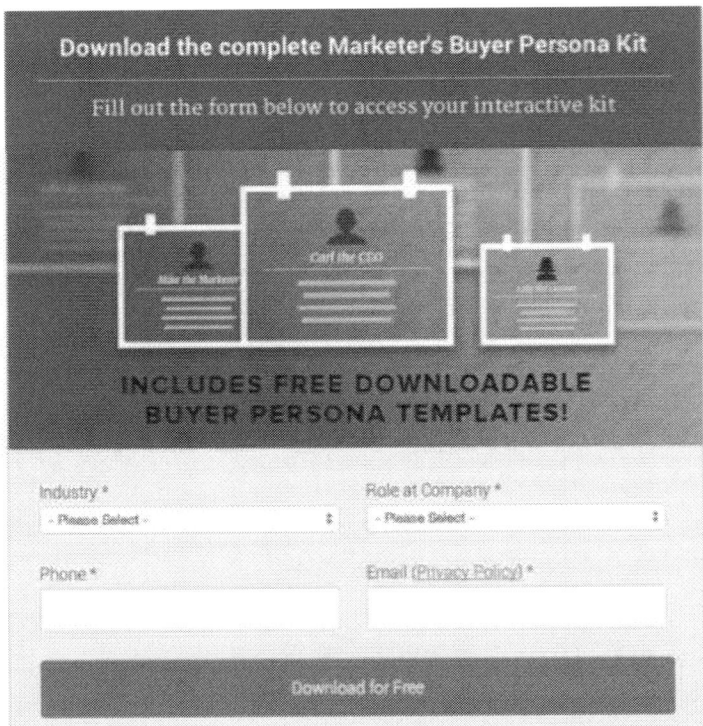

The company offered a guide to inbound marketing for free at the end of some posts. To access the book, readers had to fill in a contact form. HubSpot tested whether to provide a link to the form or to embed the form in the posts themselves.

When a form gets imbedded in that way, it's called an 'in-line CTA.' HubSpot's test found that their in-line CTA option improved the conversion rate by 71%. That's a significant boost to lead generation that any firm is sure to appreciate.

Highrise heading & subheading test

Highrise is a SaaS business specialising in customer relationship management (CRM) software. They performed an AB test to find the best possible combo of headings and subheadings for a sign-up page.

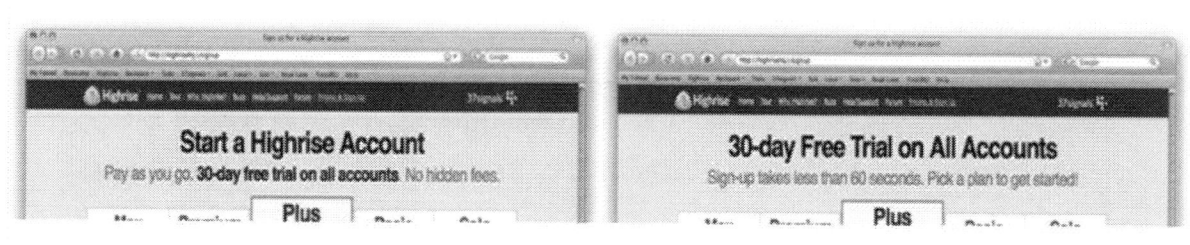

The firm developed five different headings and subheadings. They then randomised the combinations of those options and tested which performed best.

Switching up combinations like that goes against conventional AB testing wisdom. It's often better to change only one variable at a time. In this case, that would have meant changing only the heading or the subheading. You can't argue with Highrise's results, though.

Through the test, Highrise's original copy turned out to be their worst option. By trying new combos, the firm found a new heading and subheading pair that delivered 30% more clicks.

Groove landing page test

I've talked about how landing pages are critical to the success of any SaaS business. As a provider of customer support solutions for such firms, Groove understands that. That's perhaps why they performed an extensive AB test of their landing page design.

Original: 2.3%

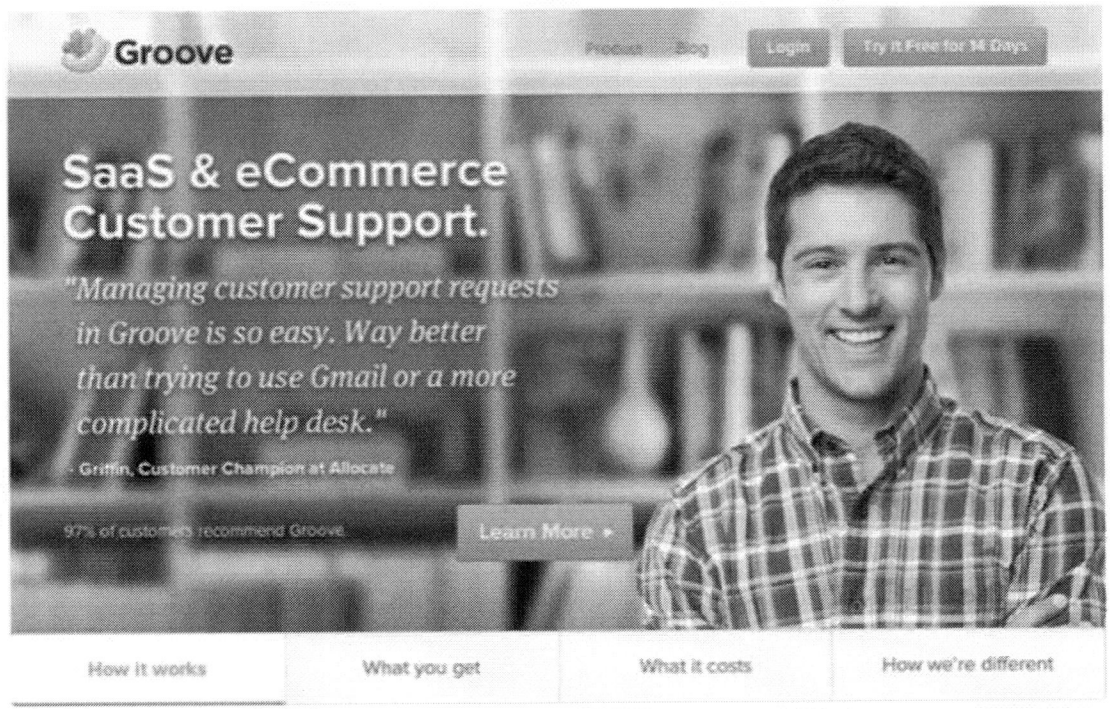

The company had a great product and blog, but a terrible conversion rate. They spoke to colleagues and experts and decided that they needed to redesign their landing page. To find out how they looked to their customers. The company talked to engaged users of their products. They found out what they cared about and how they spoke about the firm's product.

Long Form: 4.3%

Using that feedback, Groove reshaped their page. They tested many different options, all using suggestions and wording from their customers. The final result was a new page that converted at 4.3%, rather than Groove's previous lowly rate of 2.3%.

WallMonkeys homepage test

This is the first of our AB testing examples to feature a company that doesn't use the SaaS business model. WallMonkeys sell decorative wall decals online. Their homepage test, though, still offers some useful insights.

The company's original homepage had a large stock image and an overlaid headline. Their first test replaced the image. They swapped in a unique version, showing one of their actual products. The results were great. The website saw a 27% upturn in conversions. WallMonkeys, however, didn't stop there.

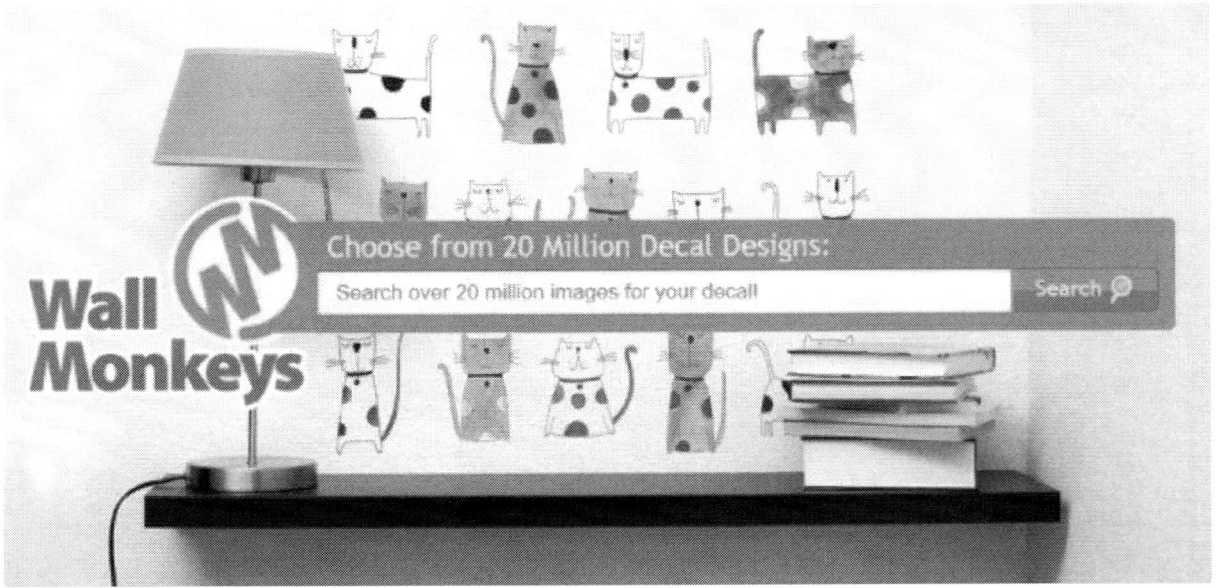

The firm followed up with a second AB test. They replaced the homepage headline with a prominent search bar. The results this time were significant, with the conversion rate rocketing by 550%. Those kinds of results display just how beneficial AB testing can be. It also demonstrates the wisdom of performing multiple tests, not only one.

Server Density pricing model test

Web design isn't all about aesthetics. It can sometimes have a profound impact on how potential customers see your products. Take Server Density, for example. They provide hosting and website monitoring on a SaaS model. Their site, therefore, has always displayed their pricing models.

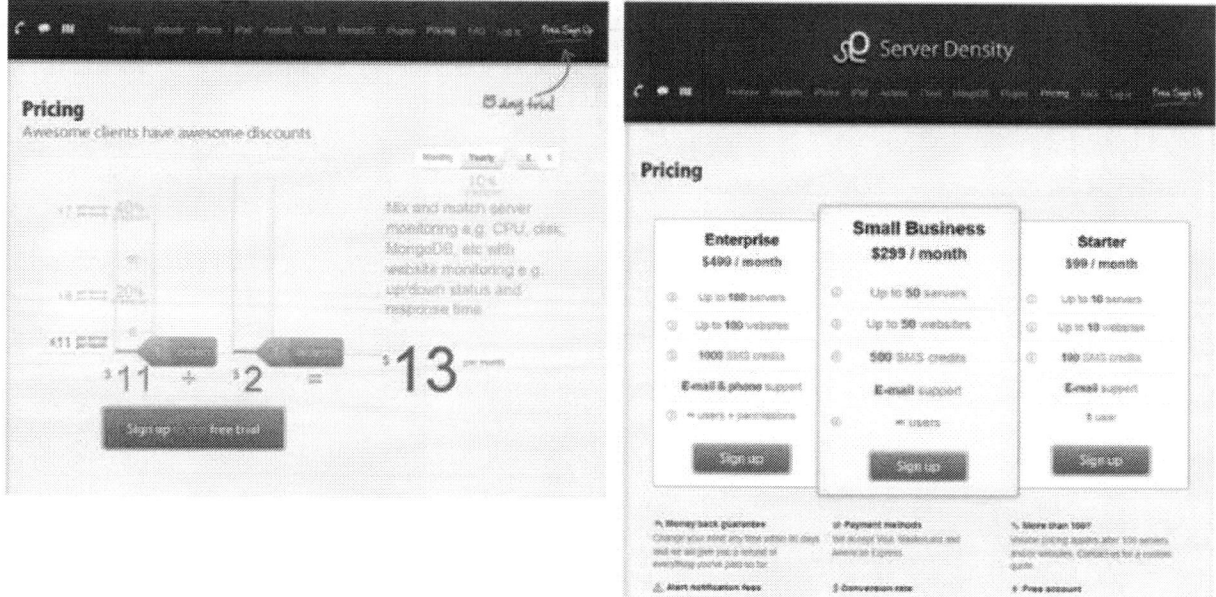

By performing an AB test, Server Density found that *how* they displayed their pricing models impacted conversions. The firm's original page focused on service *costs*. As an alternative, they tested a comparative table.

The alternative version of the page delivered not one, but two notable advantages. It led to an increase in overall revenue for the business. It also decreased the number of free trial sign-ups that didn't go on to subscribe.

Yuppiechef navigation test

This entry on our list of AB testing examples shows how simple tests can be. By only changing one small element of any page or asset, you can make considerable improvements to your site. Just like Yuppiechef did by testing the navigation feature on a landing page.

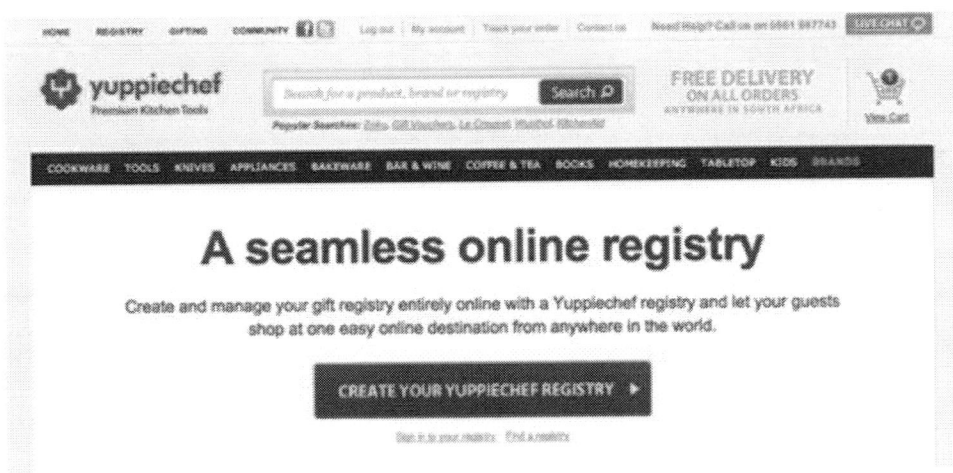

The kitchenware firm's original page included a simple navigation bar toward the top. That bar had links to different types of products and areas of the site. Yuppiechef tested the impact of removing the navigation bar.

Without the bar at the top of the page, the company's conversion rate jumped by 100%. Site users weren't getting distracted by links. This change made a massive difference to Yuppiechef's bottom line.

Humana banner test

Humana is a healthcare insurance carrier in the USA. Their AB testing example, like that of WallMonkeys, shows the wisdom of doing more than one test. In the case of the insurers, they were testing a banner advert.

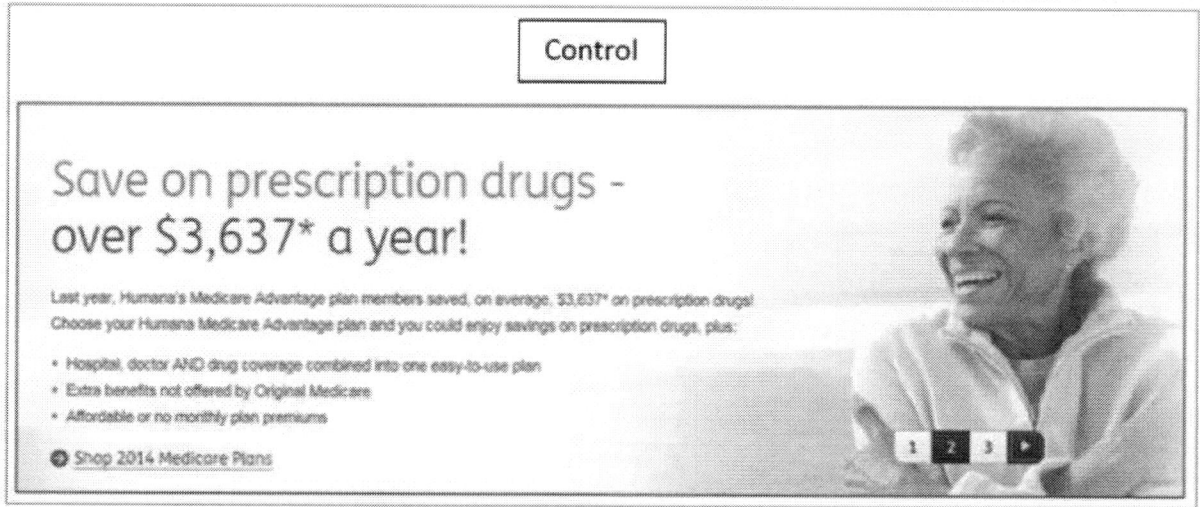

The business wanted to boost the click-through rate (CTR) of the banner. Humana's original banner had a headline, sales copy, a CTA, and an image. Via multiple, consecutive AB tests, the firm changed all those elements.

By testing each element, Humana ended up with a very different banner. The headline and copy were shorter and punchier. The CTA style was freshened up, and they made the image friendlier. By changing the copy and image, the banner's CTR jumped 433%. Adding the changes to the CTA resulted in another bump of 192%.

Sim City 5 sales page test

The world's biggest brands use AB testing. Electronic Arts (EA) are a household name in the gaming industry. They split test the pre-order page of one of their most popular games, Sim City 5.

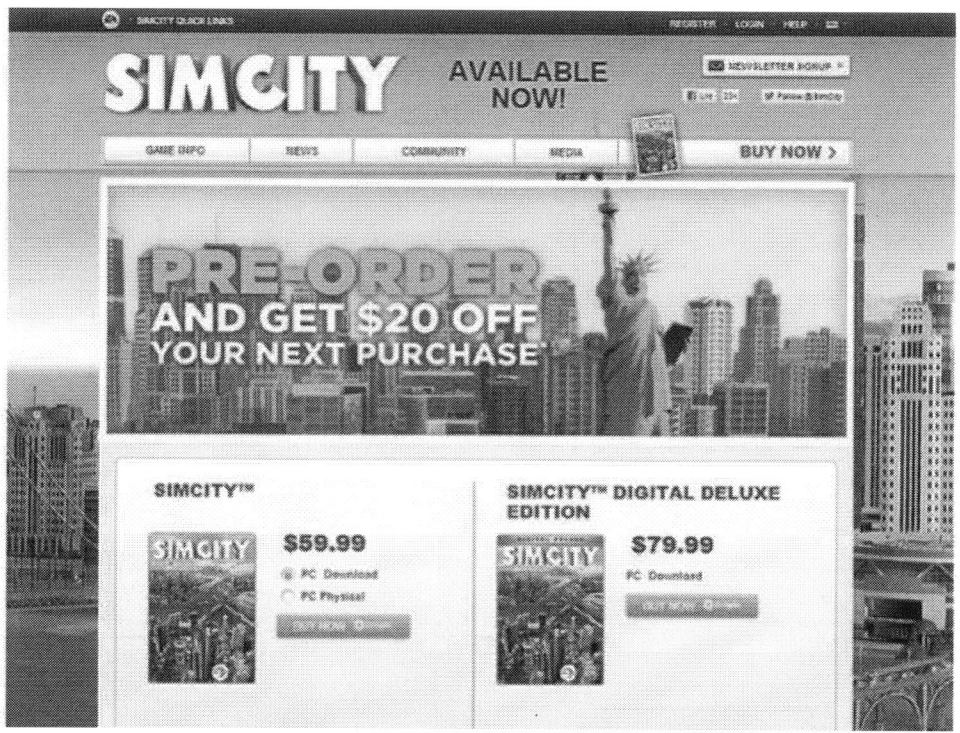

Most marketers assume that an offer or promotion helps boost conversions. As such, EA's first Sim City 5 sales page prominently featured a '$20 off your next purchase' incentive.

Via AB testing, the company found that marketing assumptions don't always hold. They tested another page, which was identical but for the absence of the promotion. That simpler alternative performed 40% better than the original.

Those people who wanted to pre-order the game weren't interested in any future purchases. The $20 off promotion didn't appeal to them. AB testing can help you avoid incorrect assumptions about your target audience.

RummyCircle Facebook Ad Test

Social media is a tool that every business owner must embrace. It can help your SEO, inform keyword research, and offer a lucrative marketing channel. If you do run social media adverts, AB testing will help you optimise them.

RummyCircle, a major Indian gambling firm, performed a simple AB test on one of their Facebook ads. They tested whether a hypothesis they had for the ad when viewed on desktop held for mobile devices.

On desktop, the firm found that users were more likely to click through the ad if they also commented on it. As such, the original ad copy included an invitation to comment.

The business's test involved one ad version that kept the invitation and one that didn't. On mobile, RummyCircle found that the option which didn't ask for a comment performed better. AB tests are also great for understanding different audience segments.

Olympic Store checkout test

The last of our AB testing examples shows that tests can also lead to significant changes. In the lead-up to the Vancouver 2010 Winter Olympics, the official merchandiser tested two types of eCommerce checkout.

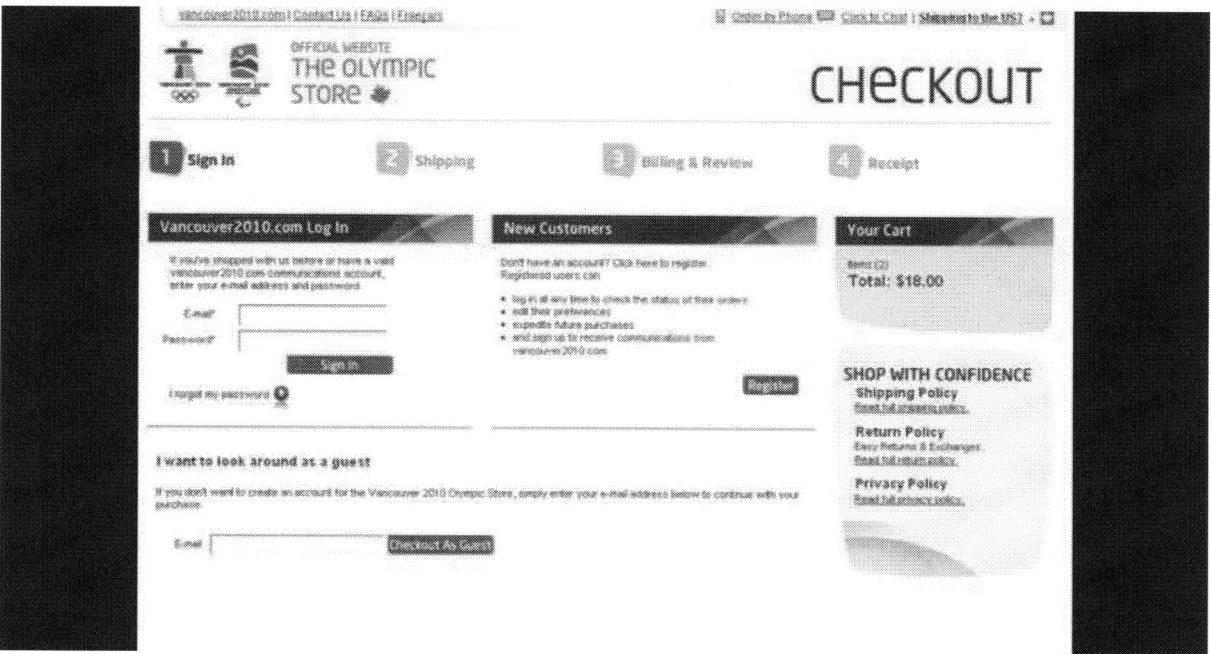

The first checkout option had multiple pages. Customers had to work through each page in turn to complete checkout. It made the process seem complicated.

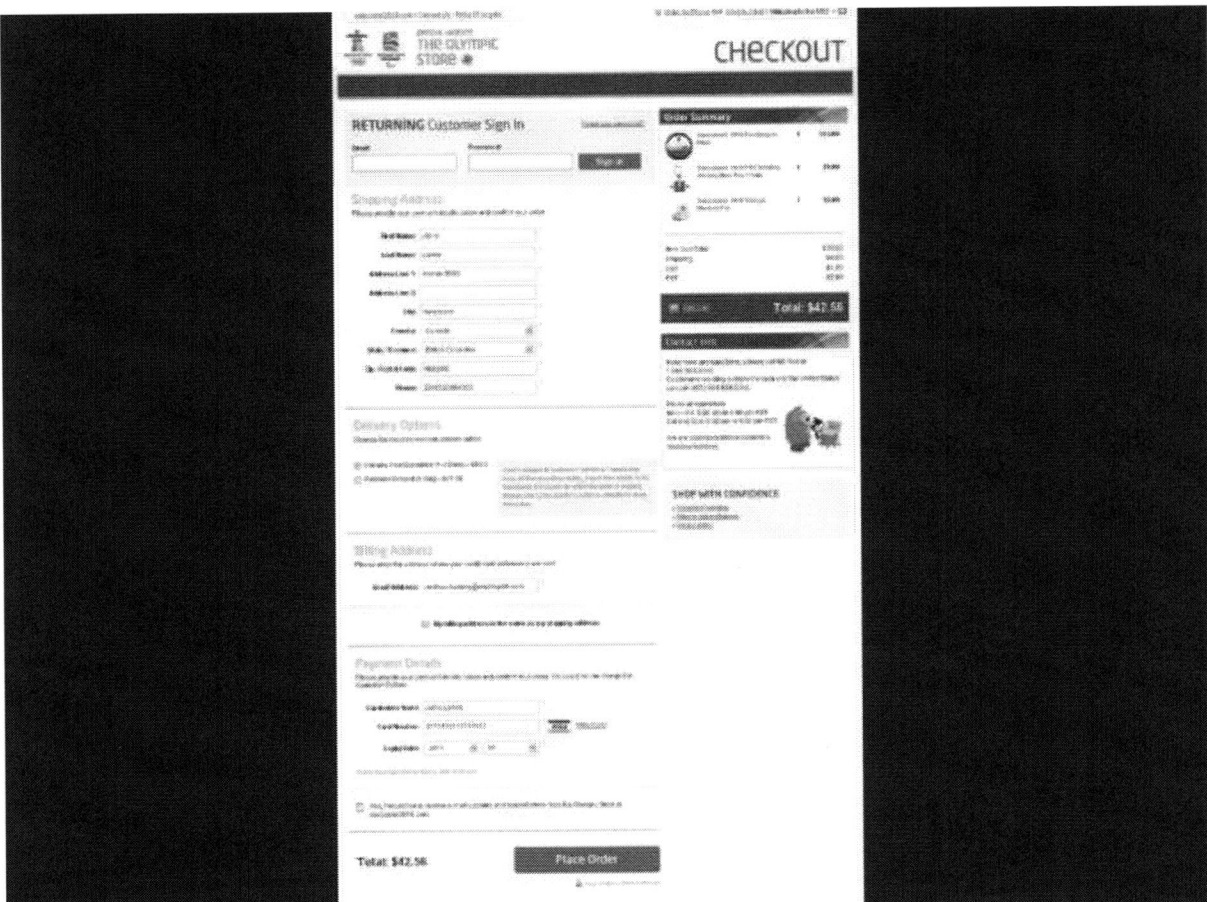

The store's alternative checkout put everything on one page. Customers could enter all the required info in one place. The new checkout also made it more evident that creating an account wasn't a prerequisite of buying something.

After only 606 transactions, the site's owners felt they could end the test. The alternative checkout had outperformed the original by 21.8%. They scrapped that original and went with the new version.

Test your way to success

Not all of the AB testing examples mentioned above will apply to your business. By learning about them, though, you should have a better understanding of the value of AB tests. They're crucial to learning what works with your actual customers or target audience.

By performing AB tests, you can optimise your content and marketing assets for conversions. You'll be sure that you're presenting pages and putting out adverts that convert. That's vital for generating those sales that will make for a healthy bottom line.

In this chapter, we have talked about how data and analytics can help inform changes to your website to improve conversion. In the next chapter, we will go over some key metrics that every employee in your SaaS business needs to know about.

Customer retention is critical to your business success and retention depends on your customer service. The next chapter will focus on how you can analyse and improve your customer retention, and in particular, how the SaaS business model is different from a standard eCommerce business.

Chapter 4: Retaining existing customers

Every business is shooting for sustainable growth. Growing your customer base, turnover, and profits in manageable fashion is the key to long-term success. The only way to get that kind of growth is if you fully understand your own company. You must know where you stand and where you need to get to in the future. You must know your current customers and your leads inside out.

The only way to have such a firm grasp on your business is by collecting and assessing data. You must track and analyse all those things that make your company and its customers tick. That's why data analytics platforms like Google Analytics are so crucial to modern firms. Those platforms let a company get to grips with the metrics that tell them how they're performing.

For SaaS companies, though, the most critical metrics differ. The SaaS business model is unique. You and your staff need to take a different view of your company and your customers. Read on, and you'll learn the essential SaaS metrics that you must track if you're going to succeed.

Success is dependent on winning new customers and retaining existing customers most efficiently and economically. We'll cover customer churn prediction and analysis in later sections, as well as how you can reduce your customer churn. First, though, we'll cover ten essential metrics we believe every SaaS employee needs to know.

4.1: 10 essential SaaS metrics every employee needs to know

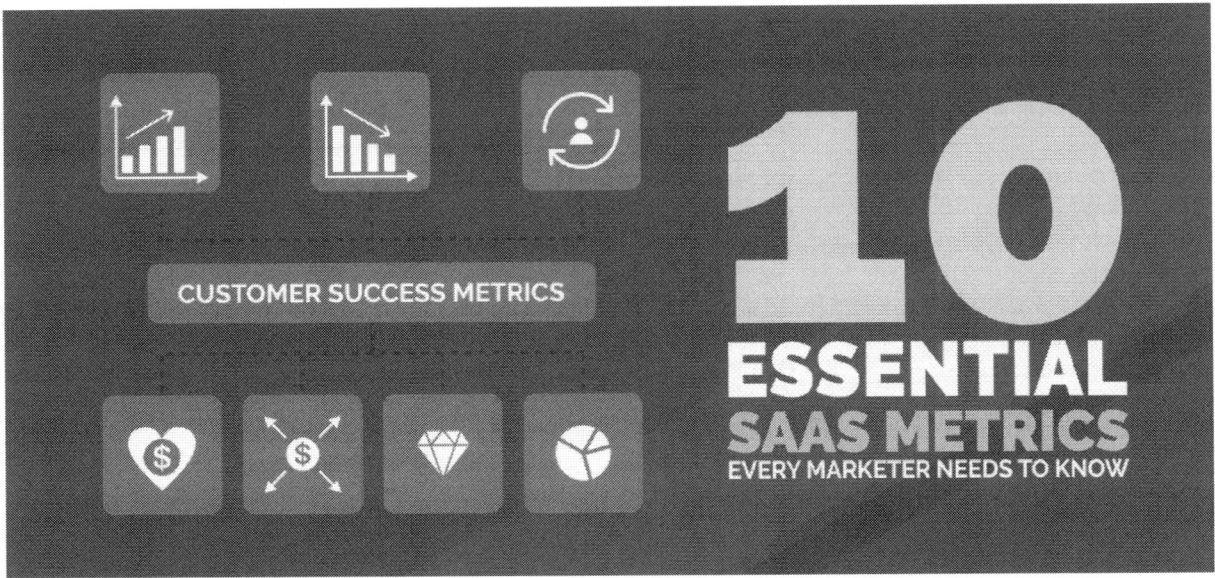

What makes SaaS different?

In most business models, the majority of revenue comes at the time of purchase. A firm acquires customers, sells them their product or service, and takes their money. The SaaS model is demonstrably different. The revenue SaaS companies get for their services comes over an elongated period.

That period is called the customer lifetime. The longer a customer lifetime your SaaS firm can foster, the more revenue you get. If a customer abandons your service earlier, you stop getting their money.

For any SaaS business, then, customer retention is vital. You must work to make every customer lifetime as long as possible. That's on top of other practical considerations, like profit margins or marketing decisions.

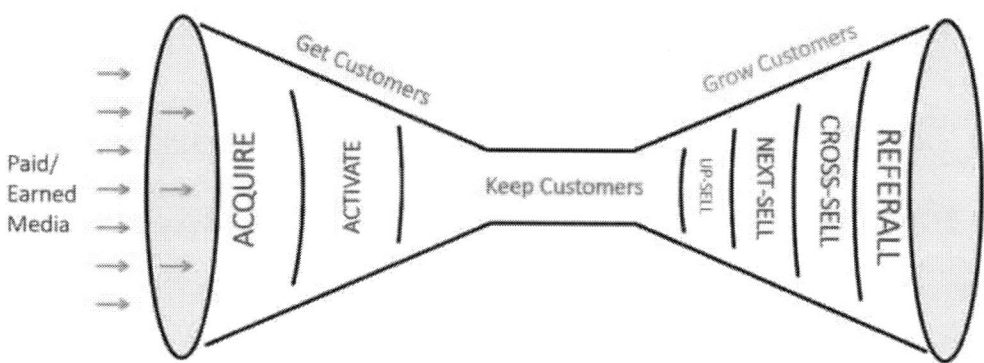

Source: Lean Case

The SaaS model, therefore, has three primary components:

1. Acquiring customers
2. Retaining customers
3. Monetising customers (getting upsells and repeat sign-ups)

Traditional business metrics don't account for the traits of the SaaS model. They don't offer the insights needed to optimise those three components of your business. That's why there are specific SaaS metrics to aid those companies.

Understanding and tracking those metrics is what will bring the sustainable growth you crave. Before you can assess the metrics and derive vital insights from them, you must know what they are. The following is a brief guide to essential SaaS metrics.

The SaaS metrics you need to understand

When your firm invests in marketing your SaaS product, you're trying to generate future growth. You're not only aiming at a one-off retail sale. As such, to make your promotional efforts effective, you need to grasp particular metrics.

Those metrics must tell you about customer retention, value, and happiness. They can't only deal with acquisition. The ten measures below are vital to understanding all those aspects of your relationship with customers.

Customer churn

Customer churn is the most important metric for SaaS businesses. It measures the number of customers abandoning your service over time. A customer churn rate, for instance, is often expressed as several customers per month or year.

No business can entirely avoid customer churn. Some people who sign up will let their subscription lapse at the end of its term. Other customers will decide to leave your company earlier. To grow your business fast, you need to keep customer churn as low as possible.

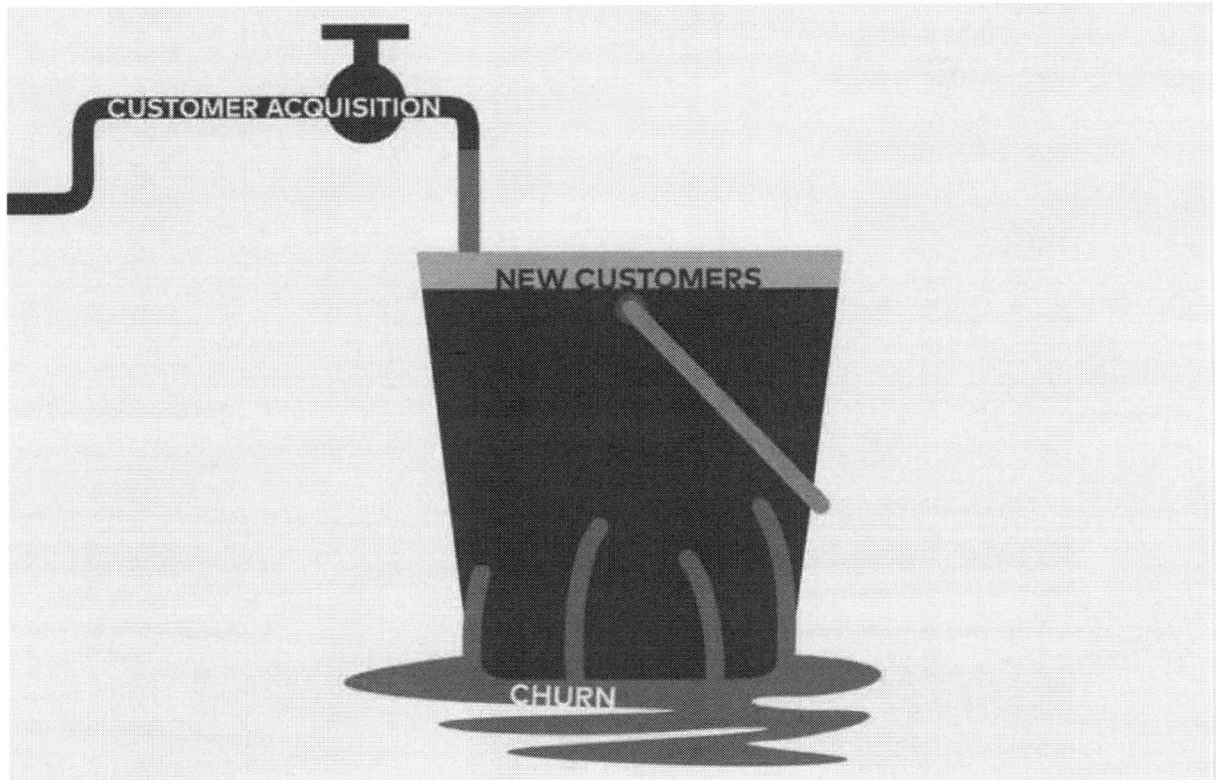

Source: Medium

As your firm relies on steady, ongoing revenue from customers, high churn can hurt the bottom line. The first step to reducing customer churn is tracking and logging your current rate.

Once you've got data on your business's customer churn, you can start digging deeper. Look at whether the customers who've abandoned your service have anything in common. That can highlight any specific issues that are making your product less appealing to those people.

Monthly Recurring Revenue (MRR)

The success of any SaaS business gets determined by the stream of revenue it has coming in. Growing a company is about sustaining and supplementing that stream. Monthly Recurring Revenue (MRR) is a metric that helps you track your success at doing just that.

Your MRR reports how much revenue your customers generate per month. Achieving high MRR is how SaaS firms stay profitable. By continually offering value to your customers, they keep paying you month on month. You can then acquire new customers and look to keep your MRR tracking upwards.

Keeping a close eye on your MRR is vital for a few reasons. Firstly, it can combine with your customer churn data to identify issues quickly. If your MRR starts falling, you know that something's going wrong.

Secondly, MRR also helps you find the ideal price point for sustainable growth. If you've undervalued your service, your MRR won't increase enough, even if you're acquiring new customers.

Customer Lifetime Value (CLTV)

Customer Lifetime Value (CLTV) is the average amount one customer is worth to your business. CLTV helps you judge the acquisition cost of new customers or the impact of losing existing ones.

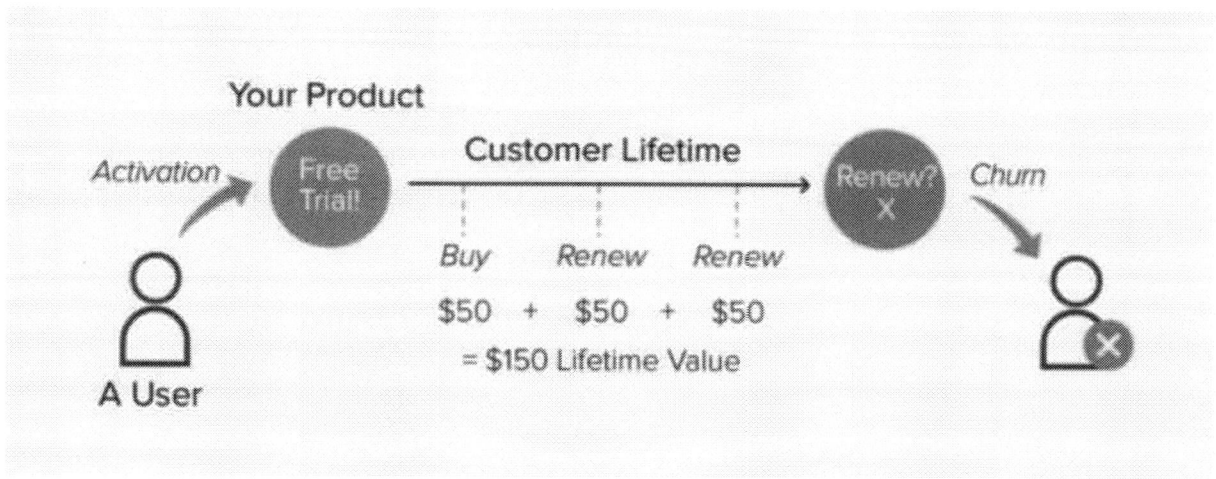

Source: Chartmogul

Working out CLTV is easy:

1. Find your average monthly revenue per account. You can find this by dividing your MRR by the total number of customers

2. Multiply the average monthly revenue by the average number of months customers that stay with you

CLTV is useful for quantifying the worth of a new customer. It tells you just how much revenue you can expect to recoup long-term for each new client you bring on board. That can help you better assess the ROI of SEO, PPC advertising, or other marketing efforts.

Customer Acquisition Cost (CAC)

Customer Acquisition Cost (CAC) is a SaaS metric that goes hand in hand with CLTV. It shows how much it costs your business to acquire a new customer. Expenses in that regard include salaries to sales staff, advertising costs, and all else besides.

To calculate your CAC, you need to work out that total expense in a given time. It's often easiest to choose a month. You add up the full extent of your spending on marketing, promotion, and onboarding.

Then, divide that figure by the number of new customers you acquired in the same period. That gives you a measure of how much it costs for you to attract each new customer. You'll then want to compare this figure with the CLTV you calculated earlier, but we'll get to that later.

Months to recover CAC

We've already talked about how crucial customer retention is to the SaaS business model. Months to recover CAC is a SaaS metric that provides the data to support that assertion. It displays how long it takes after acquiring a customer before you recoup your costs.

In other words, this metric tells you how long you need to keep a customer until you start making a profit. As you grow your business, you'll want to work to drive the number of months to recover CAC as low as possible.

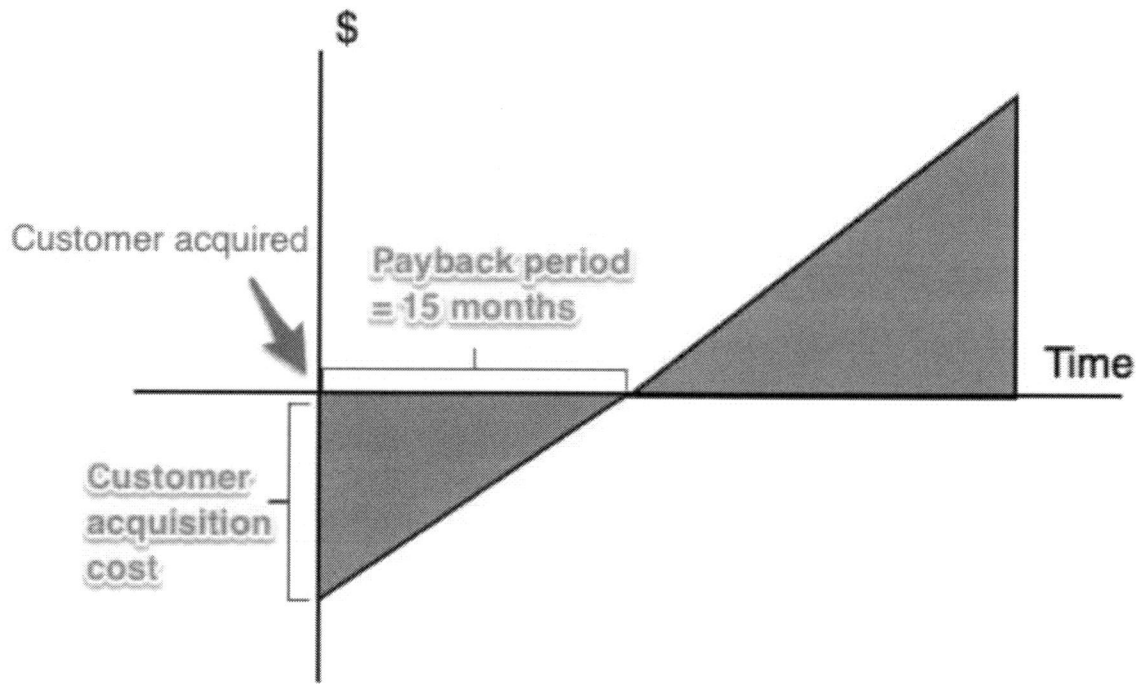

Source: Profitwell

There's a straightforward equation to figure out the months to recover CAC metric:

CAC / MRR x GM

In that equation, GM stands for gross margin. That's the profit you make after subtracting sales costs from your total revenue.

CLTV-to-CAC ratio

When you've got to grips with both CLTV and CAC, you can combine them to create a new metric. Your CLTV-to-CAC ratio is another crucial measure of the health of your business. It tells you if you've got the right ingredients in place for sustainable, long-term growth.

There's no complicated calculation for the CLTV-to-CAC ratio. You compare the two figures in question. If they're of the same value, the ratio is 1:1. If the CLTV is ten times the value of the CAC, the ratio is 10:1.

A thriving SaaS business should have a CLTV-to-CAC ratio of 3:1 or higher. If your figure is lower, you're spending too much on acquisition compared to what each customer is worth. It costs you more to bring a new customer on board than you'll ever earn from their custom. You need to either reduce acquisition costs or raise the price of your product.

Expansion revenue

Expansion revenue is the first of our SaaS metrics that deals with the third component of the SaaS business model. To refresh your memory, that was the 'monetising customers' component. Expansion revenue is a measure of any increase in MMR achieved via upselling or customers upgrading to more expensive plans.

Achieving a high expansion revenue is beneficial for any business. It's particularly useful for a firm with a comparatively high customer churn rate. That's because your expansion revenue helps to offset the drop in MMR caused by high churn.

Source: Open View Partners

It's possible to achieve a negative effective churn rate via expansion revenue. That's the name given to when a firm's expansion revenue is worth more than the negative impact on MMR of customer churn.

Net Promoter Score (NPS)

This is another SaaS metric that's useful due to its possible impact on customer retention. A net promoter score (NPS) is a value you can generate to assess the happiness of your customers.

All you need to do to create this measure of customer happiness is to give your customers a one-question survey. You ask the customers to rate from 1-10 how likely they are to recommend your product to others. You can then take an average of those ratings to create your NPS.

The higher the score, the more satisfied your customers are. The lower the score, the less they think of you and your product. If you get a low NPS, it can point to potential customer retention problems. By identifying those issues, you can nip them in the bud before they take root.

Qualified marketing traffic

Any business with an online presence should be using Google Analytics and related tools. Those platforms are excellent at helping track website traffic from different marketing channels. As a SaaS business, though, you need to take things one step further.

Due to the nature of your business, existing customers probably visit your site a lot. They might have to return to your pages every time they want to log in to your service. As you get more customers, your pages will get more traffic. That traffic isn't reflective of the success of your marketing efforts.

You need to segment your site visitors. You must separate returning customers from other leads or prospects. The latter is what's known as qualified marketing traffic. It's this traffic that you want to track. Many analytics platforms and even in-app analytics options give you ways of doing so.

Lead-to-customer rate

Our final SaaS metric to track is your website's lead-to-customer rate. This is the rate at which leads to your site converting into real customers. It's a critical metric. It reports on the success of your sales processes and lead-nurturing activities.

Like many of the metrics on this list, the lead-to-customer rate is easy to calculate. All you do is divide your total number of new customers by your total number of leads in a particular period. Then, you multiply that figure by 100.

For example, you may have had 500 leads in a month and got five new customers during the same period. Your lead-to-customer rate, in that case, would be 1% (5/500 x 100). The higher your lead-to-customer rate, the better you're converting your leads.

Master the metrics to help your business grow

As the owner of a SaaS business, you have lots of crucial decisions to make. You need to find the right path forward for your company. You must optimise your product, pricing, and promotion perfectly to achieve success. Data-driven insights into your business and its customers can help you find the right way to go.

The most pertinent metrics to inform your choices are not the same as those other types that businesses lean on. The unique nature of the SaaS business model means you must learn different things about your customers and your site. The ten SaaS metrics featured here are crucial measures of your firm's performance. Get to grips with them, and success could be just around the corner.

This section has highlighted the importance of customer churn to your SaaS business success. In the next section, we will look at predicting and analysing your customer churn rate. Keeping an eye on your customer's happiness and predicting when their opinion is turning will help you keep your business proactive and solve customer problems early before they become a reason to leave.

4.2: Customer churn prediction and analysis

Customer retention is a vital pillar of any business that works on a subscription-based model. For telecom companies and other service providers, retaining customers is important. For SaaS firms, it's key to their survival.

The SaaS business model relies on getting recurring revenue from customers. They must provide a steady stream of cash throughout their lifetime with the company. Elongating customer lifetime, then, is a crucial way for SaaS firms to scale. It's as important as marketing and promoting their site to new customers – if not more so.

Once a customer has abandoned your SaaS firm, it's tough to win them back. They've made up their mind about your service, and there are undoubtedly other options to which they can turn. The best customer retention, then, is proactive. You must look to keep customers as happy as possible. That helps remove the risk of them taking their custom elsewhere.

How do you know how likely any one customer is to take their business to a competitor? How can you find out which clients you need to focus your efforts on? The answer may be through customer churn prediction and analysis.

What is customer churn & why does it matter?

In the last section, I highlighted that customer churn is the name given to when customers – and mainly subscribers to a service – abandon a business. A customer has churned when they fail to renew the service. They have also churned if they actively end a subscription.

The customer churn metric is key to SaaS businesses. To succeed, companies must keep customer churn to an absolute minimum. Every customer that abandons the firm damages its bottom line in two distinct ways.

First, the company loses the regular income it gets from the customer's subscription. On top of that, the firm must also spend more on marketing and promotion to replace the customer. If they allow their customer base to shrink, turnover and profits will start to track rapidly downwards.

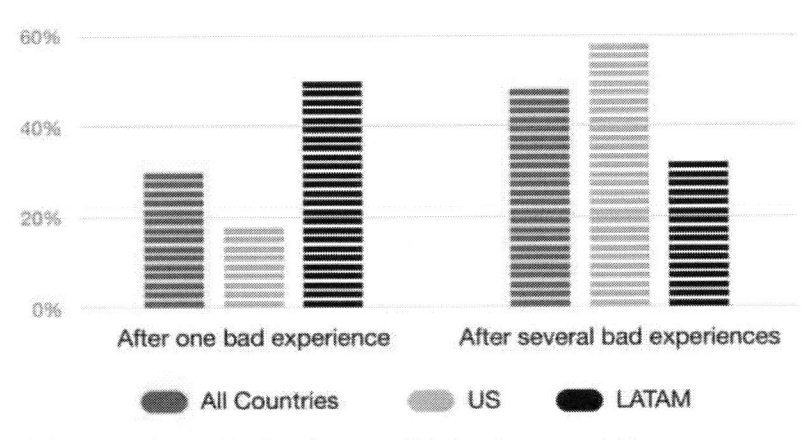

Figure 4: When do consumers stop interacting with a brand they love?

Q: At what point would you stop interacting with a company that you love shopping at or using?
Source: PwC Future of Customer Experience Survey 2017/18

Customers can churn for many different reasons. Bad experiences with your business or service will very often lead to churn. In other cases, simple service fatigue can explain churn. Service users may find over time that the service no longer satisfies their needs.

Whatever the reason, churn is something any SaaS firm must keep a handle on. Left unchecked, it can get out of hand quickly. As Michael Redbord, general manager of Service Hub at HubSpot explains:

"In a subscription-based business, even a small rate of monthly/quarterly churn will compound quickly over time. Just 1 percent monthly churn translates to almost 12 percent yearly churn. Given that it's far more expensive to acquire a new customer than to retain an existing one, businesses with high churn rates will quickly find themselves in a financial hole."

Source: Altexsoft

Wouldn't it be great, then, if you could predict and pre-empt customer churn?

The difficulties & importance of predicting customer churn

Customer retention and customer acquisition are the two options for combatting customer churn. Firms must either try to prevent customers from leaving or bring new customers on board. Ideally, they'd want to add more new customers than leave. Moreover, customer retention is often much more cost-effective than customer acquisition.

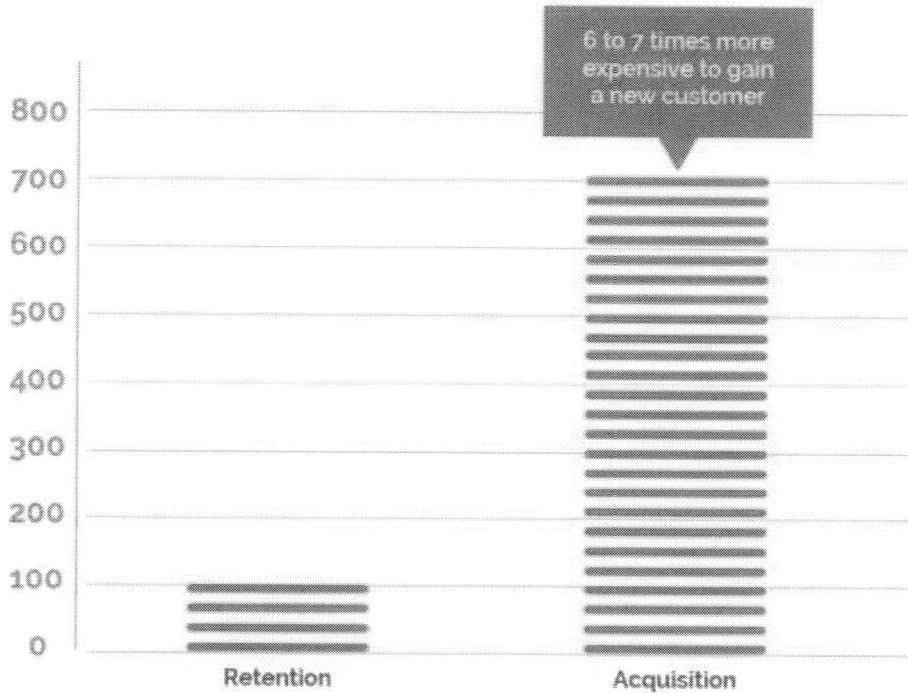

Many firms still favour acquisition, however. That's because they know how, when, and where to market their products to new customers. Understanding the best ways to boost customer retention is trickier. It takes a lot more time and effort.

Businesses can't spend that time and effort – not to mention finance – on each customer. That would not be viable. What they need to predict in advance the customers at risk of churning. They can then focus their retention efforts on those individuals.

What we've just described is customer churn prediction. It's a process made possible by cutting-edge data gathering and analytics tools. By collecting data, and developing a model from it, you can identify the customers most likely to leave. With that knowledge, you can do whatever's necessary to keep them from doing so.

Read on, and you'll learn a simple way of carrying out that invaluable customer churn prediction and analysis.

How to perform customer churn prediction & analysis

Customer churn prediction works on a straightforward premise. You can predict how likely a customer is to churn based on how they've recently used your service. You're looking to answer if a customer is going to leave within a specific period. I.e., are they going to cancel their subscription within the next month?

The result of such a prediction will be either a 'yes' or a 'no' answer. Any customers for whom the answer is 'yes,' you can then reach out to and work to change that answer. If the 'yes' or 'no' answer is the output of the process, customer data on service usage is the input. Gathering data, then, is the first step of a three-step customer churn prediction and analysis process:

1. Collecting data
2. Creating a predictive model from your dataset
3. Using the model to predict customer churn

Collecting data

The predictive model you're going to create utilises machine learning. Machine learning is an AI-based data analysis technique. The simplest way to explain the process is via pattern recognition. Models are 'trained' so that they can ID and recognise patterns in data.

The 'training' process involves presenting the model with as much data as possible. It then discerns the patterns and relationships between the data. Ultimately, the model can apply what it has 'learned' to any new data set that it gets presented. It's, therefore, able to predict possible future actions based on past patterns.

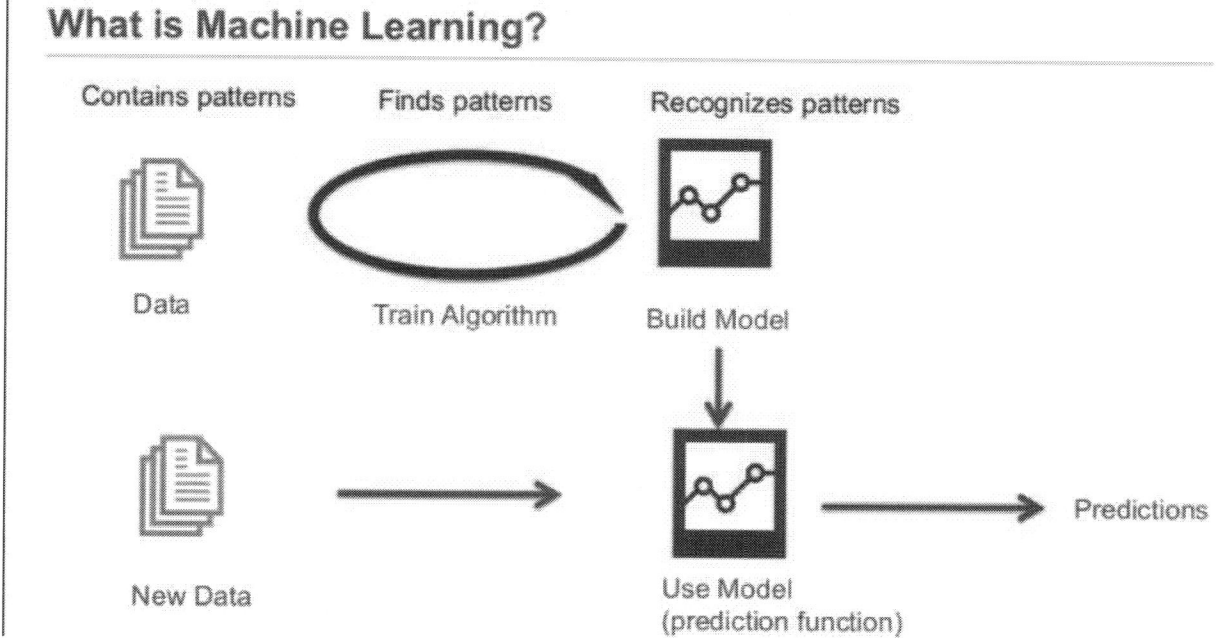

Source: Slideshare

The first step to customer churn prediction is collecting data to train your model. The data you need should relate to current or former customers who both have and haven't left your company. That way, you can compare all present and future customer data on customers who did and didn't churn.

Your data needs to contain as much information about customers as possible. Each piece of customer information is called a feature. The more customer features you can gather, the more accurate your model will be. It will, after all, be able to recognise patterns that relate to a broader range of features.

For customer churn prediction, there are four main categories of customer feature to focus on:

- **Customer features** – this is data related to the individual characteristics of each customer. It can include anything from age and gender to education level and income.

- **Support features** – information related to how customers interact with your customer support. This data can include how often they contacted your support staff or the subjects of their queries.

- **Usage features** – any data you can gather on how each customer has used your service. For instance, how frequently they log in or how long it is since they last did so. If you can collect info on how long they spend on your app or what actions they take when there, all the better.

- **Contextual features** – this is a catch-all for all other data you can gather. Do you know, for example, via which type of device they access your service? Can you identify the customer support agent they've contacted the most?

Customer churn prediction is about finding customers who may soon leave you. When collecting data, you need to quantify 'soon.' Decide what the exact question you want your model to answer. Is it:

1. Will a customer churn within one month?
2. Will a customer churn within three months?
3. Will a customer churn within six months?

The exact question you choose depends on your business. It's essential to define that so you can collect the correct data to train your model. Take, for example, question 'a)' above. If that's what you wish to answer, you need to include historical customer data.

This information can be used to predict the actions of existing customers. Your features should relate to customer activity, both past, and present.

	Account Length	VMail Message	Day Mins	Eve Mins	Night Mins	Intl Mins	CustServ Calls	Churn	Int'l Plan	VMail Plan	...	Day Charge	Eve Calls	Eve Charge	Night Calls	Night Charge	Intl Calls	Intl Charge	State
0	128	25	265.1	197.4	244.7	10.0	1	0	0	1	...	45.07	99	16.78	91	11.01	3	2.70	KS
1	107	26	161.6	195.5	254.4	13.7	1	0	0	1	...	27.47	103	16.62	103	11.45	3	3.70	OH
2	137	0	243.4	121.2	162.6	12.2	0	0	0	0	...	41.38	110	10.30	104	7.32	5	3.29	NJ
3	84	0	299.4	61.9	196.9	6.6	2	0	1	0	...	50.90	88	5.26	89	8.86	7	1.78	OH
4	75	0	166.7	148.3	186.9	10.1	3	0	1	0	...	28.34	122	12.61	121	8.41	3	2.73	OK

Source: Keyrus

To make it easy to use your data for a predictive model, you'll want to create a CSV file. That file should have a row for each customer and a column for each feature. The 'yes' or 'no' output, as to whether the customer churned should form one of those columns. The file might look something like the image above.

Creating a predictive model

Don't let all the talk so far of data, machine learning, and predictive modelling put you off. Once you've collected your data, the hard part of customer churn prediction is behind you. From here on out, you can lean on prediction services to do the hard yards for you.

There are a couple of predictive services you can choose from:

- Google Cloud ML Engine
- BigML

Both of those services create predictive models based on data that you upload to them. Upload the CSV file you've created, and they'll do the rest for you.

What you end up with is a 'decision tree' visualisation of your model. It will look something like this:

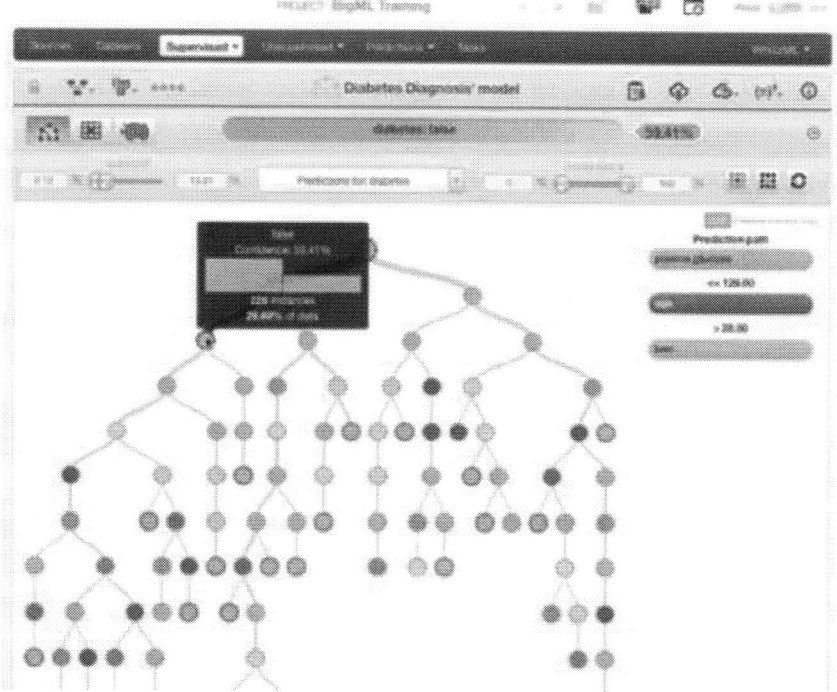

Each coloured circle on the tree represents a question related to your customer features. Every branch represents a possible answer. Work your way down to the bottom, and you'll find a circle with your final output value. In the case of customer churn, that's if a customer churned or not.

Using the model to predict churn

You now have a model that recognises and understands patterns in data on customer churn. What you need now is to use it to make predictions. For that, you first have to collect current data related to your existing customers.

That data needs to match the data used to build your model, except that it won't include the 'yes' or 'no' output for churn. You can then upload the new data to your chosen predictive service. That works in the same way as uploading your original CSV file.

From there, the way to generate predictions differs according to the service you use. To take BigML as an example once again, you need to follow these straightforward steps:

1. Access your model and choose 'Batch Prediction' from the lightning bolt icon menu.
2. You'll then see two drop-down menus. Choose your model in the left-hand one and your new customer dataset in the right-hand one.
3. Click the 'Configure' option and then choose 'Output Settings.'
4. You can then tailor how you want to view your predictions. You want to choose a CSV file output and then adapt the display of that file as you see fit.
5. Click the green 'Predict' button. On the following page, click 'Download Batch Prediction.'
6. You'll then have a file you can open with any spreadsheet program. Your model's predictions of which customers will churn in your chosen timeframe will display in the 'Churn' column.

Just like that, you've got a list of customers at risk of churning. These are the customers you need to contact. They're the customers on whom you can focus your customer retention efforts.

Persuade even one of them to stay when they might have left, and you've made a difference to your bottom line without spending nearly as much money, time, or effort as you would acquiring a new customer.

Customer churn prediction & analysis; proactive customer retention

Customer churn prediction and analysis can help improve customer retention. As a SaaS business, making such improvements can be the difference between success and failure.

Reducing customer churn is how you can keep your monthly revenue steady, even if you're struggling to attract new customers. It's also how you can get the most benefit from customer acquisition. New customers earned, after all, won't merely be replacing those you're losing. They'll be adding to your customer base and helping you scale your company.

The beauty of customer churn prediction is that it allows you to make customer retention proactive. You can learn when a customer may be about to leave you.

That allows you to take steps to keep them on board. You can reach out and solve the issues that might otherwise cause the customers to churn — all by merely collecting data and plugging it into an intelligent prediction service.

Now that you have an idea of the scale of your customer churn from the prediction process you can take action to prevent and reduce it. In the next section of this chapter, we'll provide you with a list of steps you can take to keep the customers you have now identified as at risk of churning, on board with your business.

4.3: 17 ways to reduce your customer churn

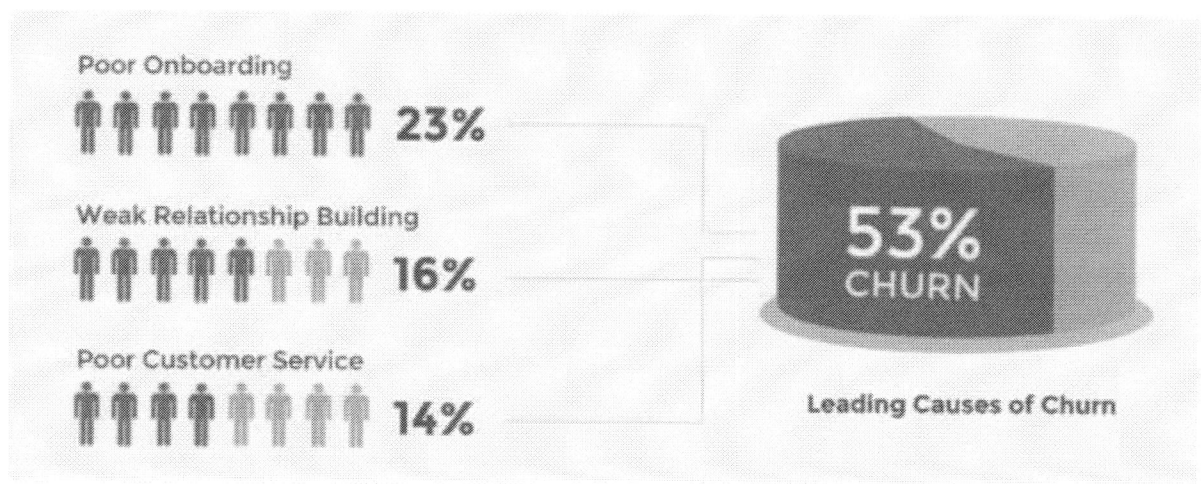

53% of all causes of customer churn are due to these 3 leading causes

There are three primary elements of the SaaS business model. Firms must acquire customers, retain customers, and upsell or resell to those customers. The second of those components, customer retention, is the most important.

In previous sections, I've talked about how customer churn is the result of poor customer retention. It's when subscribers or clients abandon your company, either at the end of a subscription or any point along the way. Keeping customer churn to a minimum is a must for any SaaS business. We're going to give you 17 hints and tips to help you reduce churn.

Why you must reduce churn

It's common sense that no business wants to lose customers. For SaaS companies, though, it's even more critical. They rely on having ongoing revenue from clients to make a profit. Where retail firms get the bulk of their money at the point of sale, SaaS businesses get paid over a more extended period.

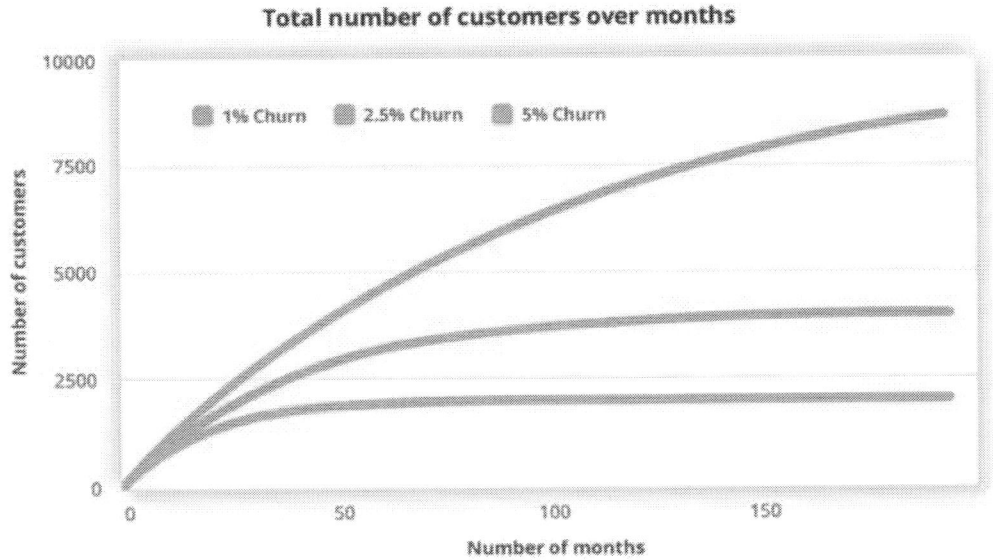

https://www.zoho.com/subscriptions/blog/how-churn-can-plateau-the-growth-of-your-subscription-business.html

The longer a customer stays with a business, then, the more valuable they are to that business. That makes reducing churn a vital process for any successful SaaS firm. It's also a key metric for any business to track. Keeping customers on board is what maintains your monthly revenue. It's cheaper to retain any one customer, too, than it is to gain a new one.

Different ways to reduce churn

Your bottom line will look a lot healthier if you can reduce churn. Keeping customers happy and paying their dues is how to get long-term growth you can sustain. The following are 17 different ways to look at the issue of reducing churn. Mix and match whichever of the hints and tips best suit your firm. Get it right, and you could both reduce churn and grow your profit margin.

Reach out proactively

The first thing to keep in mind is that reducing customer churn can't be a passive process. Customers who may be at risk of churning won't often warn you ahead of time. You need to be proactive and reach out to customers even before you know they need you.

Such proactive outreach shows customers you care about them. It tells them that you're invested in them getting the most out of your service. The best kind of outreach should also relate directly to the customer's use of that service. You may, for instance, contact customers who aren't using a specific service feature. A quick reminder about that feature and its benefits can help customers get more satisfaction from your product.

ID service weaknesses

You're proud of your business and its products, and rightly so. That doesn't mean that everything about your operation is perfect. No company has a 100% success rate in getting everything right the first time. There will always be weaknesses in your products or services. Those issues could be driving up your churn rate.

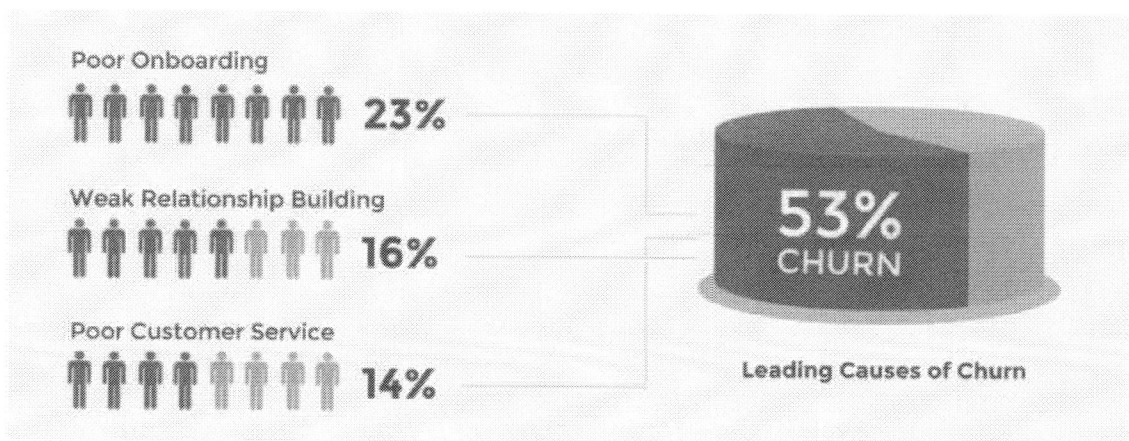

53% of all causes of customer churn are due to these 3 leading causes

https://www.retently.com/blog/three-leading-causes-churn/

The first step to solving those problems is finding them. You need to ID your weaknesses. Your current customers are your best source for finding the answers you need. Try to get as much feedback from them as you can. Ask them directly what they think you can do to improve your service.

Offer added-value elements

Reducing churn goes hand-in-hand with improving customer satisfaction. A tried and tested way of boosting customer satisfaction is by giving them more for their money. Think about different ways that you can add value to the service you provide to clients.

Added value elements don't have to be things that cost you much money. You don't need to be running promotions or providing service features for free. What you could do is to offer free tutorials on how to use your service. You may even go one step further and provide guides or resources about the wider industry your product exists within.

Segment customers effectively

So far, we've talked about general, all-purpose ways to reduce churn. Sometimes the best way to handle customer retention is to take a more targeted approach. Segmenting your customer base into groups is a super way to target them more effectively.

An individual who's been with your firm for years is a different animal to someone who signed up a week ago. You need to treat them differently if you're going to keep them happy and onboard. If you segment your customers, you can better communicate with different groups.

Use intelligent automated emails

Once you have segmented your customers, you can plan how to contact different groups. In the same way, as they're invaluable to customer acquisition, automated emails are also superb for aiding customer retention.

Need Help?

 Influencers R Us <info@influencersrus.com>
gregh@gmail.com

Influencers R Us

Hi Greg,

We haven't seen you around Influencers R Us for awhile. Is everything okay? Let us know if you're having any trouble, or would like to connect to discuss your influencer marketing strategy for the rest of 2017.

Let's find some influencers!
Megan Knisely
Customer Success Manager

Influencers R Us

https://www.evergage.com/blog/5-ways-b2b-saas-companies-can-use-triggered-emails/

Most good email clients let you set up 'trigger emails'. These are messages that go out automatically to customers in particular circumstances. They might, for instance, get sent to someone who hasn't logged in for a few days. Such emails are terrific for nudging customers back to your service or showing them how to get the most out of it.

Target customers at risk of churning

Customers at risk of churning are a crucial segment of your base on which to focus. If you can proactively solve the issues they have with your service, you may be able to keep them on board. That's an intelligent and effective way to reduce churn.

There are a few things to watch out for to predict who may be at risk of churning. Look for those customers whose use of your product is gradually diminishing. If you want to take things further, you could consider using customer churn prediction, as we discussed in the last section.

Focus most on your most valuable customers

If you have lots of customers at risk of churning, you may not be able to reach out to all of them. In that case, you should focus on those customers who are most valuable to your firm. That's at least according to Sunil Gupta, a professor at Harvard Business School:

"What's missing from traditional methods is that they focus only on a customer's likelihood to churn, but not on the overall profitability of that customer... we contend the goal should be maximizing profits, rather than only reducing churn."

Get new customers up to speed

Onboarding can be crucial to customer retention. If you help your customers get up to speed with your product and its benefits, they will get more out of using it. That will make them happier and less likely to churn.

https://blog.chartmogul.com/a-guide-to-saas-customer-onboarding/

Your onboarding process is also vital if you offer a free trial. Having got a lead as far as agreeing to that trial, you want to convert that lead into a real customer. It's much easier to do so if you help them to get the most out of their time using the product for free.

Reward loyal customers

Customers will view your service positively if you reward them for sticking with you. Setting usage milestones and incentivising clients to reach them is a smart way to reduce churn.

Incentives you choose to offer should reflect your product and your customers. Think about what's most likely to persuade clients to extend their subscriptions. Options can include discounted rates, extra features, and other bonuses.

Use feedback to inform your service

Customer churn is often a result of customer frustration. Service users sometimes become aggravated by confusion over how to use a product. They may equally get annoyed by poor customer support or assistance.

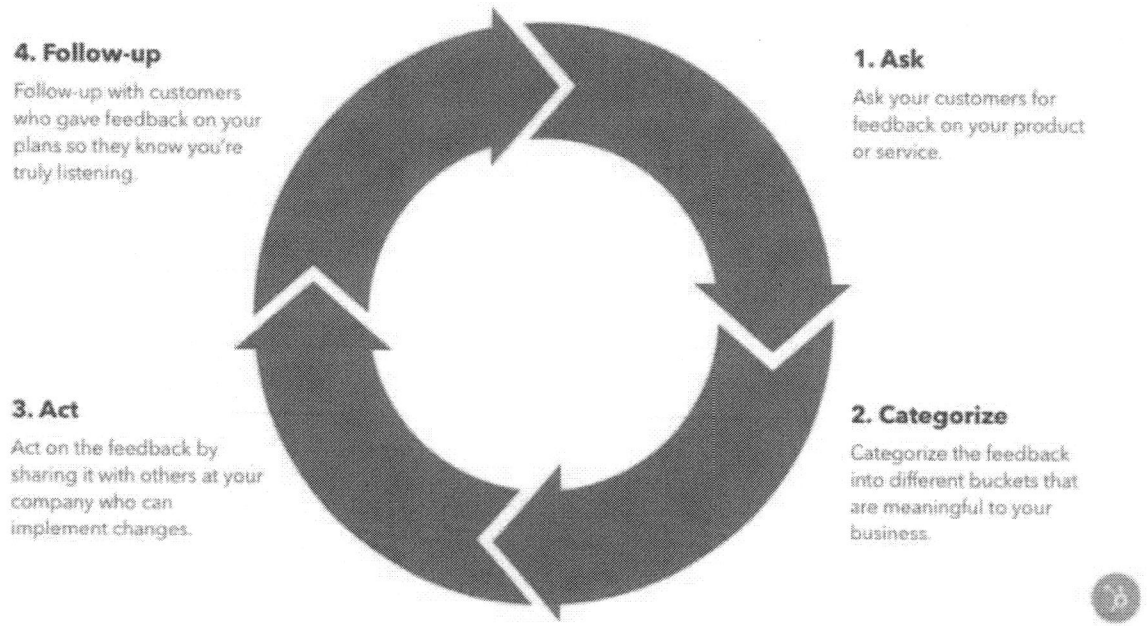

https://www.hubspot.com/customer-feedback

You need to know what it is that's getting under the skin of your customers. The best way to find out is by asking. Try to ask for direct customer feedback as often as you can. Then, make sure you do use the feedback to tweak and tailor your product or service.

Retain the personal touch

We've already talked about the value of automated emails. They're real time savers when it comes to reaching out to large numbers of customers. It's worthwhile, though, to balance the time-efficiency of automation with the benefits of personalisation.

Adding a personal touch to your messages will make each customer feel valued. They want to think that you're talking directly to them. Try to include their name in the email salutation. Also, look to send messages from named – rather than 'no-reply' – accounts.

Upsell with impunity

Promoting your products and site to new customers is vital. You shouldn't focus all your marketing efforts on new leads and prospects, though. You may find it surprising how lucrative it is to upsell new packages and add-ons to existing clients.

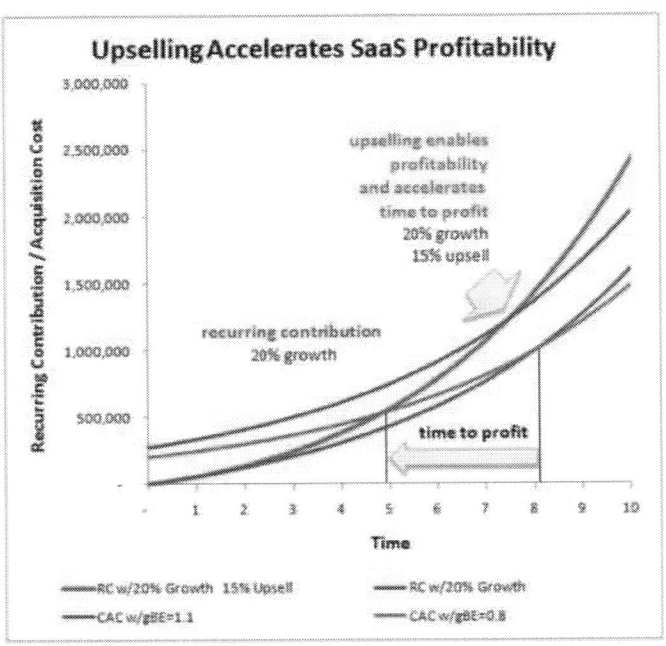

Source: chaotic-flow.com

Upselling added-value elements like eBooks or guides are also helpful for customer retention. Even though you're selling them not giving them away, such added extras can still boost customer satisfaction.

Create a customer community

People like to feel as if they belong. It's a vital part of what makes some customers so fiercely loyal to certain brands. Just ask a fervent Apple fan what they think of that company's latest release if you need any proof of that.

An excellent way to foster a feeling of belonging is by building a community amongst your customers. Add a blog to your website and actively encourage participation and interaction. Get customers talking and sharing insights. That's sure to make them think of your firm as a crucial part of their business life.

Keep adding value & tell users about it

In business, you never want to be standing still. You should always be striving to improve your products and services. Stay on the lookout for ways to add value to what you offer to your customers. When you do intro new services or features, make sure you tell customers about it.

Send customers a quick message telling them how the excellent service you offer has got even better. You may also wish to share news of how your product is helping customers. Email case studies detailing how beneficial your product is being in practice are a good idea. They will help to convince customers further that they're with the right company.

Know your rivals inside out

Competitor research is essential to many aspects of your business. You need to know as much as you can about what your rivals are offering their customers. If their products or prices are superior to yours, your customers may start looking their way.

Feature/Company	Our Product	Competitor 1	Competitor 2	Competitor 3	Competitor 4
Strengths	Faster performance due to new technology	Seamless onboarding experience, great design	Uses social media to their advantage	Great design, usability	Emphasizes security
Weaknesses	Not much social media presence	Not much interaction with customers	Documents hard to navigate	Sporadic social media presence	Language is formal, not user-friendly
Pricing	$800 per month	$800 per month	$900 per month	$850 a month	$950 a month
Social media	Twitter, Instagram	Blog posts, Twitter	Blog posts, Instagram	Blog posts, Instagram, Twitter	Blog posts
Onboarding experience	Moderate number of steps to sign up	Smooth instructions	Not much support after first step	Seamless, very few steps involved	Moderate number of steps

https://www.getcloudapp.com/blog/competitive-analysis-for-software-products

It's also useful to know how your rivals' products work. If you can get to grips with their features and offerings, you'll know if there's anything you should emulate. Equally, it's also useful to get a better understanding of the weaknesses of your rival's products. Doing so makes it easier to exemplify your competitive advantages to customers.

Lengthen subscriptions & commitments

Offering longer contracts is a simple yet effective way to reduce churn. By tying a customer to a longer deal, you're guaranteeing they won't churn for a longer period. You need to be careful about when you lengthen contracts, however.

Extending your customers' commitments works best when customers are already happy. Happy customers are more likely to want to sign up with you long-term. If levels of customer satisfaction aren't what they might be, our other ways to reduce churn may suit you better.

Learn from your mistakes

You're always going to get some customer churn. It's unavoidable, even if you cherry-pick all of our tips that best suit your firm. When churn does occur, what's crucial is to learn as much about what caused it as possible.

Try to reach out to departing customers and ask why they're leaving. Not everyone will reply. Those who do, however, can give you some vital insights. By learning what caused customers to churn, you can make changes to ensure that no others go for the same reasons. It's a classic example of the adage that it's essential to learn from your mistakes.

Combat customer churn & reap the rewards

If you can reduce churn, you're a long way toward making your business more profitable. Excellent customer retention and a low churn rate are what separate the best SaaS firms from the rest. There's no one way to reduce churn, but there are lots of different avenues you can explore.

By combining some of our 17 suggestions for reducing churn, you can do wonders for your bottom line. Whether by being more proactive, rewarding loyalty, or building a customer community, you can keep customers happy and your margins wide.

Driving traffic to your website, converting customers, improving usability and providing excellent customer service all take money. Money that can be difficult to find in the early years of your business. In the next chapter, we'll be covering different ways to source funding to take your SaaS startup to the next level.

Chapter 5: How to secure investment or a sale

As a business owner, you have to wear a lot of hats. You need to be across every significant aspect of business operation. The earlier chapters in our ebook have touched on some of the main ones. From promoting your site to getting leads on social media, we hope we've given you a few helpful insights.

One area we haven't yet covered is that of financing. To scale your company and turn it into a success, you need funding at every step of the way. Getting that necessary financing is far from straightforward. You need to know where you can turn and when to get the cash injections that will take your business forward.

The sections in this chapter cover which venture capital firms are investing in SaaS companies, how to value your SaaS company and how to pitch for funding. The first section covers the five startup funding stages. from pre-seed to initial public offering. Once you know which funding stage your company is at, you'll be able to identify suitable sources for funding.

5.1: A beginner's guide to the 5 steps of startup funding stages

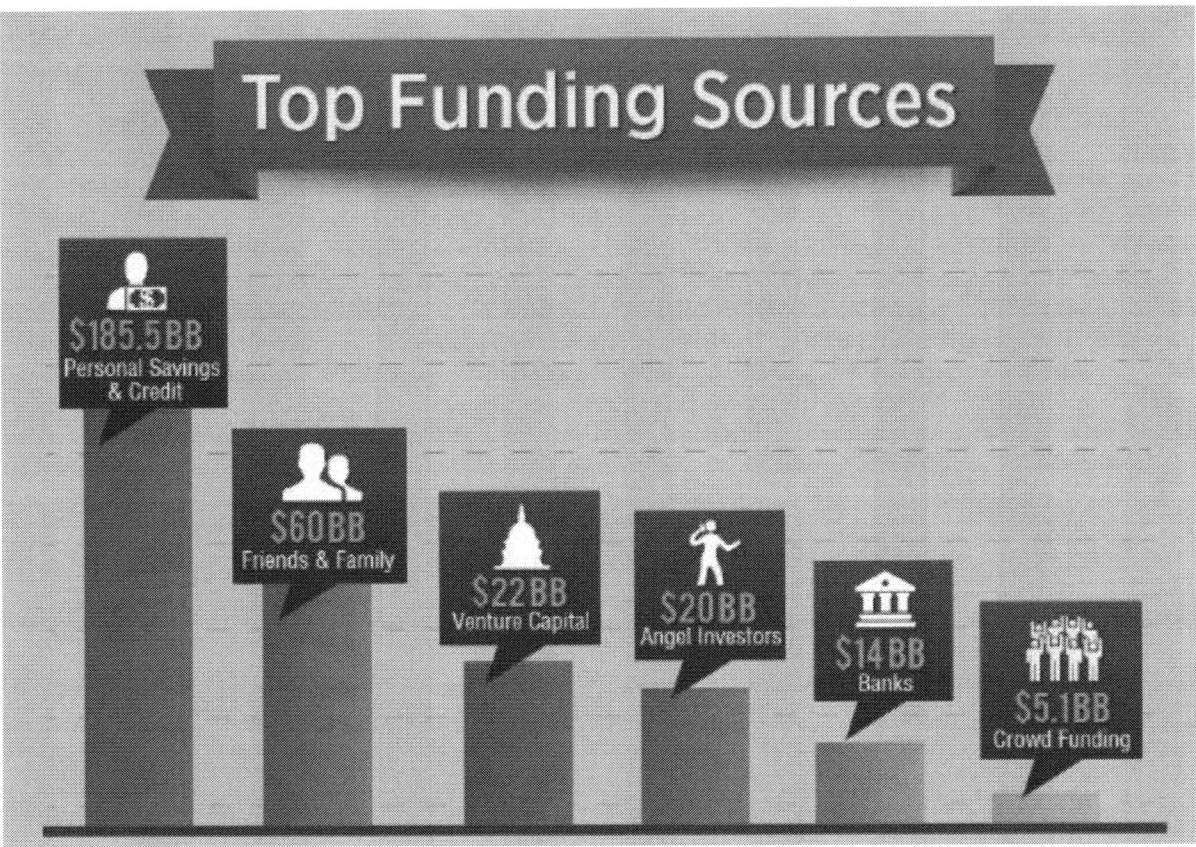

This beginner's guide will talk you through each step of what may at first seem to be a tortuously complex startup funding process. Read on, and you'll learn about the following five principal startup funding stages:

- Pre-seed funding
- Seed funding
- Series A-E funding
- Mezzanine financing & bridge loans

- Initial public offering (IPO)

We're going to explain what each of the startup funding stages entails. You'll learn the characteristics of businesses as they enter each stage. You'll also find out where best to seek finance at each different step of the process. If you need to learn all about funding your firm through its growth and development, this section is for you.

Pre-Seed funding

Some guides to startup funding neglect to mention pre-seed funding. This first startup funding stage gets overlooked as it occurs so early in a business's lifecycle. In many ways, however, that also makes it one of the most crucial parts of the entire financing process.

Pre-seed funding is the finance that startups use to get off the ground. It's the money that allows a founder of a business to get the ball rolling. In the case of a SaaS business, that may mean developing a proof of concept of the ultimate product. If you can get enough early finance, you may be able to create a beta version of your software.

Startups at this funding stage are very much in their infancies. As such, venture capitalists or other equity finance sources aren't open to them. There are a few different options for getting pre-seed funding, however.

Most startup founders have to rely on their resources for pre-seed funding. Dipping into savings, remortgaging homes, and taking on second jobs are all common routes for entrepreneurs. This reliance on your own money to fund a business is often called bootstrapping. As per the old saying of 'pulling yourself up by your bootstraps'.

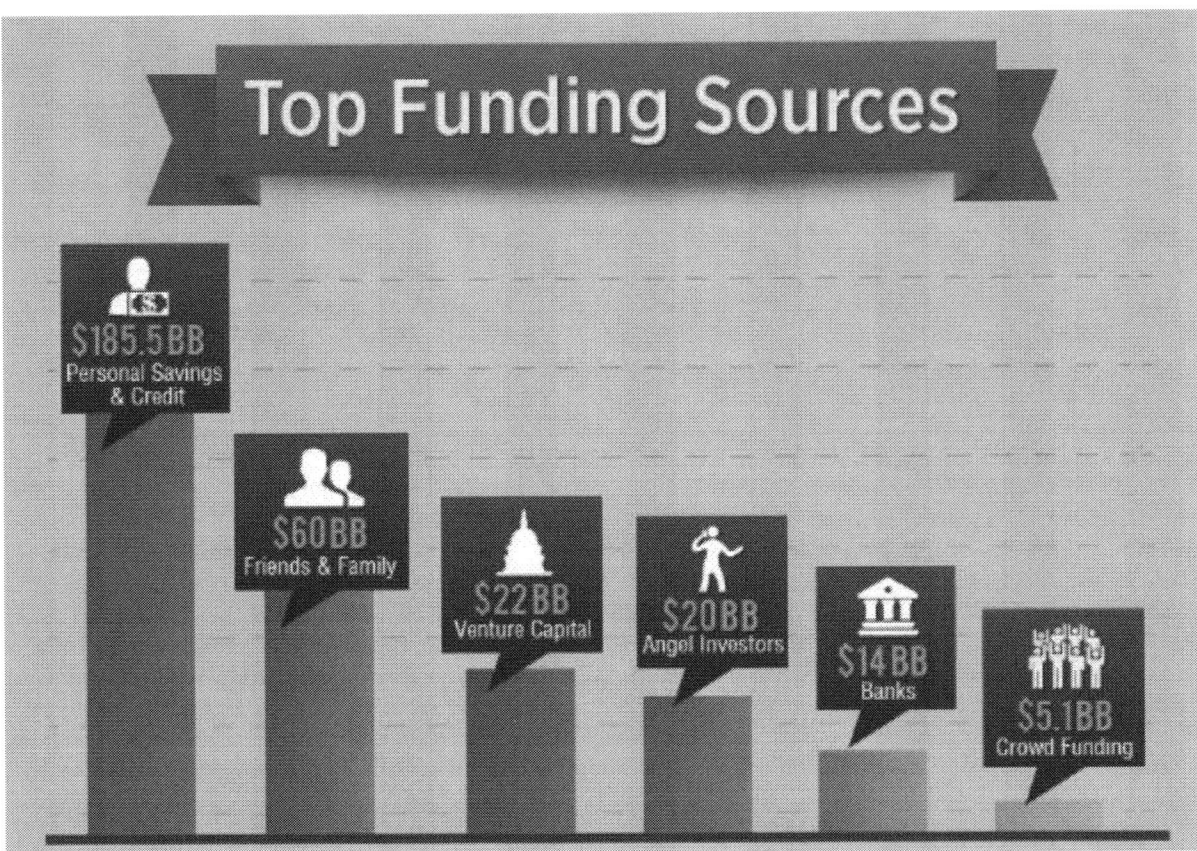

https://www.fundable.com/learn/resources/guides/startup/funding-your-startup

There are a few other options available for raising cash at this earliest funding stage. Lots of business founders look to friends and family for their initial investment.

Your loved ones won't need as much proof of the viability of your young firm to commit their investment. They will also likely agree to more favourable repayment terms. You should always take care, though, when seeking financing from relatives or friends. Problems down the road can lead to upset and disagreement.

Certain independent investors may also consider providing pre-seed funding. Some wealthy individuals and specialist funds actively invest in very young startups. Those financers get called 'Angel Investors', as their cash is such a godsend to startups.

Seed funding

Continuing the botanical theme, the second of the five major startup funding stages is the seed funding stage. This investment is what truly gets a startup growing. Seed funding is vital to any business's success, whatever the field.

According to Small Biz Trends[1], 29% of startups fail because they run out of cash. Most of those failures occur in the early months and years of a firm's operation. That means that the businesses falter as they don't get their seed funding right.

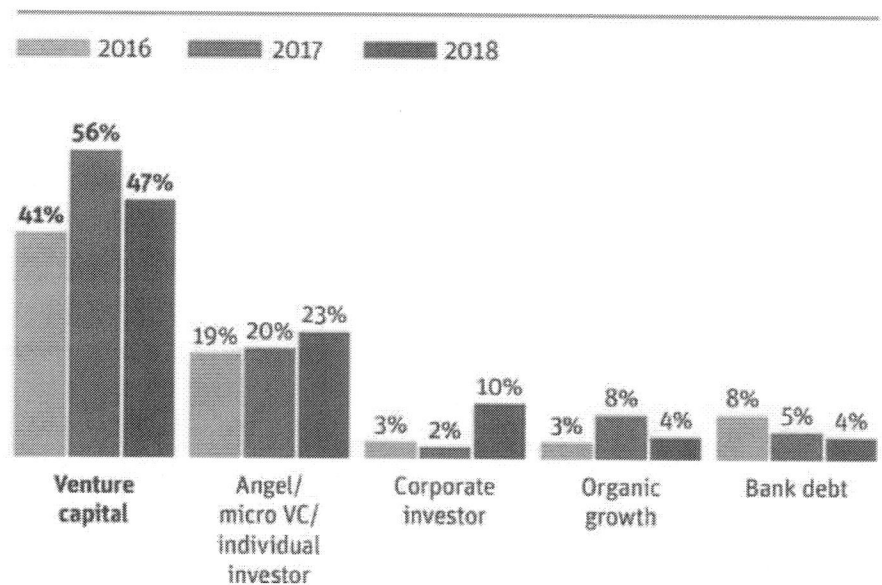

https://www.svb.com/startup-outlook-report/uk

Finance raised at this stage of a firm's development starts to turn the ideas behind a startup into reality. It's this cash that gets used to fund a product launch or to seek market research. In some cases, too, seed funding can finance the hiring of staff to move a firm forward.

The seed funding stage is the first one in which equity financing is a realistic option for most firms.

A quick refresher; equity financing

Equity financing is an investment in a business, provided in exchange for a stake in the company. Investors receive shares in the company in return for their investment. Those shares increase and decrease in value with the overall valuation of the business.

If you do go down the equity finance route for seed funding, small venture capital funds are your best bet. There are lots of specialist seed funds, like Passion Capital and Seed Camp. They work with smaller businesses to help them grow and develop.

Angel investors are also a rich source for seed funding. It's often easier for them to assess the viability of a business once it's reached this stage of development. More 'angels' will take part in the seed than the pre-seed funding stage.

It's still possible, too, for business owners or their friends and family to account for a firm's seed funding. Often, though, the extent of financing needed at this stage is beyond the budget of all but pro investors.

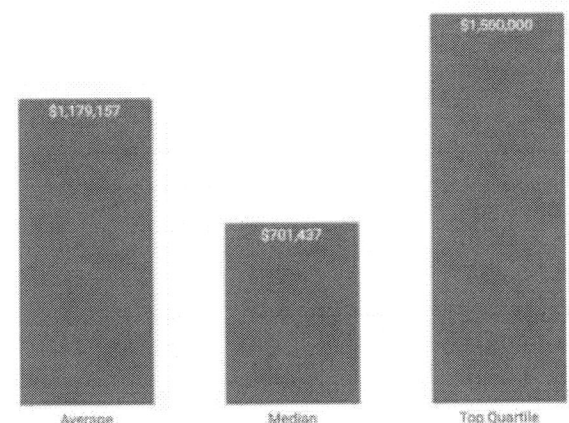

https://venturebeat.com/2018/08/22/the-european-seed-landscape-2018-so-far/

The seed funding stage is the final step of the financing process for many small businesses. Some owners fail to raise enough cash and see their businesses fold. Others raise enough money at this stage to forgo any further search for financing. That may be because their business won't ever grow large enough to need more investment. It could also be because the organic growth of the company will supply all the required cash.

Series A-E funding

The principal, middle portion of the startup funding process comprises five different 'series'. Those series are all given a letter designation from A-E. As a business moves from one round to the next, it looks to raise more money and increases its valuation.

Series A

Startups that do go through the seed funding step will begin to see some commercial traction. Their services will be picking up users, and monthly revenue will be steadily growing. By tracking key performance indicators (KPIs), you can spot when you may be ready for Series A funding. Such KPIs can include customer numbers or turnover.

Series A is where things get serious when it comes to investors. It's where the significant venture capital (VC) funds may become interested in your business. It's not easy, though, for any startup to get those funds to part with their cash.

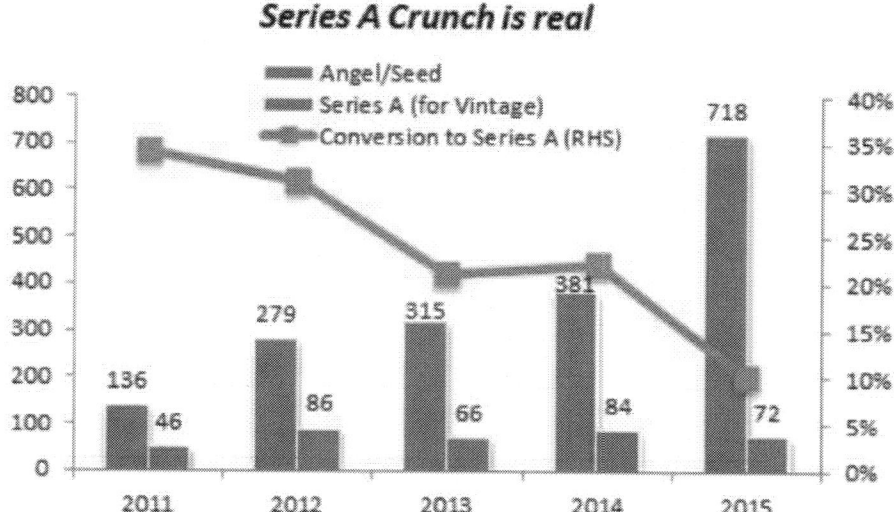

https://equitycrest.wordpress.com/tag/funding/

When you're seeking finance at this stage, you need a whole, accurate, and impressive business plan. A great idea and a few early adopters won't cut it with serious VC firms. Even with a great business plan and early signs of success, most funds will still turn you down.

Many experts cite the 30-10-2 rule for Series A. That rule states that for every 30 funds that you think may invest, only ten will show actual interest. Of those ten, two may commit funds. During Series A, therefore, you must approach investors in bulk to try to raise the finance you need.

Series B

Startups that reach Series B are significant businesses. They've captured a considerable user base, and are bringing in high monthly revenues. What their Series B funding is for is to take the firm to a new level. This finance is what they need to make their business work at scale.

In most ways, Series B is similar to the previous funding stage. A lot of the investors involved will be the same. The most successful Series B funding rounds get more cash from the original backers and add new ones.

Series C

If Series B startups are serious businesses, those that reach Series C are veritable goliaths. They've tasted significant success and are now on a path to even higher growth. This third main funding round is where the size of investments rises profoundly.

Startups looking for Series C funding are seeking real expansion. The funding is often to help them create new products, move into new markets, or even buy up other smaller firms. In many cases, too, businesses enter the Series C stage to get cash so that they can go international.

By this point, firms are no longer risky propositions for investors. As such, private equity firms, hedge funds, and investment banks all often get involved in Series C.

Series D & E

Series C is the final investment round for many startups. That startup funding stage usually puts a firm in an excellent place to think about an IPO. A business will often only embark on a Series D round and beyond, in exceptional circumstances.

A company may, for instance, need a cash injection to fund a potentially beneficial merger. If they're not ready to go public, an extra funding round can help them get that finance. On the flip side, if a business has had a tricky spell, they may need further funding just to stay afloat.

https://startupxplore.com/en/blog/types-startup-investing/

Even in the above circumstances, many firms don't turn to new funding series. For finance at this stage, they look instead to different options to carry them through to an IPO.

Mezzanine financing & bridge loans

Any startup that's moved through its seed and main funding stages is tracking towards going public. By that, we mean that the business will likely soon embark on an IPO to start trading on the stock exchange. To prepare for the final push toward an IPO, firms sometimes need one last influx of finance.

Mezzanine financing is where lots of companies turn for this final cash injection. This type of funding gets its name from the eponymous 'in-between' floors. You can find mezzanines in some large buildings, and you'll see an example in the image below.

The form of financing gets its name because it's an 'in-between' form of funding. It represents a middle way between a traditional loan and typical equity funding.

Cash lent via mezzanine financing is often subject to high-interest rates. Lenders also have the option to convert what's owed into equity in the company at a later date. That may only be if you default on repayment, or it may be after a specified period. The higher interest rate makes mezzanine financing riskier for a startup. Its purpose, though, is to speed the firm toward exit.

Initial Public Offering (IPO)

An IPO is the last stage of funding any startup goes through. Usually, an IPO is the method by which the business's founder or owner exits the stage. An IPO is when corporate shares in the company get offered to the public for the first time. The business's current owners and investors get paid based on their present stake in the firm.

IPOs can be risky for startups and their owners. There's no way to know for how much a business's shares will sell. If an IPO goes well, though, current stockholders and investors can enjoy a considerable windfall. As a public company, the business can raise more funds in the future via secondary offerings.

Finding your way through the 5 startup funding stages

Passing through the five main startup funding stages is essential for a startup. It's how business owners can steer their firms successfully from start to finish of their commercial journey. By understanding the stages, you can ID where your business sits and find the best way forward.

Having that grounding in the funding process is vital. Your business must be mature enough to deal with each funding stage fruitfully. If you were to embark on any stage too early, it could be disastrous. Armed with our simple guide, you can avert a catastrophe and take your firm from strength to strength.

In the next section, we'll supply a list of the top 25 venture capital funds investing in SaaS startups. These funds will invest in startups at any one of the five startup stages that we have talked about in the previous section. Use our guide to identify which stage your business is at and then look for venture capital partners that will fit well with your requirements from this list.

5.2: Top 25 VC investing in SaaS companies

You've got your SaaS business off the ground. You turned that inspired idea into a product that you knew customers would love. From there, you got the word out about your site and service. That helped you capture those all-important early adopters.

As customers rolled in, intelligent marketing helped you grow your base still further. If you're going to take that next step, though, you need to find some outside investment. You need the kind of financing that will help you make those bold moves that your firm needs to go to the next level.

What you need to know is where you can get that funding. If you need serious cash that you can't raise organically, venture capital funds (VCs) may be your best bet. The following are 25 top SaaS investors that might just hold the key to your business's future.

Top SaaS investors

SaaS companies typically go through five startup funding stages we outlined in the previous section. The SaaS investors listed below are VCs that may provide you with finance at any one of those stages. The VCs are based all around the world, and each have their individual investment preferences. What they all have in common is that they already work with many SaaS companies.

500 Startups

A global venture capital fund, 500 Startups calls Silicon Valley home. The fund has over $450 million worth of capital invested in helping startups grow and develop.

Focussed on tech, SaaS is one of 500 Startups' four largest investment sectors. They work with notable firms in the niche, including YayPay and Ovation. According to the firm's website, its mission is:

"...to discover and back the world's most talented entrepreneurs, help them create successful companies at scale, and build thriving global ecosystems."

83North

83North is a VC company based in Tel-Aviv. The fund's primary focus is on enterprise-related companies in Israel and Europe. Able to offer operational assistance as well as cash, 83North boasts over $550 million under management.

This fund works with SaaS firms to provide seed and later-stage financing. Cooladata and iZettle are businesses within the niche that presently work with 83North.

Accel

Accel is one of the best-known VCs across the world. Founded in 1983 by Jim Swartz and Arthur Patterson, the fund has over three decades' of invaluable experience. They have also worked or continue to work with some of the biggest names in software:

- Facebook
- Dropbox
- Spotify
- Etsy
- Slack

Working with both B2C and B2B firms at all stages of development, Accel should be near the top of any VC shortlist.

Acceleprise

Despite having only started in 2012, Acceleprise is now one of the best VC options for any SaaS firm. Based in San Francisco, USA, the fund describes itself as "the top B2B SaaS accelerator".

Acceleprise focuses on smaller B2B SaaS companies looking for early-stage funding. As well as investment, the fund provides specialist mentors to help the firms they work with. Such SaaS firms connected with Acceleprise include AdinMo and Fomo.

Andreessen Horowitz

Few VCs have a better track record on software investments than Andreessen Horowitz. The world-renowned fund has in the past invested in these tech and software goliaths:

- Instagram
- BuzzFeed
- GitHub
- Asana

The fund was founded in Silicon Valley in 2009 by Ben Horowitz and Marc Andreessen. They like to describe their VC as 'stage agnostic'. That means if a business is promising enough, the fund will invest at any stage of its development.

Atlanta Ventures

If you're looking for SaaS investors to help you raise seed funding, Atlanta Ventures may be the best place to turn. The fund specialises in early-stage funding. Not only that, according to their website, Atlanta Ventures:

"Empowers entrepreneurs to achieve their potential through community, content, and capital."

Advice and operational support, then, are also routinely provided by the fund. Firms in the SaaS niche that have benefitted from that kind of help include SalesLoft and WideAngle Software.

Battery Ventures

Battery Ventures is another VC that focuses on early-stage investment. The fund has bases in Silicon Valley, Boston, and Israel and boasts close to 40 years' worth of experience.

In the close to four decades that Battery Ventures has operated, it has funded over 300 firms. Amongst the SaaS firms on their books are customer service platform Stella Connect and Gong.io.

Bessemer Venture Partners

Even longer-tenured than Battery Ventures, Bessemer Venture Partners has been in business for over half a century. The fund is one of the biggest players in SaaS investment. Bessemer has over $40 billion of cash currently invested in close to 150 firms.

Some of the fund's most important investments were in businesses like Skype and Shopify. More recently, Bessemer has committed finance to Mambu and Claroty. Those firms, respectively, are SaaS businesses in the banking and cybersecurity sectors.

Boldstart Ventures

Boldstart Ventures is a VC fund with a primary focus on seed funding. The fund specialises in providing businesses with their first outside investment. That's why Boldstart likes to describe themselves as 'first check, lead investors'.

The New York-based VC has so far invested in over 60 startups. Some of the most successful were ultimately acquired by Google, LinkedIn, and SalesForce. Amongst their current investments are a raft of SaaS firms. Those include SecurityScorecard and BigID.

Costanoa Ventures

The next of our SaaS investors provide primarily for seed and Series A funding. That means they work with startups and firms looking to take that first big leap into VC investment. The fund in question is the California-based Costanoa Ventures.

Costanoa is a fund that's particularly interested in entrepreneurship. The decision-makers at the VC like to invest in what they describe as 'disruptive ideas'. Costanoa's existing SaaS investments span niches, such as cybersecurity and scheduling.

Draper Esprit

First and foremost a pan-European fund, Draper Esprit has a presence that extends around the globe. According to the fund's website, they have a network that spans "...the US, Europe, Asia, South America – and everywhere in between".

Innovation is at the heart of Draper Esprit's operation. In 2016, they broke the VC mould and went public so that they could offer more flexible funding. One of the highest-profile firms the fund worked with is review business Trustpilot. In the SaaS field, Iceye and Conversocial have both received funds from Draper Esprit.

Eight Roads Ventures

Taking a particular interest in healthcare and tech, Eight Roads Ventures is a genuine global VC. The fund has offices in ten countries, including significant bases in China, the UK, and the USA. Since its foundation in 1969, Eight Roads has funded over 300 separate businesses.

In spite of that high number of investments, the fund is very selective. Businesses that do get Eight Roads funding also get advice on recruitment, marketing, and operations. In the past, the fund has worked with Alibaba and Avidity. It also has an active SaaS portfolio, featuring firms like Silot and ForceClouds.

Frog Capital

Any European SaaS business could do worse than to hop on over to Frog Capital's website if they need finance. The fund works almost solely with European software firms. It also offers investment at every stage of the startup funding process.

Frog Capital boasts a global network of connections and plenty of industry expertise. Those things allow the fund to offer long-term partnerships to firms in which it invests. SaaS companies already enjoying such partnerships include Dealflo and Dynamic Action.

Frontline Ventures

This entry on our list of SaaS investors caters only to a particular kind of company. If you're a B2B SaaS firm looking for seed funding, Frontline Ventures could be the fund for you. According to the fund's site, it seeks to invest in "...ambitious seed-stage B2B founders".

Headquartered in Dublin and London, Frontline works mostly with UK-based businesses. The fund specialises in speeding those firms toward expansion in the USA. Data workflow platform Astronomer and marketing and analytics firm Localisto are among the fund's existing SaaS partners.

Insight Venture Partners

While the fund calls New York home, Insight Venture Partners has a global reputation. It helps firms the world over and is flexible in the finance it offers. The fund prefers to work with market-leading outfits. It will also, though, provide smaller deals for the right companies.

Insight Venture Partners has over $20 billion under management. Much of that investment is committed to the SaaS niche. The fund's impressive SaaS catalogue includes a good number of firms. Good examples include Email marketing platform, Campaign Monitor, and workflow tool DrillingInfo.

New Enterprise Associates

Like some of our other SaaS investors, New Enterprise Associates (NEA) focusses on healthcare and tech. NEA started working with clients in 1977 and has since invested over $19 billion. The fund has also accounted for over 350 mergers and acquisitions, and more than 200 IPOs.

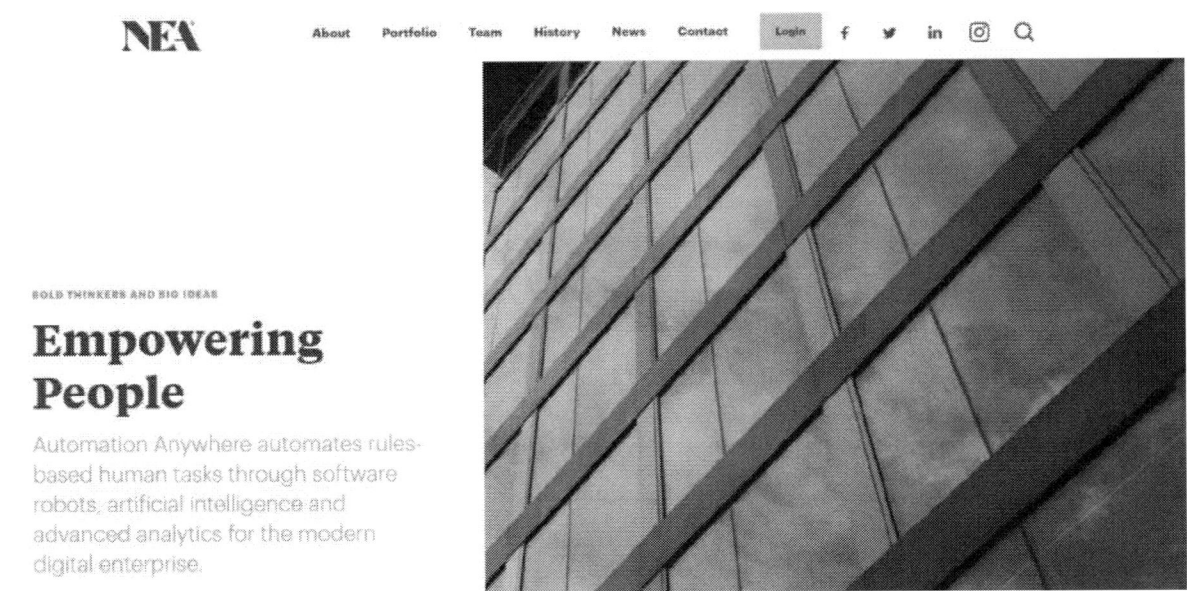

NEA is a live option for any SaaS business searching for late-stage funding. The fund has already backed many companies with SaaS models. Those firms include cloud-based training platform CloudTickle and Indian HR system greytHR.

Northzone

Northzone is a VC that calls Stockholm home. As such, it's a live funding option for any European SaaS business. The fund first started investing back in 1996. In the ensuing 23 years has financed lots of significant companies, including:

- Spotify
- com
- Trustpilot

Today, Northzone likes to focus on firms that develop disruptive technologies. The fund offers seed and early-stage finance. Current Northzone partners include HappyOrNot and Aevy.

OpenView Venture

This VC tailors to established software companies, looking to expand. OpenView Venture specialises in taking such firms to the next level in their development. As well as finance, it offers an 'Expansion Platform'. That platform aids in hiring talent, growing customer bases, and finding industry mentors.

OpenView has helped a few SaaS firms to expand successfully. Deputy is a prime example. The employee management tool used finance and help from the fund to go from strength to strength.

Point Nine

Describing itself as an "Angel VC", Point Nine specialises in seed and early-stage financing. The Berlin-based VC also sometimes gets involved in the latter part of the funding process. SaaS firms and the digital marketplace account for much of Point Nine's portfolio.

Investing all over the globe, the German VC works with a few exciting SaaS companies. Those firms include both Factorial and Zanaton, providers of small business software solutions.

Prime Ventures

Prime Ventures is a VC fund focussed on the European market. It has offices in the UK and the Netherlands and manages over 700 million Euros in investments. SaaS investments of the fund include stakes in Perpule and Falcon.io.

According to Prime Ventures own website, the fund is:

"...a leading venture capital and growth equity firm focused on investing in European companies in the technology and related industries."

PROfounders Capital

The London-based PROfounders Capital is a VC pitched at entrepreneurs. The fund enjoys investing in dynamic and forward-thinking business founders. It then uses its resources and expertise to help founders make their firms viable.

PROfounders often focusses investments on SaaS firms that aim to solve enterprise problems. One of the fund's biggest success stories is the social media data management tool, Tweetdeck. After working with PROfounders, Tweetdeck got acquired by Twitter in a significant deal.

SaaS Venture Capital

As its name suggests, SaaS Venture Capital is a VC with a specific interest in SaaS businesses. The fund views the SaaS model as the most likely to succeed in the software niche. That's why it describes itself as;

"a seed-stage venture capital fund focused on enterprise tech."

SaaS Venture Capital works with a few prominent SaaS companies. The fund's current projects include those with Huntress and Balto. Respectively, those are firms in the security and call centre software niches.

Sequoia Capital

A giant in the VC industry as a whole, Sequoia Capital is also one of the most prominent SaaS investors. Don Valentine founded the fund in 1972, and it has been based in California ever since. The fund caters to investments in finance, energy, enterprise, healthcare, and the internet.

Sequoia has invested in well over 1000 companies. Those businesses include world-famous names like Airbnb, Zoom, and Drift. It's not easy for smaller firms to get the fund's attention. The VC, though, does invest in some of the world's fastest-growing SaaS startups.

The SaaStr Fund

The SaaStr Blog was an online resource to help founders launch and scale SaaS firms. From that blog, the SaaStr Fund was born. The fund takes things a step further than its parent blog by investing in promising SaaS startups.

The SaaStr Fund is now a $90 million VC. It provides not only finance but also expertise to assist and market companies. Some SaaS startups that have partnered with this fund include Mixmax and Automile.

VenTech

VenTech is a Series A specific VC. The fund will often only invest in startups that have already received between €2 million and €5 million in seed capital. VenTech started in 1998 and mostly limits itself to investing in European firms.

The fund is only interested in the tech sector but will invest in either B2B or B2C firms. In its 21 years of operation, VenTech has worked with many SaaS enterprises. At present, 365talents and Albacross are among the fund's SaaS portfolio.

Getting the investment you need

Starting and then scaling a SaaS business isn't easy. In the early going, you have to think about all manner of promotion and marketing. You need to get your name out there and grow your customer base. Then, once you're established, the biggest challenge becomes seeking funding to take that next leap.

Securing VC investment for a startup is a tricky proposition. The majority of VCs you reach out to will turn you down. That's why you need to know about as many funds as possible, that might be interested in SaaS investment. Our list has introduced you to 25 of the best SaaS investors around. The rest is up to you.

To approach a venture capital fund, you will need a clear idea of what your company is currently worth. In the next section, we'll provide a guide for how to value your SaaS business using your annual earnings potential and a valuation multiple. Once you have a figure of value, you can begin to consider the future of your company, whether that is further rounds of finance or an eventual sale.

5.3: The definitive guide on how to value your SaaS company

The SaaS business model is growing in popularity at an extraordinary rate. Organisations of all shapes and sizes increasingly get their apps and software solutions from SaaS firms. The SaaS market has grown year-in and year-out for around the past decade or more. That growth isn't slowing, either. The SaaS market is predicted to grow by a further $60.36 billion[1] by 2023.

The success of the SaaS model, however, doesn't mean that it's easy to make each business flourish. Delivering SaaS presents unique challenges at every stage of a firm's lifecycle. Due to the uniqueness of the business model, owners must be careful in their approach to promotion and marketing. It's imperative to get those things right in the early days of a SaaS company. Doing so is the only way to grow a customer base sustainably.

Different metrics must be tracked, too, to keep a growing SaaS firm on track. You need to assess a SaaS business differently to an enterprise that adopts a simple retail model, for instance. Finally, when it comes time to sell a SaaS business, things are once again a little divorced from the norm.

If you're looking to sell, you first need to know how to value a SaaS company. You can't adopt precisely the same approach as you would when valuing another firm. Read on, and you'll learn all the dos and don'ts of valuing your SaaS business. That ensures that when the time comes, you'll get the very best deal for your firm.

The two primary components of valuing your business

The principle calculation you must make when valuing a SaaS business is a simple two-step one. You need first to calculate the annual earnings potential of your company. Then, you must work out a reasonable multiple by which to times that revenue figure. The resulting number will be a fair representation of your firm's value.

Your calculation, then, would look a little like this:

Valuation Multiple (Annual Earnings Potential)

So far, so simple. Where things get a little more complicated is when it comes to putting a real figure on both your earnings potential and the multiple.

There are numerous factors to consider when putting a figure on your valuation multiple. You then must make a judgement based on those, as to a reasonable level at which to set the multiple. We'll discuss all the pertinent factors in depth a little later.

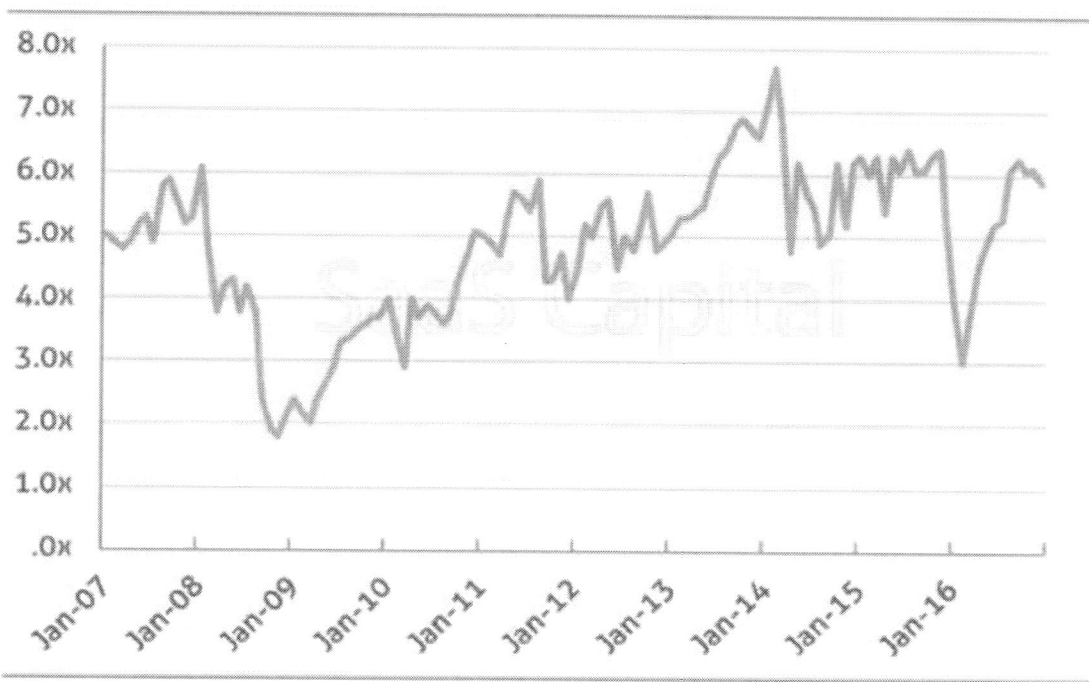

https://www.saastr.com/saas-valuation-multiples/

When it comes to figuring your annual earnings potential, there are three different options available to you. You can apply a Seller's Discretionary Earnings (SDE) formula. You can alternatively employ the Earnings Before Interest, Depreciation, and Amortisation (EBITDA) method. Finally, in some cases, you may choose to predict revenue based on projected growth.

Let's take a look at each of those methods a little more closely. By doing so, we can see when they may or may not be appropriate. That way, you'll be able to take your first step in learning how to value a SaaS company.

SaaS businesses; SDE, EBITDA or Revenue

The first part of valuing your firm is assessing its annual revenue. Or, more accurately, the company's annual earnings potential. You have two main choices – and a third, less common alternative – for doing this. These are to calculate your firm's SDE, EBITDA, or a projected revenue based on future growth.

How to value a SaaS company using SDE

SDE is a relatively straightforward way of calculating your firm's yearly earnings potential. It's the method that's most suitable for all but the largest SaaS businesses. If your company's estimated worth is anything lower than around £4m, the SDE method is likely the one for you.

The first step to finding your SDE is to take the gross revenue of your company. From there, you subtract the cost of goods sold and all other non-discretionary operating expenses. Finally, you add the owner's (your) compensation back on to reach the final figure. That last step assumes that the company is owner-operated, as many firms worth less than £4m will be.

Your SDE calculation, as a result, looks like this:

Gross Revenue – Cost of Goods Sold – Operating Expenses + Owner Compensation

Put simply, SDE is the profit left to an owner after the deduction of all costs and expenses. The formula is the most trusted for small business valuation. It's effective in displaying the true earnings potential of more modest, owner-operated firms. Things change when you start dealing with bigger businesses.

How to value a SaaS company using EBITDA

Valuations of SaaS firms with an estimated worth of over £4m are more complicated. These firms are not typically owner-operated. At least, not many are solely operated by one owner. As such, an SDE calculation is no longer valid. Instead, you may look to the EBITDA formula.

https://www.educba.com/ebitda-formula/

This formula is the industry standard for valuing companies larger than around £4m. It's trusted to give an accurate picture of any business's earnings potential.

In the vast majority of cases, using either SDE or EBITDA will give you an accurate snapshot of earnings potential. For some SaaS companies, though, neither will prove an entirely precise measure. In those circumstances, you need something else.

Growth-projected revenue

For a young but fast-growing SaaS firm, SDE and particularly EBITDA can be misleading. An EBITDA figure, for example, could easily come out at zero or a negative value. That's not a fair reflection of the company's value. The firm's growth potential may still make it attractive to possible buyers. That growth potential, then, can get factored into the valuation.

You can estimate a firm's earning potential based on projected growth. That gives a better picture of the *value* of the business, even if it doesn't reflect the raw worth of its current assets. This kind of valuation, though, is risky as it relies on often volatile growth predictions.

Calculating the earnings potential of your SaaS firm, then, is a delicate issue. You need to use your judgement to assess the method that best suits you. In some cases, it may even be worth combining all three options. What you need to do, after all, is to take the most accurate value snapshot possible.

With earnings potential figured, you can then look to your valuation multiple.

Your valuation multiple

Once you've got your annual earnings potential, you need to find your valuation multiple. That's the figure that you're going to multiply your earnings potential by, to reach a final listings price. Multiples differ significantly according to the companies in question.

The largest, most successful firms will need to apply a high multiple. In general, valuation multiples for smaller SaaS businesses sit within the range of three to ten.

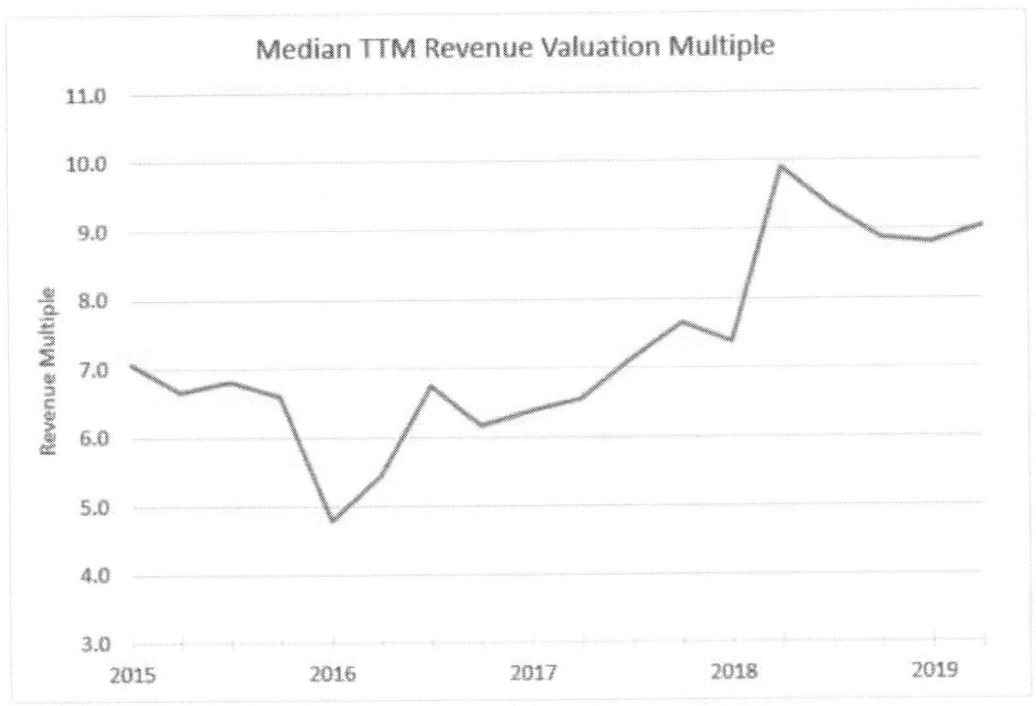

https://www.saas-capital.com/blog-posts/private-saas-company-valuations-2019/

Finding the correct multiple to sell a SaaS business is no easy task. You need to assess and analyse a vast number of factors. To get as accurate a multiple as you can, you must consider every data point possible. You need to look at everything that reflects your firm's health. You're seeking to use all measures on offer to you to judge your firm's scalability and sustainability.

Many different things impact any business's overall health. You need to consider things like the size of your customer base and how many visitors your site is getting. You must look at your revenue streams and the ROI of your SEO. There are also a multitude of external factors to consider.

To give you an idea of the types of factors to give most weight, let's look at four of the main ones. If you afford this quartet of elements lots of attention, you'll get to an accurate valuation multiple.

Age of business

Few things are better at revealing a firm's potential sustainability than its age. Businesses that already have a track record for survival have better prospects moving forward. A more extended history of prior performance also makes it easier to predict future growth. You have a larger sample size of data from which to work.

It's unusual to sell a SaaS business that's younger than two years old. By that stage in development, most firms are yet to get truly established. From the age of two years up, the older a company is, the higher a value multiple it can apply.

How involved an owner needs to be

Some SaaS companies require a lot of input from their owners. Smaller firms primarily rely a lot on the time and effort of their owners. Certain companies also need a good deal of technical input from the founder.

When it comes time to value your business, the more owner input needed, the lesser the multiple. A higher number of prospective buyers will be interested in a company they don't need to do a lot with. A reliable revenue stream with little input required makes a firm far more valuable. A business that needs the new owner to commit lots of time and expertise is worthless.

Company, market & industry trends

When you sell a SaaS business, the valuation isn't all about where the firm presently stands. It's also about where the company is going to be in the ensuing months and years. As such, how the firm is trending is essential to your valuation multiple. If the firm is growing consistently, you can up the multiple. If growth is stagnant or the company is shrinking, its value is less.

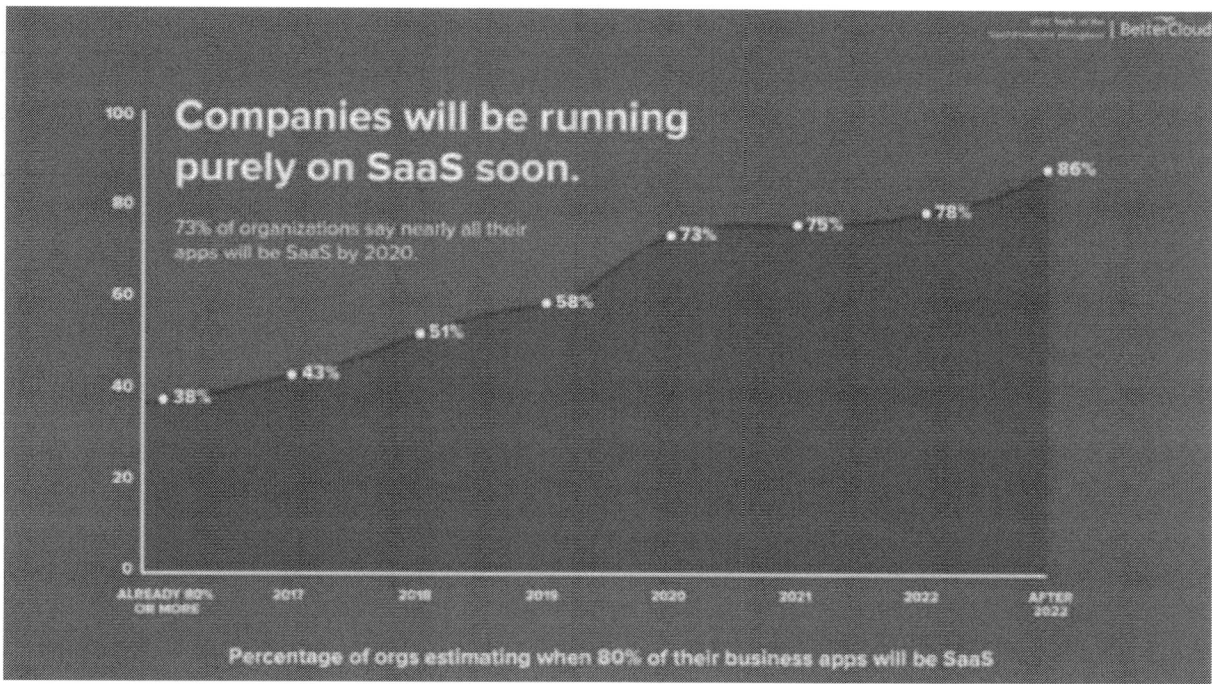

https://financesonline.com/2018-saas-industry-market-report-key-global-trends-growth-forecasts/

Market and industry trends also impact your valuation multiple. The ultimate value you put on your firm, after all, needs to reflect how much someone may pay to buy it. In a time that the market in which your firm exists is growing, you can up your multiple. That's good news for SaaS firms, as the SaaS market is one that's enjoying consistent year-on-year growth.

Key SaaS metrics that determine your multiple

The general health of your business is also key to your valuation multiple. There are a handful of key metrics to keep track of to assess the vitality and viability of a SaaS firm. The following are four of the most crucial:

- **Customer churn** – customer churn is the rate at which customers leave your business. It's a vital metric for any SaaS firm. The revenue of SaaS businesses relies on customers sticking around for a long time. The higher your customer churn, the lower your valuation multiple. A firm that rapidly loses customers has less value than one with good customer retention.

- **Customer Acquisition Cost (CAC)** – a firm's CAC is how much they have to spend to bring each new customer on board. The figure includes all marketing, promotion, and staffing costs related to acquisition. For a higher valuation multiple, you need as low a CAC as possible. A low CAC means a business is more sustainable for any new owner.

- **Customer Lifetime Value (CLTV)** – the value of a customer to a business over the whole time they're signed up, is the CLTV. SaaS businesses want to achieve as high a CLTV as they can. If your CLTV far exceeds your CAC, it will have a positive impact on your valuation multiple.

- **Monthly Recurring Revenue (MRR)** – the MRR is the amount of reliable revenue your firm brings in each month. It's the amount that all your combined customers pay to use your services in a calendar month. The higher your MRR, the more optimistic you can be with your valuation multiple.

How to value a SaaS company – in summary

You've now got both your yearly earnings potential and a valuation multiple. All that's left is to multiply the two, and you get a listing value for your firm. That's the amount that you can realistically hope to sell your business for. Once you know how to value a SaaS company, you're well on your way to a successful sale. By calculating a true earnings potential and a reasonable multiple, you can pitch your firm at the right level.

That will ensure that you won't put off otherwise interested buyers. It also helps you to avoid underselling your business. After all the hard work you put in building the company, you don't want to do yourself out of the best possible deal. Follow all the above advice, and you give yourself the best chance of selling your SaaS business successfully.

Not ready to sell yet? The sale of your company may not be the primary reason for seeking a valuation. If the purpose behind valuing the company is to inform further rounds of funding, you're now well-placed to move onto pitching for funding. In the next section, we'll show you some unbeatable pitch deck templates to use when approaching venture capital funds for investment.

5.4: 27 unbeatable pitch deck templates you can use for your startup

There are many different stages of your SaaS firm's development at which you may need to raise funding. If you need to reach out to a VC to get that critical finance, your first step is to create a pitch deck.

A pitch deck is a short presentation aimed at convincing investors to part with their cash. The presentations are often ten slides in length or shorter. In spite of their brevity, they're crucial to persuading an investor of your firm's potential and viability.

It's essential, therefore, that you get your pitch deck right. To give you an idea of how to do that, let's look at some examples of real pitch decks. The following are 27 pitch deck examples that worked wonders for the businesses that created them.

1. **Facebook**

It's hard to imagine a world in which Facebook isn't a household name. That was the case back in 2004, though, when Mark Zuckerberg was looking for funding to get his social network off the ground.

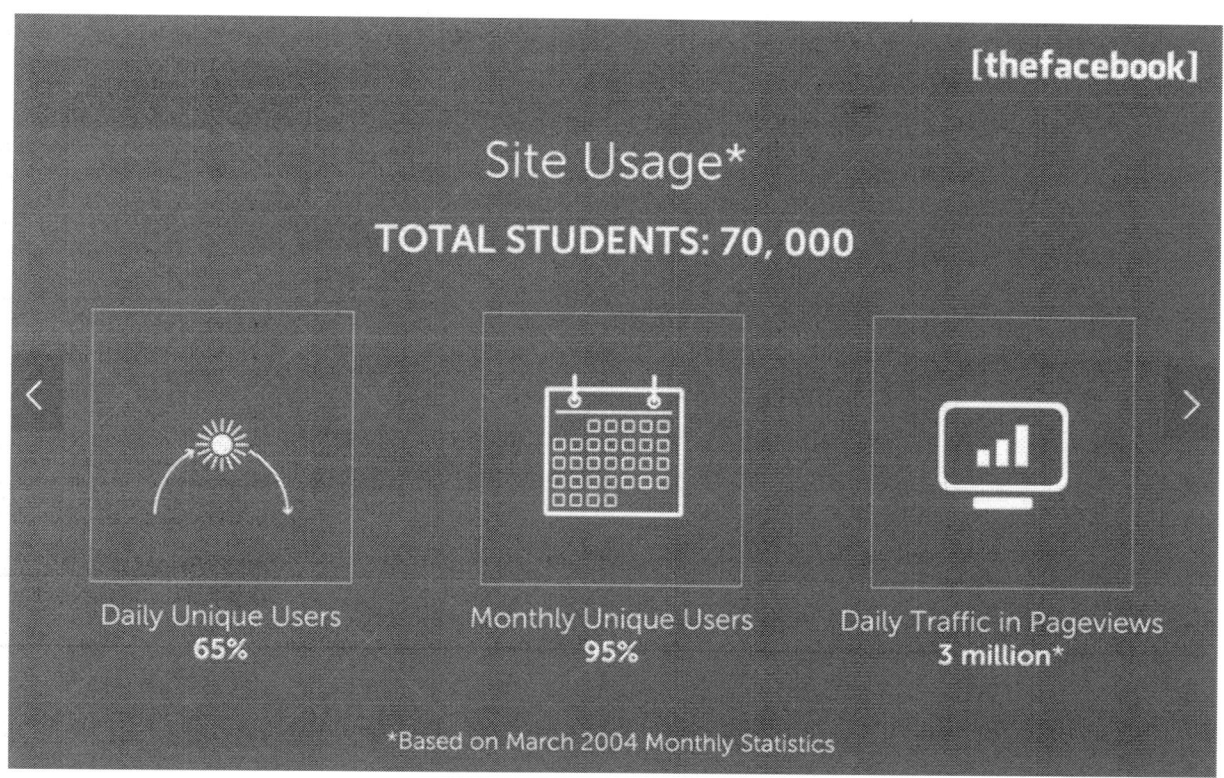

The original Facebook pitch deck, available on pitchdeckexamples.com, is an excellent example of using quantitative data to convince investors. Many of its slides focussed on traffic, users, and user engagement. Those kinds of measures displayed the site's potential.

2. **Airbnb**

Today, we're all pretty used to the idea behind Airbnb. Before the business got up and running, though, the concept was almost unthinkable.

Problem   2

Price is an important concern for customers booking travel online.

Hotels leave you disconnected from the city and its culture.

No easy way exists to book a room with a local or become a host.

The pitch deck Airbnb used to get finance is a widely shared example, and is available on SlideShare. The magic of it was how effectively it established the key principles behind Airbnb.

3. **Buffer**

Buffer is a platform to help users schedule social media content. It works with the likes of Facebook, Twitter, and LinkedIn. After the Buffer pitch deck, available on SlideShare, had helped net the firm $500,000, the startup's owner made it available as an example for other business owners.

As with the Facebook pitch deck example, Buffer used compelling numbers to make their argument. The slide titled 'Traction' succinctly showed how the platform was succeeding in getting a foothold in the market.

4. **Square**

Square is a modern payment provider. The business lets merchants accept mobile credit card payment for goods via a dongle. Amongst our pitch deck examples, Square is notable for how the firm highlighted its management team.

Management Team

The team has the background, proven track record and vision to succeed

The startup rightly identified its management team as one of its main strengths. They'd held positions at firms like PayPal, Twitter, and Google, after all. The pitch deck, available on SlideShare, put that impressive prior experience front and centre.

5. **LinkedIn**

The next of our pitch deck examples was used by LinkedIn, available on SlideShare, when they were looking for Series B funding. It succeeded in netting the social network significant funding, two years after its initial launch.

Google: Search for Things 2.0

Search for Things 1.0:
Altavista

alta^{vista:}

Rank search results by looking at **each individual page in isolation**

Search for Things 2.0:
Google

Google

Rank search results by looking at **network of links between pages**

August 2004
CONFIDENTIAL

7

The main crux of this pitch deck was to set up LinkedIn as 'Professional People Search 2.0'. To drill that home to possible investors, LinkedIn used a range of analogies. They showed how many successful firms represented the second generation of previous tech or solutions. As such, LinkedIn aligned themselves with those earlier success stories.

6. **Mint**

Mint is another company from the financial services industry. The tool offers a new way for users to track spending and so save money. Their pre-launch pitch deck, available on SlideShare, was never actually used to get investment. It was, however, a notable entry in a major competition.

Exit Calculation

Multiples Analysis for MyMint
Dollars in Millions (MyMint in Thousands)

Company	Ticker	Enterprise Value	2007 Sales	2007 EBIT	EV/Sales	EV/EBIT
PlanetOut.Inc	LGBT	$61.9	$76.0	($7.2)	.8x	N/A
DealerTrack	TRAK	$940.2	$219.8	$57.3	4.3x	16.4x
Synchronoss Technologies	SNCR	$490.8	$101.8	$24.0	4.8x	20.5x

1 High	4.8x	20.5x
2 Average	3.3x	9.4x
3 Median	4.3x	16.4x
4 Low	.8x	N/A

MyMint	2007	2008	2009	2010	2011	2012			EV
Sales	751.3	1,513.6	2,914.3	5,377.1	9,532.4	16,278.8	Sales Year	3	$25,914
EBIT	38.1	326.3	1,090.1	2,562.9	4,994.7	9,223.1	Method	1	$52,414

Cash Flows	(3,000)	$49	$164	$6,259		Assumptions		Average EV
						Investment	$3.0M	$39,164
Reinvested IRR	25%					Stake	15%	
						Hurdle Rate	5%	

The most interesting aspect of this example is how it speaks directly to investors. The pitch deck addresses many of an investor's prime concerns. Most notably, it suggests to them a range of possible exit strategies.

7. MapMe

If you're looking for successful pitch deck examples, a presentation that raised $1m seed funding fits the bill. That's just what the MapMe pitch deck, available on SlideShare, achieved. It helped get the accessible map creation tool to get rolling.

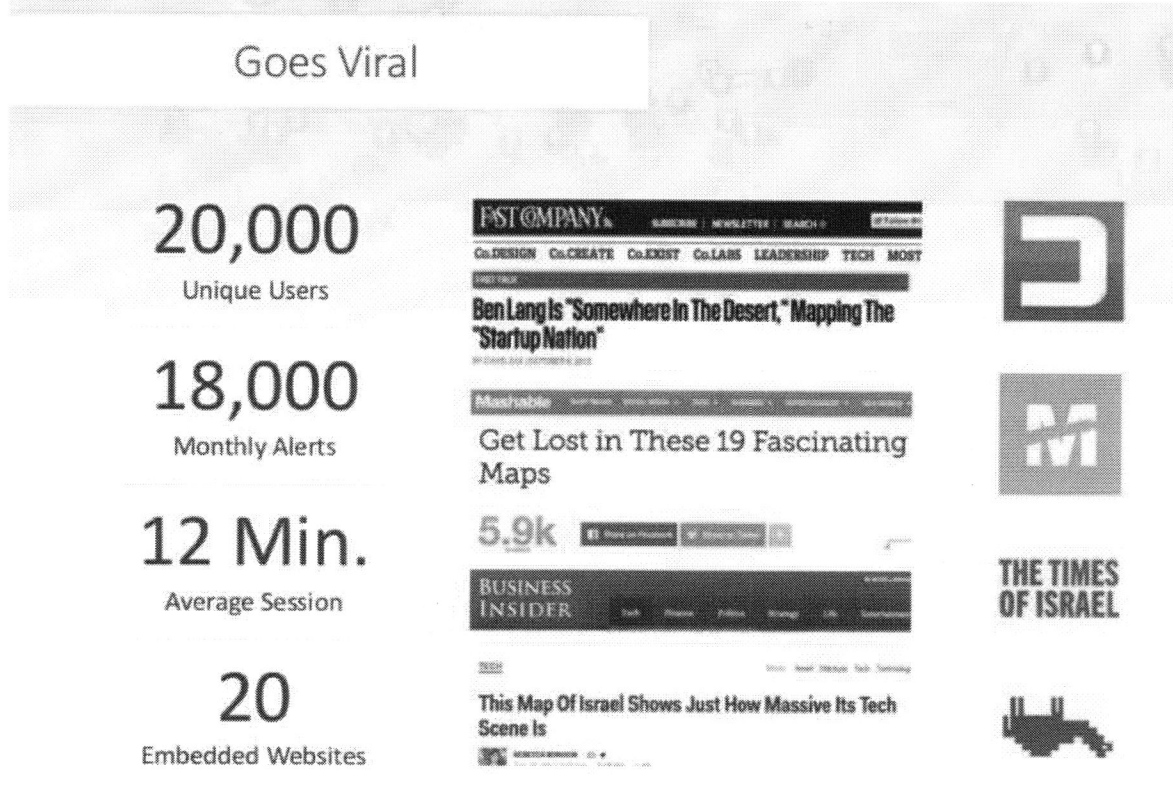

What made this pitch deck so successful was how well it leveraged social proof. The presentation displayed clearly how the news of the tool had gone viral. That succeeded in demonstrating the existing interest in the business. It also showed how it could grow, given the right investment.

8. **LaunchRock**

LaunchRock is a tool to aid the promotion of websites. It helps startups build landing pages and market themselves via social media. Their pitch deck, available on SlideShare, is one of the most aesthetically pleasing on our list of examples.

As well as being easy on the eye, LaunchRock's presentation also put their product front and centre. In just a few slides, the pitch deck managed to explain how the product worked and why that made it a good investment.

9. **Mixpanel**

An advanced analytics platform, Mixpanel works on both mobile and desktop. The tool lets users measure pageviews and assess users' on-page actions. They used this Series B pitch deck to raise more than $65 million.

> **COMPETITIVE ADVANTAGE**
>
> In 2010, we built the most sophisticated analytics database engine to answer questions that existing technology could not answer. It's the reason we are winning.

The presentation used a simple concept but delivered it exceptionally well. It first presented a problem, being that site owners often guess their analytics. The pitch deck then explained how Mixpanel helped solve that problem, as well as how it did it better than its rivals.

10. **Moz**

If you're in any way familiar with SEO or content marketing, you'll know the name Moz. Starting as only an SEO firm, Moz later pivoted toward the broader world of marketing. To support that move, they used a Series B pitch deck, available on SlideShare.

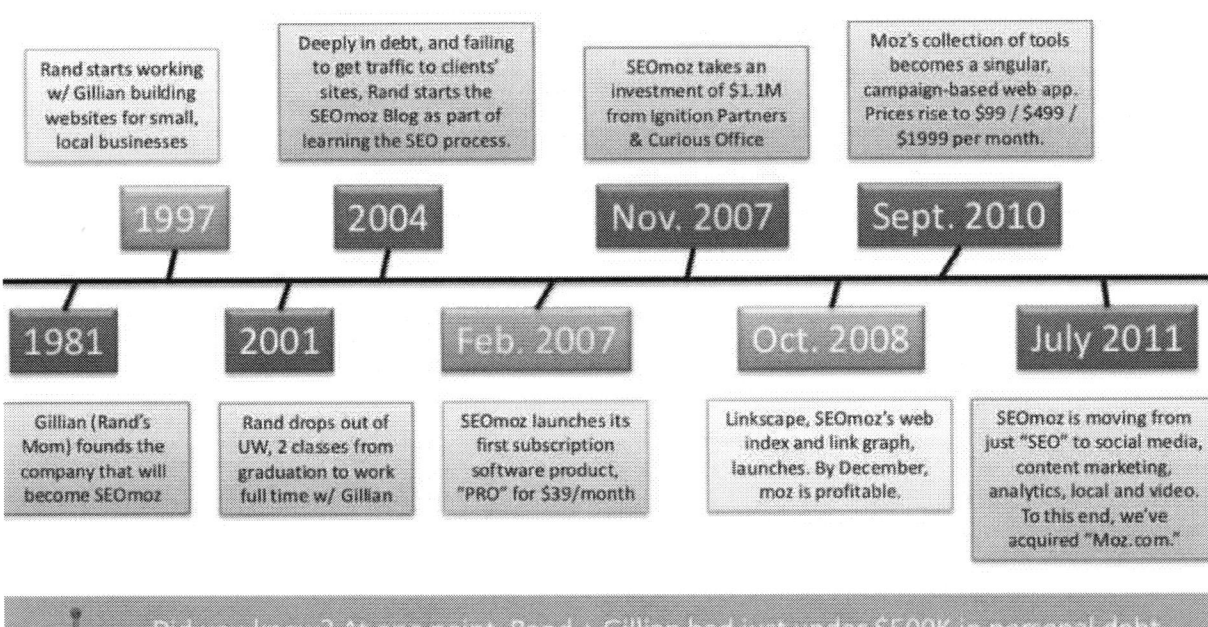

One of the longest of our pitch deck examples, the presentation is packed with info. It lays out a vast amount of detail about the first five years of Moz's operation. If yours is a more established SaaS firm, this example may be the best template to follow.

11. **BuzzFeed**

One of the most recognisable names on the net, BuzzFeed has enjoyed massive fundraising success. Through various pitch decks, avalable to view on SlideShare, the firm's managed to secure over $240 million.

As you may expect from BuzzFeed, the key to their success comes from social proof. Their presentation exemplifies the website's millions of monthly users. It also showcases a quote from CNN in support of the company.

12. **Manpacks**

Manpacks is one of the lesser-known startups on our list of pitch deck examples. Via a unique and effective presentation that you can view on SlideShare, though, the firm managed to raise a cool $500 million. That's a lot of cash to help them sell their products pitched at men!

What stands out about this pitch deck is its tone. Manpacks applied the humorous, informal tone it uses to market its products. That was a risky move, but it paid off as it showed investors that the firm had a clear identity.

13. **Foursquare**

Foursquare's first pitch deck, also available on SlideShare, from 2009 is another example of the utility of social proof. The mobile platform helps users to find local attractions and places to go. In their presentation, Foursquare used screenshots of Tweets from users of the platform.

The effectiveness of those screenshots was two-fold. Firstly, it demonstrated that people were already engaged with the platform. Second, it proved that the platform did work in practice as it was designed to do.

14. **Dwolla**

In just 18 well-designed slides, Dwolla managed to snare $18.5 million of investment. The business provides a new kind of payment solution. That solution lets users send, receive, and request funds from one another. check out the presentation on SlideShare.

As is the case for many startups, the idea behind Dwolla came from its founder's personal experience. What this pitch deck did well was to tell the founder's story and explain how it helped shape the company.

15. **ZenPayRoll (Gusto)**

Gusto is a cloud-based solution to help SMEs to pay staff more efficiently. Back when the firm was still called ZenPayRoll, it used a simple pitch deck to raise $6 million of investment.

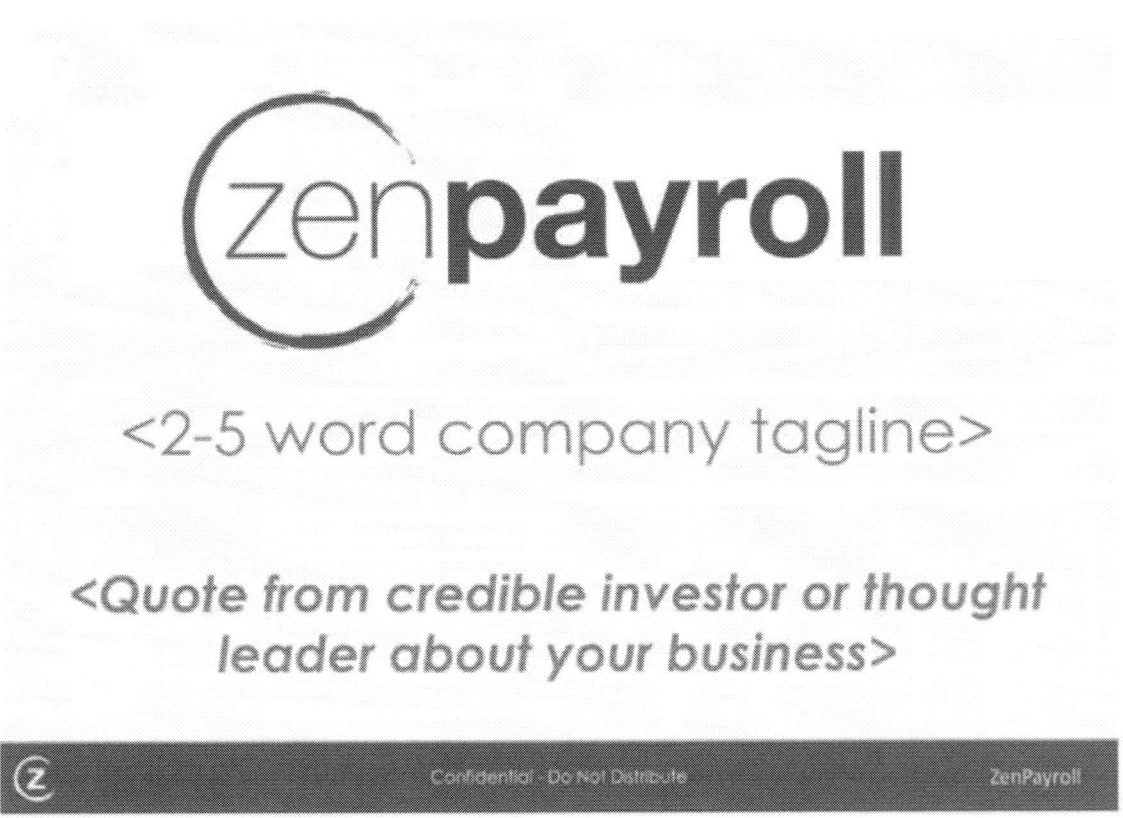

After the success of its presentation, Gusto shared the slides they used. Rather than showing the exact content it used, the firm put out an informational template. Check it out on SlideShare if you need ideas for how to structure and arrange your pitch deck.

16. **Bliss.ai**

In 2015, Bliss.ai used a 14-slide pitch deck, view on pitchdeckexamples.com, to persuade investors of the viability of its service. Bliss offers both metrics and a community for pro-coders. The presentation used by the company helped it to accrue $400,000 in investment from a group of 61 investors.

What made this pitch deck so compelling was its perfecting pitching. It was clear from the content that the decision-makers at Bliss were experts. They understood both their users and the investors to whom they were presenting.

17. **Adpushup**

AB testing is a vital process for any firm with an online presence. Adpushup helps businesses boost ad revenues by applying advanced AB testing. The company kept things simple with their pitch deck and reaped the rewards.

Eleven slides in length, the Adpushup presentation followed a format that it's easy to copy. It featured an introduction, and then presented problems faced by advertisers. Then, the presentation showed how Adpushup solved those problems. Finally, it displayed current products, traction with users, and plans for the future. See more at SlideShare.

18. **Wealthsimple**

The first of our pitch deck examples from Canada, Wealthsimple's slides were superb at swaying investors. The online investment management firm brought in over $2 million in 2.5 weeks from 15 investors.

The investment industry is transforming

Industry transformations by decade

1980s	**Mutual funds** transform the way investors save for retirement
1990s	**Discount brokerage** creates an easy, low cost solution for DIY investors
2000s	**ETFs** become a credible, low-cost, liquid alternative to mutual funds
2010s	**Online solutions** democratize access to sophisticated investment management

A significant part of why this pitch deck was successful was due to how it displayed the firm's expertise. In only a few slides, Wealthsimple showed a firm grasp on its industry, its products, and its customers. View on SlideShare.

19. AppVirality

AppVirality is a toolkit for aiding mobile apps to grow and develop. The slides of the company's pitch deck, view on SlideShare, keep things simple when it comes to design. As far as content goes, they delivered precisely what was needed.

The pitch deck does a great job putting investors in the shoes of potential customers. It lays out the needs and desires of app developers. It then works through how AppVirality can satisfy those needs.

20. SteadyBudget

Our list of pitch deck examples has included lots from firms in the financial sector. That should come as no surprise, given the financial expertise of those businesses. SteadyBudget offers budget management software for PPC analysts.

Their seed funding pitch deck from 2015 is an excellent template to follow if your startup has got good early traction. Available to view on SlideShare. SteadyBudget used the initial interest it had generated to convince investors of the long-term viability of its app.

21. **Podozi**

An eCommerce company from Nigeria, Podozi sells beauty products for women. It's well worth taking a look at the pitch deck on SlideShare that was used by the company to raise investment in 2016.

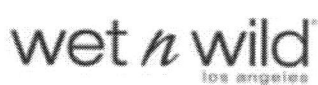

Podozi's presentation is a testament to the effectiveness of keeping things simple. Their whole pitch lasts only ten slides. Many of those slides include very little text and a reasonable degree of white space. Still, the firm manages to display its main strengths. Most notably, Podozi highlights the valuable commercial partnerships the firm has already secured.

22. **Fittr**

Fittr is an online platform to support users' efforts to get fit. It designs custom workouts to best suit each individual and their circumstances. The firm's pitch deck from 2012 offers some great clues for any other SaaS companies looking for smaller investments. It's available on SlideShare.

Unlike many of our pitch deck examples, Fittr's slides tell investors how much funding they want. More importantly, the company also lays out what it plans to do with the finance. That helps to show prospective investors that their money won't be wasted. It also displays clarity of thought and planning from the company.

23. Swipes

The task manager app, Swipes, gives yet another example of how a simple pitch deck, can be viewed on SlideShare, can bring success. The firm used its app's design elements and colour scheme for the presentation but kept the text to a minimum.

The copy that did get included exemplified all that was good about the platform. Key features and metrics displaying traction played a big part. Notably, too, Swipes was able to include positive quotes from both Lifehacker and Next Web.

24. Canvas

If you own a SaaS startup that uses disruptive technology, you need to check out the Canvas pitch deck on SlideShare. Canvas is a SaaS firm that helps replace traditional, paper-based processes. Instead, it offers easy-to-use mobile apps and forms.

In 2014, Canvas succeeded in raising $9 million via a simple but stunning presentation. The firm shared ten of the most important slides from that presentation. What many of those slides have in common is a scarcity of text. Canvas used loads of images and infographics to make info as digestible as possible.

25. **Ooomf (Crew)**

The firm now known as Crew had the name Ooomf when it presented a pitch deck (on SlideShare) that netted over $2 million in finance. The mobile freelancer marketplace secured that cash by creating a presentation with a natural flow.

As you navigate Ooomf's slides, you get the sense of being told a story. The presentation takes you step-by-step through a tale. That tale ends with the conclusion that you should invest in the company.

26. **Cubeit**

Founded in 2014, Cubeit is a mobile app for aggregating and sharing content. The company used a much-admired pitch deck in 2014 to secure the seed funding it needed to grow. Check it out on pitchdeckexamples.com. Comprising only 13 slides, Cubeit's presentation got them $3 million in finance. That came from Accel Partners and Helion Venture Partners.

One of the best things about this pitch deck is its first slide. That slide captures the attention and hits potential investors between the eyes. In no time at all, it sets out the raison d'être of Cubeit and explains the issue it solves.

27. **Castle**

Detroit-based real estate startup, Castle, is the last of our pitch deck examples. The Castle web app offers property owners a new way of listing and managing those properties. The firm's pitch deck was equally innovative. See more on SlideShare.

A great deal of effort and expertise went into the design of the presentation. The real estate themed slides were easy on the eye without detracting from the company's message. The pitch deck, as a result, was compelling and easy to digest.

Your Perfect Pitch Deck

You shouldn't seek to copy any one of the pitch deck examples discussed above. Looking at all the different types of presentations that have brought funding success, though, is worthwhile. It can help you to pinpoint the different styles and alternatives that will work best for you.

Cherry-pick a slide style from here and a design element from there, and you can build your perfect pitch deck. With the presentation in place, you're well on your way to getting the vital investment your firm needs and deserves.

This ebook provides an overview of a marketing strategy for your SaaS startup. We have discussed getting traffic and paying customers to your website through content marketing and paid advertising.

Once you have gained interest, you need to continue to engage potential customers and convert visitors to prospects with email campaigns and webinars. The design, layout, and wording of your landing pages is critical to conversion.

Website tools need to collect data so that your sales teams can continue to serve existing customers to the best of your ability. All of this sales activity takes time and money, so finding funding can make the difference to your success or failure.

There is so much to do when you're starting and growing a SaaS startup! We have one last word of advice: seek support when you need it. If you already know you need help, your next step is to call us on 0117 336 1103 or email us hello@accelerate-agency.com. Find us at accelerate-agency.com.

Appendix

Chapter 1: Getting traffic to your site
[1] Nestor Gilbert, 2019, *62 SaaS Statistics You Must Learn: 2019 & 2020 Market Share & Data Analysis*, https://financesonline.com/saas-statistics/

1.1 12 tried & tested SaaS marketing strategies that just work
[1] Rosie Murphy, 2018, *Local Consumer Review Survey 2019*, https://www.brightlocal.com/research/local-consumer-review-survey/

1.4 Essential guide to guest posting
[1] Brian Dean, 2016, *We Analyzed 1 Million Google Search Results. Here's What We Learned About SEO*, https://backlinko.com/search-engine-ranking

1.5 Best social media channels
[1] J. Clement, 2019, *Number of social network users worldwide from 2010 to 2021*, https://www.statista.com/statistics/278414/number-of-worldwide-social-network-users/

Chapter 2: How to get paying customers
2.1 How to run retargeting ads
[1] Wilco de Kreij, 2019, *These Stats Will Convince You to Retarget and Improve Your Campaigns*, https://connectio.io/facebook-retargeting-stats/

2.2. How to set up email marketing campaigns
[1] Jordie van Rijn, 2015, *DMA National Client Email Report 2015*, https://www.emailmonday.com/dma-national-client-email-report-2015/

2.3 How to run webinars
[1] Amber Tiffany, 2017, *The Essential Webinar Cheat Sheet*, https://blog.gotomeeting.com/essential-webinar-cheat-sheet-infographic/

[2] Shelby Britton, 2014, *Webinar Engagement by Numbers*, https://blogs.adobe.com/adobeconnect/2014/03/webinar-engagement-by-numbers.html

Chapter 3: How to keep visitors on your website
3.1 11 SaaS landing page examples and why they work
[1] Kara Pernice, 2017, *F-Shaped Pattern of Reading on the Web: Misunderstood, But Still Relevant (Even on Mobile)*, https://www.nngroup.com/articles/f-shaped-pattern-reading-web-content/

Chapter 5: How to secure investment or a sale
5.1. A beginner's guide to the 5 steps of startup funding stages

[1] Matt Mansfield, 2019, *Startup Statistics – The Numbers You Need to Know*, https://smallbiztrends.com/2019/03/startup-statistics-small-business.html

5.3 The definitive guide on how to value your SaaS company

[1] technavio, *Software as a Service (SaaS) Market by Deployment and Geography - Global Forecast & Analysis 2019-2023*, 2019, https://www.technavio.com/report/software-as-a-service-saas-market-industry-analysis

Authors

Nick Brown - SEO Specialist

"I founded Accelerate because I'd had enough of seeing hard-working companies provided sub-par SEO for premium prices."

Nick started his career as a Zoologist. He has over 12 years of experience in digital marketing, first starting up an e-commerce business in 2007. It grew to a turnover of £500,000 in one year. He works with leading brands advising them on SEO, CRO and content marketing.

Phil Pearce - Analytics Specialist

"I founded Accelerate because I was tired of seeing one of the most powerful marketing tools, Google Analytics, not being used to its full potential."

Over the past 15 years, Phil has helped clients improve their analytics and search engine marketing through the introduction of new tools and disruptive techniques. "Fail Fast – Succeed Faster" is the motto behind Phil's approach. Phil is renowned for his in-depth technical skills and the ability to solve business challenges through innovative technological solutions.

Find out more at accelerate-agency.com.

Printed in Great Britain
by Amazon